ARCHITECT ERRANT

By the same author

RECONNOGRAPHY
ENGLAND AND THE OCTOPUS
BUILDING IN PISE
THE ARCHITECT
SIR LAURENCE WEAVER - a biography
THE ADVENTURE OF BUILDING
TOWN AND COUNTRY PLANNING
ON TRUST FOR THE NATION (2 vols)
PORTMEIRION, THE PLACE AND ITS MEANING
ROADS IN THE LANDSCAPE
AROUND THE WORLD IN NINETY YEARS
THE FACE OF THE LAND (edited)
BRITAIN AND THE BEAST (edited)

with Amabel Williams-Ellis
THE TANK CORPS (A WAR HISTORY)
THE PLEASURES OF ARCHITECTURE
HEADLONG DOWN THE YEARS

with Sir John Summerson
ARCHITECTURE HERE AND NOW

CLOUGH WILLIAMS-ELLIS

ARCHITECT ERRANT

PORTMEIRION LIMITED
PORTMEIRION • GWYNEDD • LL48 6ET • WALES
1991

First published in 1971 by
Constable and Company Ltd
Orange Street, London WC2

Copyright © 1971 by Clough Williams-Ellis

ISBN 0-216-91023-4 (limp)

Reprinted 1980, 1991, 1995

Printed in Finland by WSOY

To Amabel
for everything

Contents

1	VOCATION–ANTECEDENTS–CHILDHOOD	1
2	BOYHOOD	24
3	SCHOOL AND HOLIDAYS	43
4	CAMBRIDGE AND A CAREER	56
5	FLIGHT TO ARCHITECTURE	66
6	EDWARDIAN GLITTER	78
7	MY OWN HOME	92
8	WAR	108
9	BACK IN LONDON	135
10	THE NEO-GEORGIANS	151
11	A SPECTRUM OF CLIENTS	159
12	WRITING AND RUSSIA	176
13	ISLAND HUNTING	190
14	PORTMEIRION–CONCEIVED AND BORN	203
15	PARTLY ABROAD	214
16	WAR AGAIN	228
17	BUTLIN, STEVENAGE, TRAVEL AND THE FIRE	243
18	KALEIDOSCOPE	263
19	ADDING IT UP	273
	APPENDIX: LIST OF BUILDINGS DESIGNED	277
	INDEX	285

Illustrations

The author at Portmeirion, armed with litter-picker, 1970   *(front cover)*
Amabel Strachey arriving at her wedding to the author, with her father, St. Loe Strachey, in his Surrey Guides uniform
Welsh Airs sung to welcome the author and his bride (leaflet damaged by fire at Plas Brondanw, 1951)
The Watchtower, Plas Brondanw
The Garden, Plas Brondanw
Plas Brondanw, entrance front
Plas Brondanw, an interior, as rebuilt after fire
Romney's House, Hampstead
Chatham House, Stowe
Stairhead, the Butterfield and Swire Residence, Shanghai
Llangoed Castle, Breconshire
First Church of Christ Scientist, Belfast
Entrance front, Bishop's Stortford College Chapel (the first building in England by a living architect to be scheduled for preservation)
The Library, Oare House, Wiltshire
Cold Blow, Oare
Paper model for Dunwood House, Yorkshire
Piers by Wren, gates by the author, Wroxall Abbey, Warwickshire
Cornwell Manor, Oxfordshire
New Village Centre, Cornwell
King George VI and Queen Elizabeth at Pen-y-gwryd, with the author showing them the proposed extent of the Snowdonia National Park
Unveiling by the Prince of Wales of the memorial tablet in Westminster Abbey to David Lloyd-George designed by the author, 1970. From the right, the group includes the Prince of Wales, the author, the Sub-Dean of Westminster, Earl Lloyd-George of Dwyfor, Sir Dingle Foot, the Right Hon. Edward Heath, the Right Hon. Jeremy Thorpe
A crystal goblet, by Laurence Whistler, presented to the author by its trustees on the fortieth anniversary of the foundation of Portmeirion
The Town Hall at Portmeirion from Battery Square
The author speaking from the Gloriette at the anniversary celebrations
The Lloyd George grave, designed by the author

Illustrations

Telefoto picture of Portmeirion from across the estuary, with Snowdon in the background
The author at work, 1970

Acknowledgements

I should like to thank the *New Yorker* for permission to quote from the description of the Lloyd George grave by Lewis Mumford on pp. 147–8 and from his description of Portmeirion on p. 210; also for the poem quoted on p. 265; and the Oxford University Press for an extract from *Russell Remembered*, by Rupert Crawshay-Williams on pp. 212–13.

Of those who have helped in other ways, I would like to thank, first and foremost, my wife, and also my granddaughter Rachel Wallace, Franziska Becker and Peggy Pollard. I would also like to thank *Country Life* and the Architectural Press for producing photographs that have precoriously survived from long ago, more especially because so many were destroyed in the London blitz, and almost all the rest, along with other records, when my home was gutted by fire after the last war.

The woodcuts at the opening of each chapter are reproduced from *The Universal Penman*, a collection of engravings by George Bickham issued between 1733 and 1743. A copy of the original collected edition was the only book in my library at Plas Brondanw to survive the fire in 1951, and a reissue of it is still available from my publishers, Constable—to whose helpful patience over the present book I should also like to pay tribute. For the frontispiece, the photograph of the Town Hall at Portmeirion and the portrait facing page 277 I am indebted to Mr. Bruno de Hamel's skill. The photograph of the Lloyd George grave is reproduced by courtesy of the *Radio Times*, and that of the unveiling of the Lloyd George Memorial tablet is the property of Fox Photos Ltd. The Illustration Research Service kindly traced the photographs of Romney's House, Hampstead, which originally appeared in the *Architects Journal*, and of Chatham House, Stowe, supplied by the British Travel Association; and the excellent photograph of Portmeiron with Snowdon in the background is by Mr. Tim Gell. I am more than grateful to Mr.

Acknowledgements

Minhinnick for providing a copy of his spirited cartoon which appears on p. 272.

Finally, and not least, I would like to thank my secretary, Miss Mary Roberts for patiently typing out a voluminous scribbled manuscript and reducing it to order.

Chapter One

Vocation–Antecedents–Childhood

*And hence one master-passion in the breast
Like Aaron's serpent, swallows up the rest*

Alexander Pope

It will have been deduced from the book's title that I am an architect.

The fact is central. Building therefore comes into my story both directly and as inevitably conditioning my reactions to issues and happenings of all sorts both public and private, as well as to persons and places. Although much else that has befallen me in the course of a long and varied life seems quite irrelevant to my master passion, yet even as scientist, engineer, soldier, amateur sailor, country landowner, traveller and writer, the architect within me has been ever-present, no matter how heavily overlaid by more immediate concerns. Being well aware of this bias, it seems only honest to begin by declaring my interest and revealing the mainspring of my whole career and prefacing even my birth with a brief note on 'vocation'.

Given my *architectural* life to live over again, I' should live it very differently, particularly the first few years; though to be sure there is always something to be said for youthful folly and for gaily curveting up blind or crooked alleys. For one thing, you discover what it is you really want, while how badly you want it can be roughly gauged by the sort of obstacles you smash through or clamber over to reach your heart's desire.

Certainly, had I not been possessed by a real passion for architecture—a passion that I can remember as quite strongly developed by my sixth year—I should never have become an architect at all. But I believe without any shadow of doubt whatever, that I was born to be an architect and nothing else. If mortar was ever in anybody's bones, I know it is in mine.

My mistake was that finding myself thus born, I did not see to it that I was also well and truly and quite thoroughly *made*. With (as I feel in those bones) an acute inborn instinct for architecture, I still remain in some respects half-baked as a technician—a handicap that can only be repaired, and that cumbrously, by the hiring of fully trained and technically proficient experts whenever either instinct or experience may fail.

Thus I have lamented that, being born an architect, I was not also thoroughly made. There are doubtless others in a like case; but the more usual condition is to be made an architect without having been so born. This is an omission and an oversight that nothing whatsoever can repair, and most of our more important architectural infelicities are from the brains and hands of such 'synthetic' architects.

I was born on 28 May 1883 in a rather gaunt old rectory at Gayton, in Northamptonshire, where my father had retired to a college living after giving up his Cambridge Fellowship on his marriage, as was then compulsory. It has always seemed to me that there had been altogether too much compulsion about his career: he had been obliged, for instance, to take Holy Orders that he might qualify for the tutorship of his college. He never questioned this authority: he was of his age—he expected to obey as he looked to be himself obeyed.

I grew up under a different *zeitgeist*, and with a definite reaction *against* obedience, and was inclined to suspect and question orders of any sort, whether Holy or otherwise. There was nothing architecturally distinguished about my birthplace. We left Gayton when I was four, but I remember an excess of plate-glass and much lugubrious plum-coloured paint. What I can recall vividly is the moss-grown end of a terrace wall under a great cedar, the massive roof trusses of an old barn where I used to hide, the archway in the garden wall between the rectory and the church, and the fiery glow of the sunset on the mullioned windows and mellowed ironstone gables of the old manor house across the road.

But the earliest of all my memories is of Queen Victoria's first jubilee in 1887, not through any innate infant loyalty, but because the treat to the Gayton school children that my parents were giving in celebration was interrupted by a crashing thunderstorm that gave me my first remembered fright.

Thoroughly scared, I prudently sought shelter from the expected thunderbolts in a dark recess under the monumental dining-room sideboard, and lightning still has to me a faint smell of musty wine.

I think I must have been a rather selfish little boy intent on my own interest for I recall, at a neighbour's Christmas Tree the following year, deserting the party as soon as I had secured my presents, and starting off homewards through deep snow, clutching my loot, until the hue and cry caught up with me and I was dragged back to say goodbye and thank you.

Also I had a tendency to 'know best' that later, in Wales, resulted in a variety of misadventures such as sliding down a haystack followed by a pitch-fork that luckily went through one of my ears instead of my still softish skull; laying open a knee with an unwieldy felling axe; being rolled on and badly kicked by my pony through attempting a silly jump; falling overboard at a regatta at about the age of seven before I could swim; later still being far more nearly drowned by being sucked down under a sluice when learning to and dislocating minor joints through over-estimating my agility or foolishly trusting to inadequate branches or to rotten ropes. All this quite failed to induce caution and simply intensified my innate belief in luck and that in the end things usually turned out well enough and that it was anyhow silly to fuss.

Fortunately for her sons (we were six originally, of whom I was the fourth) that was also my mother's general attitude, so that absences and adventures within reason were accepted as no more than natural.

There came a day when suddenly, and as it seemed to me without the slightest warning, we were all of us—parents, little boys, household, horses, pets, toys and furniture—whisked right away from our familiar English rectory to North Wales, to what seemed to me a strange and desolate country where there was no architecture and scarcely any building.

I remember how queer it seemed not being in a village like (surely) everyone else in the world. It might be rather grand, but it was also rather bleak. Even in a largish, rambling, old country-house with all kinds of meandering dependencies, one felt alarmingly alone and defenceless against the miles and miles of empty Welsh lowland country, all doubtlessly teeming with bears and banditti.

I remember soon after we had thus moved to Glasfryn, our home in Caernarvonshire, my father asked me if I would like to go with him to look at Gors Marchod (which in Welsh means the 'Horseman's Marsh'), a new plantation—nothing to do with 'Market' or 'Gorse' as I had misheard it. I suppose I had a colony in mind, but anyway it was clear to me that I was to have the rare treat of visiting a settlement of some sort, presumably as it was called 'new', with building still in progress or only just completed. I tried hard not to expect too much. I was determined to be as pleased and surprised as possible by what I had convinced myself was to be an architectural outing. I remember saying to myself that it would be silly to expect any of the houses to be more than two stories high in that out-of-the-way place, and that they would probably be quite small and plain and much alike, though if I were in luck one or two might be washed with colour instead of with ordinary whitewash.

I hoped that their doors might be either glossy with many coats of tar, or else peacock blue, and anyway opening in two halves like a cowhouse door, as I had discovered was their engaging habit in the older cottages of the neighbourhood.

If there were a shop (there might well be just *one*, and I had a penny in my pocket), would it be too much to hope that its window would belly out in a fatly smiling bay with twinkling little panes? This would be the way to make it look big and busy, and the wares within mysterious and seductive, like the half-revealed glories within a network Christmas stocking.

Somehow I never visualized a church: churches as a general rule never interested me as much as houses, and I was already a little contemptuous of the north Welsh variety, which I had found to be low, barn-like affairs with ugly new slate roofs, no coloured windows, and pitch-pine pews glistening with yellow varnish which I knew to be hard and believed to be ugly. I had at that time had my fill of churches, both from within and from without.

One thing, however, I did most earnestly hope for, and that was a little market square, surrounded by houses except where the four ways entered it, preferably at the corners.

There was another thing, which, if not utterly essential was certainly very, very desirable. The market-place should be paved with smooth, rounded cobbles, the smaller the better, and following the camber of the square like the scales on the foolish roach I had just learnt to catch in the lake.

Would it be market-day? Hardly. One could scarcely have such luck as all that. Or, if by chance it were, one would anyway be too late, as it was well after tea-time and already darkening into twilight. But they might still be clearing up? Even if only one man remained just sweeping the cobbles, the bustle and romance of the day would be lingering on with him, and the dusk would have brought out yellow squares of candle-light in the dim, whitewashed walls perhaps, and that would be nearly as exciting as the market.

Only what would they buy and sell in a market in such a place? There seemed to be nothing but furze bushes, and my small legs were already full of their prickles.

Yes, gorse was clearly the staple of the place; it would be gorse that they trafficked in—no doubt chopped fine in a chaff-cutter and bundled up like great Christmas puddings in sacking, only surprisingly light for their size and smelling of almonds. Buyers would open these bundles and handle the stuff to gauge its quality: it would be scattered about the square and between the little cobbles. Even now, it was their dark-green, pungently-smelling spines that the besom of my imaginary scavenger was flicking out from between the tight-packed stones, here and there stained greeny-black by the juice of the trodden gorse.

A very, very long way to this village—or with its market-place surely almost a little town—but worth it. And not tedious, because of thinking of it. Perhaps I was thinking about it too much—I dawdled, or at any rate moved short and rather tired legs without much spring or judgement.

But my father had stopped, and was jumping straight up and down in a patch of dejected-looking young larch trees. Good, he had found some transplants loosened by the wind, and was treading them into the boggy soil as his habit was, and if there were enough of them I should have time to catch him up.

'Father, how far is it now . . . to the — the — plantation?'

'Oh—we're there now—this is it. Not much the matter—and now we must hurry home or it will be dark.'

I can find no parallel to the bitterness of that homeward march. It was my first experience of the cruel gulf that is fixed between the ideal and the real.

As a child grows, its awareness of people increases and it begins, without formulating, to be aware of an immediate circle and then to differentiate between individuals. I suppose that I became vividly aware of my mother, as a person and not just as a benevolent and helpful presence, when I was about eight.

I was, or rather felt, a good deal alone about then, my two elder brothers being too grand for me, and I too grand for my younger ones. Neither they nor my father got much pleasure through their eyes and to go out with my brothers meant very often to kick a ball about, or else to follow the guns with my father and the keeper and whoever were shooting.

I suppose I was barely twelve when I became possessed of an old sixteen-bore pin-fire gun of my own and my father, the keeper, and my big brothers were all very kind in encouraging me to use it like a man.

'Like a man'—that was the lure that betrayed my now long, but unreliable legs into all-day tramps across a seemingly boundless terrain of stubble and turnip fields, mountain and bog. Only now and again did these expeditions take us into what I considered 'scenery'. I was oddly unresponsive to wide-open horizons and to the sky except at sunset, and indeed demanded some element of the dramatic, even the theatrical, or failing that a certain intimacy or perfection of detail. I positively detested ploughland with its leg-tiring potato ridges, its stumbling-block roots and boot-soaking cabbages. There was little corn land, and that mostly oats, but I did admit to an admiration for the golden smoothness of September stubble fields, without which mitigation my agricultural agoraphobia would have been complete.

Rather a hard fate, it seemed to me, this being a little boy; these day-long trudgings over tedious farmlands with a too-heavy gun, the shame of missing easy shots, the poor satisfaction of fluking hard ones.

How different it was to go out with my mother, about whom there was so much for me to guess. How and where for instance, did she manage to satisfy her instinct for beauty of form and colour in this altogether too large and too empty country? A few leisurely, meandering walks in her company opened my eyes—quite literally.

The things she saw! The queer little things she would stop and exclaim over, so ordinary, so to-be-taken-for-granted and unremarkable as they had previously seemed to me. Old grey boulders in a wall under a windblown beech, golden lichen on the worn steps of an old stile, the red and russet mosses of some quaking bog with the many-coloured cranberries scattered upon them as though spilt from an overflowing basket.

I clearly remember a feeling of superiority and condescension mixed with my surprise—these inconspicuous quiet unheroic little things—how childish compared with the tumbling waterfalls, the precipitous crags, the ruined castles and blood-red sunsets which were what *I* considered noteworthy!

Yet quite quickly and imperceptibly the little things seduced me, and I began to be happy in their company.

It was my mother, too, as a second stage in the keying down of my demands on the picturesque, who revealed to me the almost 'natural' beauty of the old Welsh cottages that she was so fond of sketching. To begin with, I would not allow that they had any merit or interest at all. How could a mere hovel of only two rooms with no upstairs, no stone-mullioned windows, no arched doorway even, be called beautiful or even interesting?

She would not debate the question, but would quietly and very deftly make another picture. By degrees these sketches began to interest me, and I came to think them beautiful. It was not long before the attributes of interest and beauty that my mother had somehow contrived to make manifest in her pictures attached themselves to the originals, and I was soon protesting that she should not waste her time sketching animals and children when she might be so much more profitably employed in bringing out the faint yet subtle architectural flavour of the traditional 'folk-building' of our still primitive countryside.

For that matter, I would do it myself—to set her a good example—and she must therefore instantly teach me just exactly how one made these engaging and revealing pictures. I can still remember that first architectural drawing lesson and the rapture with which I repeated again and again my mother's ingeniously simple formula for drawing a cottage—invented for me, I believe, on the spur of the moment. One started ever so easily with the just comfortably familiar capital 'T', and drew yet another nice long straight line as the ground for it to stand on. Then a short line upwards for the other end of the cottage with a curve at the bottom—rather harder—for the brick oven. That done, you put on the curve of the thatched roof—harder than it looked—finished the chimney top and put in two windows and a door *au choix*.

Then—with a little shading to show the shadows—the thing was done—all ready for its path, its two apple trees, the curling wood-smoke (how hard to get it 'real-looking') and the water-crock beside the door. Timidly and very gradually, I developed this primordial little house into all manner of more evolved variations, but it was months, I know, before I could start my creation without the well-tried aid of that magical, protoplasmic, and literally initial T.

A little later I went through a phase of copying pictures out of our old bound volumes of *Punch*—particularly Tenniel's cartoons, which I admired for their clear, incisive line—a preference strongly commended by my mother, though as a great drawer of horses, she herself had a warm affection for Leech and had illustrated *Black Beauty*, one of my earliest books. Though she attended the Slade School of painting and Ruskin's lectures and was urged to make art her career by her admired friend Ralph Waldo Emerson, she opted for marriage and a family, though only accepting the declaration of my father-to-be whilst high up a ladder at work on a mural. I have an idea that the choice (and hence my very existence) may well have been quite a near thing.

It chanced that a more than usually enterprising ride to and along the coast had brought me to the one really distinguished old church in the whole country—Clynnog Fawr. No, it was not chance I suppose, for having heard of it, I set out to find it. And having found it—this noble, weather-stained old fortress of a collegiate church, by far the grandest piece of architecture I had ever yet seen—I vowed a great vow (therein forswearing myself) that I would assuredly become a parson.

This resolve I immediately announced on my excited return; but though one Ellis at least in every generation time out of mind had been a clerk in Holy Orders, the announcement of my own call was received a little doubtfully in view of my past record. I was tolerably obedient and rather markedly honest, as little boys go, but devout—no. If I shone at all, it was quite notoriously not in church or at family prayers—which I cut whenever possible, though that was distressingly seldom.

Moreover, it appeared that my clerical ambitions began and ended with the repair and embellishment of the great church in which I had just been worshipping—worshipping Architecture. I indignantly supposed that its then forlorn and ruinous condition was the fault of its callous and obviously criminal rector, whose job it surely was to set his House of God in order.

I would show him! *I* would build up again the ruined chantry, and repair the broken rood screen—*I* would reglaze the windows, mend the leads, and transform the greenly mouldering chancel into a dramatic climax of glowing colour, banners and tapestries, crimson and gold, answering to the deep and rich vibrations of the mighty organ—also put in by me.

Me! So that was the call! Fun for Me! Wherefore it was patiently pointed out to me that it was not so much a clergyman that I wanted to be as an architect. An architect! Somewhere, hidden but within recall, that idea ever after remained with me. For though I overlaid it with other ideas so far less acceptable and so far less truly mine, and though I obediently made to smother it with borrowed common-sense, in the end it would not be denied. So I became what (as I firmly believe) I was predestined and designed for, if only by the shuffle and deal of the forty-six chromosomes that made me, like everyone else in the world, unique. Somehow or other, and do as you would about it, the hand dealt out to me would make sense in no other way: it would spell out A-R-C-H-I-T-E-C-T clearly and emphatically, or failing that, just gibberish. Not necessarily a good architect, not even a successful one; but for better or worse an architect of sorts. That was my destiny, that my desire . . .

It must have been in the spring of 1891, three or four years after our migration to Wales, that my father ultimately set about what he had long intended, the rebuilding and enlargement of our old home.

As I first remember it, the house, low and couchant, spread its inordinate length of low-pitched gables across a wide lawn bounded by immense beech trees ending at a ha-ha above the lake. It was a queer, rambling old place enough, with no architectural pretentions whatever earlier than the Gothick revival, and even these of a rather half-hearted order. Yet it should have been otherwise, for in his 'town house' in Bangor, Archdeacon Ellis had designed and built charmingly in the classical tradition of his time, a neat, elegant little box, far more answerable to his own fastidious person than the sprawling shapelessness of his country-house, which from small beginnings he had considerably enlarged.

The Archdeacon was, from all accounts, a man of many parts with a passion for science, especially chemistry and metallurgy, some of his laboratory equipment surviving at Glasfryn to this day.

In 1809, when the Archdeacon's son had succeeded him, Edmund Hyde Hall described Glasfryn as:

... the seat of the Reverend Thomas Ellis, near a small lake of the same name. In this are several rushy islands and haunts of wild ducks and other than this place I scarcely know of a spot within the county more susceptible of rural beauty and polish.

A substantial body of correspondence between this father and son has lately come to light, mostly dealing with business and public affairs and all in an advanced form of shorthand, which at that date, very few others could surely have deciphered. With so many strings in his hand, it was no doubt a very prudent precaution.

Since his day other Ellises seem to have had their go at the house, and pretty wildly, and even after my father's drastic efforts at rationalization, the layout and internal planning showed small regard for any logical sequence and was indeed chaotic. Starting at the extreme south-western end and working northwards round two or three right-angle bends with turns this way and that, the several rooms and offices succeeded one another thus:

Gun room, bailiff's bothy, laundry, boot room, coal house, back entry, scullery, lavatory, larders, backstairs, kitchen, pantry, servants' hall, side entry, main staircase hall, business room, drawing-room, entrance hall, front porch, great hall, cloak room, dining-room, study, conservatory, school-room, third staircase, bathroom (with heating chamber under), lavatory, another entry, wine cellar, dairy, store-room, yet another and final entry, old saddle room and ultimate lumber room. The two floors above were neither so extensive nor so incoherent, yet, apart from the dairy and laundry maids and the coachman who (reluctantly) carried coal and cleaned boots—all had to be serviced by an indoor staff that never exceeded five.

Yet no one of us at the time, staff, family, nor anyone else, seems ever to have blamed the haphazard planning for any inconvenience, unnecessary work or needless running around. In the 1950s and '60s, amputated at both extremities and twice ingeniously further reorganized, first by my elder brother and his wife, and then by his eldest son and his, the old house still retains its familiar character, but none of its former intimidating drawbacks, and is well adapted both for family life and entertaining.

But even when I was a child, my father's ambitious reconstruction had greatly improved the place's amenities, central heating, more or less realistic plumbing and electric light being amongst his innovations. On the whole, and considering it was nearly eighty years ago that the major operation was performed, the final result was surprisingly painless, largely owing to the wise censorship of my mother. Certainly we were given a battlemented tower, but this romantic gesture is in fact a good deal less baronial and daunting than the architect's drawings had threatened, due to my mother's feeling for plainness and propriety and her valiant intervention.

I well remember myself joining in a debate about some wrought iron scrollwork with which it was proposed to crown the turret that gave access to the leads of the tower, and vehemently pleading for its suppression. To my delight it was actually omitted, though it was probably the blacksmith's estimate rather than my infant protests that settled the matter so satisfactorily. But I had, for a seven- or eight-year-old, pretty decided views about building, especially considering that never before had I seen one stone laid upon another. I recall reproaching my parents for substituting pitch-pine for oak on the upper floors, for putting plate-glass in the stone mullioned windows, for crowning the roofs with glazed ridge tiles, for using hard, lobster-red bricks for the back chimneys and cast-iron drainpipes to support the back door porch. Their plea of economy or 'architect's orders' I grandly pooh-poohed. Altogether I must have been rather a tiresome little boy, rather indulgently treated, a sort of architectural Infant Samuel. None the less, I felt cruelly defrauded and ill-used at being removed for the two or three years of the rebuilding to another house of ours about twelve miles away—which was with the roads and vehicles of those parts and at that time equivalent to a hundred miles today.

This other house was architecturally quite vacuous, and though it was on a (then) lovely part of the coast with a yacht and boats and nets, and islands to visit, yet nothing would please me because only two hours away *building* was going on, and I was not there. Also I constantly bewailed the absence of any proper trees. I missed the great beeches and their rooks almost as much as the building, and to this day I am never altogether happy out of the sight of trees, unless, indeed, out of sight of land.

But there were compensations and adventures peculiar to Abersoch. I bought a small tin of sardines at the village shop for a halfpenny (because it was rusty) and ate them up one of the rare trees without ill-effects. On one occasion I was given a hot-news verbal message to take up, along with some newspapers, from my father's yacht to the St. Tudwals Island lighthouse-keeper. It was 'Parnell is dead.' When they asked, 'Who is Parnell?' I didn't know and felt foolish.

Dust, glare and headaches are a part of my memories of these seaside years—perhaps they were unusually hot summers—but something at any rate has caused the word 'tree' to sound in my ears very like the word 'content'.

Buildings and trees, trees and buildings are still, to me (with sailing ships) the most exciting things in the world. Indeed I cannot so much as look at a house that will bear looking at without grouping or rearranging imaginary trees about it, or see even a pair of elms without visualizing the sort of house that would become them as a background.

Once on one of my rare visits to the building at Glasfryn I saw the great one, the architect himself, and smelt the delicious fragrance of his portfolio of tracings: two or three times I had the supreme felicity of clambering about the scaffoldings with the contractor or his foreman. Not even excepting a circus, a menagerie, a trip in the lifeboat and the descent of a lead mine —it was the happiest memory of a not unhappy childhood.

Imitative, as are all children, I sought to soften my seaside exile as best I could by building on my own account. It would give me considerable sentimental pleasure, I confess, to come upon my first drawings for the house I really intended to build for myself at that period—about my eighth year.

The site I chose was on a gorse-covered bluff, high above the river, a south gable with its single little window towards the sea, the door (divided into upper and lower halves, a style I greatly admired) opening on to a ledge of rock, and though I slaved like a little ant painfully and slowly assembling my heavy materials, once I got my walls above the trenches of their foundations, these walls would by no means rise up in obedience to my will. Slowly I would build up a corner to so respectable a height that quite soon one would have to consider fetching a soap-box to work from as a scaffold, and then, just one more stone, and down would rattle my whole day's work.

Less skilful and persistent than the ant, I was perhaps more intelligent, and knew when I was up against something too big for me. Philosophically I decided to cut my loss and abandon the intractable thing defeated.

I had, however, accumulated a building fund of nearly five shillings for the financing of this venture, and now, suddenly I was fancy-free again with all my capital untouched. For a week or two I bargained anxiously for a crossbred Airedale puppy that had seemed to me to show both sympathy and good sense in daily inspecting my excavations and apparently approving. But the long negotiations came to naught. It appeared that the creature was too nobly connected on the female (Airedale) side to be had for my five shillings.

Very soon, though, I was glad enough to be still a capitalist without encumbrances—animal pets were not really in my line— and one of my village friends told me that a firm offer of half-a-crown would probably secure the remains of a little flat-bottomed canoe that lay rotting amongst the thrift where the river met the sea. Very carefully and hesitatingly we estimated that the other half-crown should buy enough canvas, tintacks and pitch to patch her holes and make her seaworthy. It turned out that we were half right. All the obvious holes—the sort of holes through which fingers or even small fists could be poked—were duly sealed up; and one memorable Saturday, on the flood of a high spring tide, we launched her, all shining black and sticky with pitch and Stockholm tar, smelling divinely, free of debt.

Proudly the owner and master stepped aboard. How voluptuously the warm pitch, soft and toffee-like, caressed and embraced the toes, how magic-quick were they suddenly awash in cold sea-water—how soon indeed, one by one, did the lovely, heart-breaking, gleaming rills of bubbling water along every seam, disappear beneath the calm inexorable blackness of the rising water within her hull!

Clearly the launch had been premature, the reconditioning imperfect; such were the findings of our immediate court of inquiry on the disaster. More capital must be raised, and more radical repairs must be put in hand forthwith. Thanks to an approaching birthday my credit stood high, and accommodation to the extent of a shilling or two was arranged without difficulty. But alas! the more tow and pitch we pressed into the seams, the more they gaped, and the more we hammered, the more the nails worked loose in the rotten planks. And—most ominous of all—more than once the hammer itself went right through the precious hull so quietly and so easily that one was reminded, in a way that made one feel sick with apprehension, of damp short-bread.

It would be pleasant to recount how dogged determination and eight-year-old steadfastness triumphed, and how one by one, many and daunting obstacles were surmounted and difficulties overcome, by pluck, foresight, and good management. But in actual fact, I gave up my salvage project as I had given up my house, as a bad job, or rather, as a job beyond my powers, which at that time I would seem to have consistently over-estimated, or at any rate over-taxed. But a little later the lake at Glasfryn tempted me to yet another bit of naval architecture.

I invented, designed, built and launched a wonderful 'roller-boat' with which to astound the world by skimming about the lake at hitherto undreamt-of speeds. The great secret was a row of casks on axles supporting a frame or chassis that carried the deck. The idea was that as the barrels were rotated by power derived and elaborately transmitted from the commander's legs, the vessel would roll silently over the water with practically no friction and consequently without appreciable effort and with remarkable velocity.

There was a grand launching ceremonial, I remember, only slightly marred by my smashing up a good deal of my ship in unsuccessful attempts to break a bottle of wine on some part of her delicate structure. However, I merely supposed I had just happened upon an indestructible bottle (one must surely, once in a while) and that part of the christening ceremony was quietly abandoned, with regret but no superstitious misgivings.

Even when, on taking the water, she would only float unstably with a steep list to one side or the other, I was not greatly cast down about my ship, for I reckoned she should at any rate float dependably and level if turned upside down. This theory of the designer was at once vindicated by experiment, and in its capsized state the boat displayed admirable stability.

Alas! it had few other qualities. The revolutionary character of the roller-boat had indeed gone quite beyond my intentions. One stood ankle-deep in water on the underside of the deck, the machinery was upside-down somewhere below that, and could only be worked indirectly by turning the barrels round with one's hands. This, it appeared, was very easily done—all too easily as it soon proved, for though one paddled round the dripping barrels at a fine rate, their turning left the boat unmoved.

Then only did I admit defeat and, quitting marine engineering for ever, I proceeded to re-establish my broken credit and self-esteem by a series of easier structural triumphs on land. A jetty, a diving-board, a two-storied wooden 'house', and an ambitious water-power scheme survived for a year or two as monuments to this period of rehabilitation.

Not infrequently I would be laid up, damaged, either actually cut, bruised or strained, or merely bone-tired through attempting some feat of enterprise beyond my strength or skill. When I was about nine I was ill enough for the doctor to be sent for. He did his round on horseback and wore breeches, top boots and a top hat.

I was growing rather fast, being at that time, indeed, both in time and space, roughly half-way between my original inaugural jelly speck and my full-grown six-foot two.

Of course, my mother did her best to discourage such projects as she deemed beyond me, whenever she heard of them, though her policy generally was one of wise non-intervention.

I myself was never much cast down by failure as I was sustained in adversity by a sort of inner fatalism—I took it for granted that the odds would always be against me and accepted it as a law of nature. Being thus resigned, I was I think a rather sober child, by no means unhappy but not often merry either. I was not as strong or as tough as my exploits really required me to be and got too easily tired. But I was truthful and honest and reasonably obedient, there being no reason to be otherwise—and—except in an almost fierce independence—an altogether mild and uninteresting little boy. I liked doing things alone and being on my own and if my employments could be kept secret, so much the better.

I was so self-sufficient, perhaps selfish, that brothers and even parents were not much more than figures in the background of my own absorbing personal life. I had, as I say, done my best to rid myself of expectations, and, rather strangely, I seem to have been without ambitions of any kind beyond quietly surviving, to no particular end. A certain timidity might have been expected to go with all this, but for some reason it did not, and I was physically brave enough and indeed pretty reckless in the running of risks and the taking of chances. Certainly I was not self-satisfied as to my physical make-up. Why should I be pale and freckled and loose-limbed with curly brown hair and a turned-up nose, when I longed to be compact and ruddy with straight black hair, a Roman nose, and slightly bandy legs that seemed to me so much more reliable looking than my own. That was my then ideal—no doubt a composite figure made up from various admired contemporaries.

When I saw my first negro (off a schooner discharging her cargo at Abersoch) I thought how fortunate he was and how very distinguished to have been born black. Yet, I was not envious, I was just quietly resigned to being a rather unlucky person and resolved never to expect too much so as to avoid the cruel pangs of disappointment—such as almost overwhelmed me when a visit to a circus was called off at the last moment because of rain. Nor would I let my affections become engaged too deeply lest I suffer again the agony of returning after a day's carefree sailing with my father to find my guinea pigs' hutch overturned and its six inmates scattered bloody and dead about the lawn.

So, thenceforward, I never kept pets again until middle-aged. But, despite my infant philosophy of not giving hostages to fortune, of not expecting too much from life, I was none the less enterprising and adventurous enough with all sorts of ploys, mostly secret.

Until I went to school I had scarcely been exposed to architecture even in picture books—but had I been, I think it would have provided an instant and absorbing interest to a childhood otherwise devoid of any over-mastering preoccupation. I liked messing about with boats on the lake. I tried a little later, to care about shooting and fishing, but I really liked the idea and its grown-upness rather than the fact, though I did enjoy hunting, largely as exploration. My fatalistic outlook reconciled me to any adverse circumstances clearly beyond my control—that I had been born a boy for instance instead of a girl, and that I had been christened Bertram Clough instead of Reginald or George—two vain and puerile regrets that I well remember.

I was, I should say, a cool and equable child with rare and only moderate attachments—one, for a time, to our gamekeeper Watkin, a boisterous buffoon at times, very strong and agile and devious in his ways, with an admirable talent for the long-range squirting of tobacco juice through his teeth and for subversive comic songs.

I remember my Aunt Hilda teasing me long afterwards by imitating my earnest avowal, 'I believe on Watkin.' Then there was, again briefly, Peggy, the, for the moment, adored six-year-old, whom I had met once and once only, at a rare children's party, and for whom I remember declaring my love on the long drive home in the dark in the family wagonette.

To give a few further clues as to my hereditary make-up: the Clough part of me derives from Denbighshire—my paternal grandmother being the ultimate heiress of Sir Richard Clough of Plas Clough and so on in the Vale of Clwyd—originally a glover in Denbigh and finally Queen Elizabeth's agent in the Netherlands and concerned with Sir Thomas Gresham in the founding of London's Royal Exchange. Michael Burn, in writing a book on the history of spying (*The Debatable Land*) tells me that his researches have discovered top-scret correspondence in cipher between Sir Richard and his Queen's chief minister Cecil, that show him to have been up to his neck in secret service work—as I suppose most crown agents and ambassadors really are even now —and ever have been.

Anyway he apparently did very well for himself as well as for his Queen—spent a lot on building, which of course endears him to me, and was a great one for masques and pageantry of all sorts.

One of his Denbighshire houses, Bach-y-craig (long demolished) in the Dutch style had a cupola on its high-pitched roof from which he studied the stars through a telescope, but where local report insisted, to his embarrassment, that he was communing with the Devil. He married the much-courted Catherine de Berwyn, the second of her four successive husbands, whence her title, of 'Mam Cymry'—'Mother of Wales'.

The next Clough of any celebrity was Arthur Hugh the poet—best known for his somewhat cynical revision of the Ten Commandments into his own decalogue:

> ... Thou shalt not kill, but need not strive
> Officiously to keep alive.
>
> Thou shalt not swear, for by thy curse
> Thine enemy is none the worse ...

and so on.

Also for his poem 'Say Not The Struggle Naught Availeth'—quoted by Churchill at one of the worst crises of the last war.

He was Florence Nightingale's chief confidant and his sister, my godmother, Annie Clough was the first principal of Newnham College, Cambridge.

The Williams part of me is Merionethshire pure and simple—anyhow simple—of Plas Brondanw where my forebears had the good sense to establish themselves some four centuries ago and where I still live. None of them did anything at all notable though my great-grandfather's tombstone at Llanfrothen Old Church records that 'he was the first to introduce sea-banks into Wales'. That was at the end of the eighteenth century and preceded the far more ambitious reclamation works of William Madocks. They both gained quite a lot of poorish land but at the expense of the landscape and for my part, I wish they had left well alone and not meddled.

Thomas Love Peacock evidently agreed with me when he wrote in *Headlong Hall* some hundred and fifty years ago:

They beheld a scene which no other in this country can parallel, and which the admirers of the magnificence of nature will ever remember with regret, whatever consolation may be derived from the probable utility of the works which have excluded the waters from their ancient receptacle. Vast rocks and precipices, intersected with little torrents, formed the barrier on the left: on the right, the triple summit of Moelwyn reared its majestic boundary: in the depth was that sea of mountains, the wild and stormy outline of the Snowdonian chain, with the giant Wyddfa towering in the midst. The mountain-frame remains unchanged, unchangeable; but the liquid mirror it enclosed is gone.

The Ellis part of me is from Glasfryn, Caernarvonshire, where I was brought up and where the most interesting of my ancestors was probably John—born 1721—who seems to have done well for himself by marrying the Brondanw (Williams) heiress, whence Williams-Ellis and the merging of the two estates. Proceeding to collect ecclesiastical benefices he became a proper eighteenth-century pluralist, rector of this and that—vicar of Bangor, archdeacon of Merioneth and so on, and, apparently, managing director of the diocese of Bangor—in the absence of the Bishop, who like so many of his period, was largely an absentee, preferring life in London. From the full-length portrait we have of him—in flaxen wig, saffron coat, lace ruffs, diamond buckles at his knees, he looks far too dandified and fashionable to be the cleric he undoubtedly was, though apparently more of an administrator than a divine. Yet unlike many of his contemporaries he was said to be both just and incorruptible though his own affairs do seem to have benefited substantially from his exertions, along with those of the diocese he so ably ran.

His favourite diversions outside his official duties seem to have been litigation and science—especially geology—the first exemplified by years of acrimonious and expensive law suits with a neighbour and kinsman to determine whether the Lloyds of Trallwyn or the Ellis's of Glasfryn were the rightful occupants of the front pew in Llangwbi Church. I don't know how this grave matter was settled—if at all—but there was a period when each house would send servants along well in advance of the services to occupy the disputed territory if they could against the coming of the rival claimant.

As to his geological knowledge, this led him to suspect that there might well be worthwhile copper deposits around Amlwch in Anglesey, whither he despatched his factotum with metal rods or anodes to test his hunch by suspending them in a nearby spring and bringing them back for his analysis—the result of which was entirely negative. When, some while later, the famous Parys Mountain copper strike was made, he sent for his man to find out exactly how his instructions had in fact been carried out and the wretched fellow confessed that he had gone no further than Clynnog Fawr where he had hung up the rods in St. Benos holy well, and gone off on a two days' drinking spree.

Well knowing of the enromous wealth that the Parys Mountain bonanza had brought to the few lucky families who were in on it, even my father, when feeling poor, would exclaim, 'Oh! If only that rascal had obeyed his orders.'

My maternal grandfather, John Whitehead Greaves, also geologically minded, did better, and was one of the luckier prospectors who were hopefully scratching for slate all over North Wales in the early nineteenth century, to its considerable disfigurement. His reward was the Llechwyth quarries at Blaenau-Ffestiniog which continue to this day, though now in nothing like their former prosperity—a decline shared by most other slate quarries.

On the whole, a harmless, active, rather scholarly lot of ancestors, if, with few notable achievements to their credit, then also with few black sheep, though no doubt with a good deal of friendly nepotism, an amiable enough failing not yet quite extinct, I think, amongst us clannish Welsh.

For example, two of my uncles happening to be the Lords Lieutenant of Merionethshire and Caernarvonshire respectively, it was merely a toss-up as to which of them would first think to make his young nephew a magistrate. I had property qualifications in both their territories—but it was to the Merionethshire County Bench to which I found myself surprisingly elevated whilst I was just beginning my professional career in London with no prospect, near or distant, of actually functioning. That, however, did not seem to matter and anyhow it was a nice cosy avuncular gesture.

In fact I never once sat and was ultimately thrown off the Bench by my younger brother who had become its Chairman, not for neglecting my duties, but because I had reached the age limit, seventy-five or whatever it was, in short for senility. Not a very good record of responsible citizenship it may be thought, but the fact was that for most of the time I was fully occupied with other matters both public and private about which I did really know something, whereas I was then quite out of touch with local Welsh affairs and moreover could not understand or talk the language.

The Anwyls of Parc, adjoining the Brondanw estate, and whose land up the Croesor Valley is now part of it, were amongst my forebears. The last heiress of the place (not my ancestress I would stress) married an Irish baronet Sir Thomas Prendergast. (It was quite a local industry in Georgian times—Irishmen coming over to snap up Welsh heiresses.)

Anyway, someone ferreting through old letters at the British Museum some years back sent me copies of two that he thought might interest me as a family sidelight. They did. The first from Lady Prendergast to H.R.H. the Duke of Cumberland in which she said, 'There was a time when you would deny me nothing. Now you could really please me if you would. I have learnt that the Postmaster Generalship of Ireland is falling vacant. Please, please secure the post for my husband, Sir Thomas.' From him— her once devoted Royal Highness—in response, 'My dear but of course, I have already fixed it.'

It seems that the not too scrupulous Sir Thomas continued to live very cosily withdrawn in his flighty wife's old manor house up our valley on his official salary, presumably employing some wretched underpaid hireling in Dublin to do the actual work.

Those were certainly the days! The Georgian days, when corruption flourished no doubt in Wales as throughout Sidney Smith's England. I wonder how my sober Ellis forebears thought of such goings on—they tending to be university dons and, in later life, parsons or rather squarsons—almost automatically— as was my father.

My grandfather and my great-grandfather too used to ride up to Cambridge every term by leisurely stages on Welsh ponies that they there sold, to return by coach. Maybe the practice was general—and not their own bright and economical idea—I don't know—but it anyhow showed a typically Welsh determination to acquire culture, a determination that—long after their day—resulted in the founding of Wales's own university.

Though considering my ancestors' addiction to lawsuits absurd, can it be that I too am just a little tainted with the same litigiousness? I hope not. Highly allergic to rows of any sort as I have ever been, I none the less do seem to have had an unfortunate capacity for precipitating them, simply through saying or writing too bluntly what I felt to be the truth. Whether in a speech, an article or a review, I would now and again let myself go in an uninhibited tirade against something or someone, generally barbing my well-intentioned shaft with the unsportsmanlike poison of ridicule.

It was that, it seemed, that usually most rankled and engendered threats of actions for libel or slander or whatever, or letters of protest, that had all, somehow, to be most tiresomely dealt with. Yet, knowing all this, I would none the less again write or say something well calculated to provoke someone into violent reaction, as though impelled by some malign imp dedicated to the task of keeping me simmering in perpetual hot water.

Brisk reaction was of course what I wanted—but I did *not* want to be myself further involved which is what too often happened—meaning time-consuming correspondence. I have just come across a mass of old letters surviving from long ago, that illustrates the sort of thing I would let myself in for, the way in which I would get myself tangled up in affairs that were really right outside or only marginally within my anyhow ill-defined province of 'amenities agitator' to the neglect of issues of far greater moment where my intervention might have had some effect. I shall burn and forget them.

Chapter Two

Boyhood

My mother was, most blessedly, the very queen of non-fussers, but where she did try to 'interfere', though unsuccessfully, was in the matter of lessons which from the time I was eight, began to fill all too much of my day. Lessons, given by a series of governesses or occasionally to my older brothers by my father himself, were deemed to be his department.

It may seem odd to later generations that five little boys should have been taught up to the public school stage by governesses, but any accessible elementary schools were then very sub-standard indeed and this was not in fact such an eccentric decision on my parents' part, especially as our governess-in-chief, Miss Skinner, was a graduate of Newnham, in fact, a female tutor.

There was one that came before her, Miss Barker. She, poor gentle thing, suffered cruelly from sick headaches, what today would be called migraine, and no wonder, considering how we treated her, always calling her among ourselves 'the Carcass'. Miss Skinner was utterly different and almost excessively robust, though I never made real friends with her and indeed on one occasion, after a sharp quarrel, made a vow that I never, never would forgive her.

But she had her merits, among others, a brother. I well remember our first sight of him, for it coincided with that of the first safety bicycle that I had ever seen. Always fascinated by construction I realized that Mr. Skinner had ridden into my life all the way from Cambridge on, of all things, *air*, in fat indiarubber tubes pumped tight round spindly wheels. I think Miss Skinner's forte was mathematics, which appealed to my father far more than to any of us children, and I believe she had also read botany—but I can recall no instruction therein or indeed in natural history of any sort from anyone.

From the old-fashioned teacher's point of view I think it very likely that my father had himself been a model pupil—eager and quick to learn, with a good memory and unflagging industry. Certainly he carried off every possible kind of prize and scholarship, both at school and university. First he had learnt to work, then, for years, he had recklessly overworked. To him 'work' was the highest virtue in its own right, and thrift not far below. Therefore we must all learn the meaning and habit of work as early as possible, especially as we were so numerous and would need to earn our several livings without undue delay.

And so it was enacted that our governess should even inject what instruction she might into our empty, sleep-giddy heads for half an hour each morning before our stomachs had been revived and set going by our achingly-longed-for breakfast, between us and which also yawned (*mot juste*) the gulf of family prayers. To all intents and purposes we worked on all through the morning; and though, in spite of my impressions, it cannot have been solid schoolroom, no useful change was left out of it for our own employments.

In the afternoon, work again—after lunch in the summer, in the winter after tea. Oh! those interminable, leaden hours of half-learning and blank not-learning! The bitter contrast between the dead-alive, snuffy hush or drone of the dim schoolroom and the blithe bustle of out-of-doors! That, no doubt, is a memory common to my generation, but in my case the imprisonment was for so cruelly long a term—for a child of eight; and looking back I am clear that for years I was partially stunned and appreciably retarded and upset both physically and mentally by the inordinately long hours we were made to work, or rather, that we were kept from playing.

Unfortunately, my father's great success as tutor of his college and as a coach had turned him, as it happened, into a most dangerous director of studies for his own numerous, not unintelligent, but slowly-maturing children. Very well, if we were dull and slow at our lessons, clearly we must work the longer to make up for our unfortunate natural dilatoriness and backwardness.

That irrelevant mathematical logic of the wrangler overbore the sound psychological instinct behind my mother's protests; and long and firmly were our miserable little noses held down to that drearily trundling grindstone—the schoolroom—which instead of sharpening mine at any rate, gave it a bluntly calloused end that has made it, I fear, needlessly insensitive in some respects and inefficient in others.

Sundays were clouded by fine raiment and religious observances. Sometimes the church services were in English sometimes in Welsh, sometimes justly blended according to the congregation. I attended hundreds, attended *to* very few, and so far as I can tell, was directly affected by none. I merely thought them a nuisance and regretted them as a sad waste of precious out-of-school time of which there was so little.

But we had our Saturday afternoons off, and now and again in the hunting season when there was a meet near by, we would get a Wednesday, too; and on these hunting days, lessons, such as they were, were squeezed in as best they could.

Yet I have an odd memory of really working and really learning on those exciting short-time days. Partly, I suppose, as in honour bound in return for the boon of early release, but mostly, I suspect, because one was so generally alert and stimulated before setting out, and, at the day's end, so contented and fulfilled.

Our ponies were really the principal figures in the landscape or my middle boyhood, which might well be divided into four periods; that of yachting with my father and of sailing and contriving our own boats on the lake; that of hunting and reconnoitring on our ponies; that of the bicycle and more extended exploration, and lastly, that of shooting and of comradeship with the keeper.

Of organized games we had none, nor did we miss or want them. Young cousins and 'neighbours' all seemed to be a half-day's drive away, and the youth of the surrounding villages, being born in Nonconformity, were then forbidden ball games and could anyhow only respond in broken English to our no less mangled Welsh. Thus, though we were geographically and traditionally exactly where we should have been, in the old home of our Ellis forefathers, socially we were extraordinarily isolated and self-sufficient.

It was exactly what my father liked—this retiring to the home of his youth with his active work finished and behind him, and with nothing more exacting to attend to than the rather scattered estate, the home farm, a moderate amount of county business and the bringing up—or rather the schooling—of his five surviving sons. Yet I remember him as by no means notably free from worries, which were often financial and usually groundless. Temperamentally he was exceedingly careful and inclined to regard money spent on anything except the estate or the acquisition of further land as more or less wasted. This caution was tempered by occasional bursts of quite startling recklessness, on the whole, with good results.

On resigning his College living, for instance, he had bought an elegant seventy-ton yawl in addition to the steam launch he already had and seldom used, and then built grand shore quarters for the considerable crew near our seaside house at Abersoch, and did things *en prince* generally for a season. But the yacht's draught was too great to allow of her using the local harbours, the running costs were out of all proportion, and he quickly decided to cut his losses and escape from these inordinate commitments as best he could.

No doubt he really lost money in buying land, as he certainly did on farming, but it was his occasional dabbling in industrial and mining ventures that brought the most painful reverses—whether real or imagined.

'We shall end in the workhouse, depend upon it,' was a favourite phrase that, apparently soothing to my father in some fatalistic way, filled my young imagination at least with a quite real foreboding of coming disaster and destitution. How, at nine, could I possibly support myself—how, for that matter, *ever*?

It became, indeed, an abiding anxiety; and not until I actually found myself on the brink of becoming an architect had I any real confidence in ever being self-supporting.

It was an understood thing that allowances, if any, would be small once our several educations were complete. That 'if any' was the ominous, unnerving and quite unnecessary clause. It seemed to debar all the learned professions and artistic callings save to such precocious brilliance as I clearly lacked.

I am sure it never occurred to my father that his well-intentioned thrift propaganda or his oratorical workhouse flourishes were planting groundless worries in the necessarily literal minds of his children. That with nine hundred and ninety-nine children out of a thousand this very worry was then by no means groundless, was to me a desolating thought.

Though not really rich, I would seem none the less to have inherited or picked up from my father the classic rich man's attitude to money that carefulness of pence and disregard for pounds that often characterize the capitalist. But to have the rather ungracious foibles of the millionaire without the sanctifying millions is liable to irritate one's friends and may seriously embarrass oneself.

I can seldom bring myself to hire a taxi without a twinge, save in extreme emergencies. Liking good food, well served, I am yet inclined to wince at the high cost of high living, and am unable entirely to stifle the kill-joy thought that I have perhaps spent on a dinner for two, already eaten, as much as a mason earns in a week or the price of a thousand bricks. On the other hand, if it is land, or a house or yacht, or car, or furniture or embellishments of any sort, the question of cost is apt to be airily swept aside altogether. I can only quote in extenuation what a very rich tycoon once said, 'Alas! my dear fellow, habits of economy early acquired are so hard to shake off.'

Perhaps this apparent discursiveness needs some categorical justification, so I will sum up as best I may such permanent effects as my childhood seems to have had upon my habits, my character and psychology.

Certainly my apparently inborn instinct for construction was fostered and strengthened, partly by an intoxicating contact with actual building at home, partly by my own always hopeful but generally abortive efforts. In these I was only thwarted by my own lack of strength, experience and resources: my family's attitude being one of benevolent neutrality. Even the tantalising exile from home for those marvellous 'might-have-been' years when the incantation of masons' hammers and carpenters' saws wrought an enchantment on the place that I could scarcely bear to think of—even that poignant 'loving and losing' probably sharpened my desire and made the act of building seem more magical than ever.

I have recounted some of my childish failures, but I must confess that what chiefly impresses me in retrospect is my enterprise. Certainly it was about all I had, save perhaps a certain naïve ingenuity, but it was something. It was in judgement that I failed, as how could I not?

Indeed, this sudden and unpremeditated looking back into my own infancy makes me feel a new tenderness towards the blundering contrivances of the very young—those irrational, messed-up botches, so ludicrous, even irritating to the mature, if one only regards them with the eye of common sense. I begin to see how crushingly the odds are tilted against the child in its struggle with material things, with the elements, with gravity, with ideas. Everything is so inconsiderately big and heavy, everywhere is so far from everywhere else, the intractability of matter is a staggering obstacle to almost every enterprise, yet the child is not daunted.

It might be that the great men of this world are just those who contrive to keep the sublime valour of their childhood. They could scarcely add to it. Also, if I can take myself as anything like the norm, the child is surprisingly philosophical in adversity. Somehow I was never heartbroken at my recurring failures to realize my multifarious projects—merely crestfallen, and that not for long.

In retrospect I catch myself regarding the spectacle of my eight- or nine-year-old self, repeatedly struggling to achieve this or that cherished design with so little success, as pathetic, but that is mere grown-up sentimentality. True I was constantly getting hard knocks, both physical and spiritual, but I was learning things, and on the whole to be learning is to be happy. Anyway, I do trace to these and other early failures a certain ability to take disappointments easily, and the faculty, which has its drawbacks, of quickly forgetting what it is not pleasant to remember.

To what extent, if any, excessive lessons may indeed have taken the edge off my intellect it is clearly impossible to say, but if there is that to debit them with, there is this to their credit—I did learn some patience with unpleasant tasks and the power of application if not of concentration.

Not that I exercise such patience unless I must—unpleasant tasks are still unpleasant, and I am liable to defer them lest they may haply turn out to be no longer necessary, or in case my sudden death or some other contingency may honourably relieve me of any obligation in the matter.

Our isolated prairie-like existence of this time is probably rich in effects if one could only trace them—our Swiss Family Robinson life in what was practically a foreign land with a foreign tongue. My father could talk Welsh perfectly, as was the family tradition that alas! ended with him, he indeed being created a bard with the title 'Sean Pentierch'. My mother learnt it tolerably well, but I and my brothers had but a smattering picked up from Welsh nursemaids and servants, which severely restricted our social contacts outside the family. Within it I should say that, whilst harmonious enough, we all rather tended to be self-sufficient and to go our several ways. In the way we respected each other's rights and liberties—not to mention eccentricities—I should say we were a rather civilized community, though in the political rather than in the cultural sense.

My father could not abide what he called 'strangers' in the house, so that the grand new spare bedrooms were very rarely opened, nor did he at all approve of 'gadding about', so hardly ever did we see anyone even outside. I remember aching and aching for a sight of someone besides the family, even of some old professor of astronomical mathematics from Cambridge. I recall the visit of an Archbishop as a long-looked-forward-to and long-remembered treat.

Something, at any rate, has produced in me so oddly mixed a social complex that I cannot well define it. I like and do not like being with people—I like and do not like being alone; and these conflicting desires and their converses interweave and co-exist in so confusing a fashion that I am seldom sure what I really want in this regard. My impression is that, broadly speaking, I like seeing people for short periods at reasonable intervals—with solitude in between. Domesticity I merely regard as a heightened, superior sort of solitude.

But this question of how much and how often and how long I want *people*, and just who and when and why, is that which I find the hardest of all to answer. The Spanish, less ambivalent than I, have a rather brutal saying, 'Guests are like fish. After three days they stink.' Still, I do not know what they mean.

Our empty and far-away Welsh countryside offered few spectacular opportunities for enterprise, with a pony ride as the limiting radius of our activities which, however, luckily just included the sea at two points, one small town, half a dozen minimal villages, three or four minor mountain tops and a couple of other country houses.

Thus circumscribed one observed the happenings within one's little world with minute attention and the comings and goings and doings of all its few inhabitants and their rare visitors from outer space.

One such that I rather took to was a bearded and beery sea captain who was courting my nurse, but of whom my mother disapproved, incautiously referring to him within my hearing as 'no better than a barrel on legs'. I thought this a splendid description and tactlessly asked my nurse if she didn't think so too. Most emphatically she did not—nor he—and to my dismay the affair ended explosively in tears and lamentations, my own mingling with my nurse's. My first of many failures in tact.

A few—a very few—recollections of the far-away world in which we lived belong to this time.

I occasionally went with my mother to the village school. This was a single classroom where all the children large and small sat with their slates on a sort of wide staircase chanting their lessons. Then I was aware of the holy wells, where clothes were still held down by stones for 'purification'.

Certainly I was not made blasé by precocious dissipation. I went to two Christmas Trees, one circus, one menagerie, two children's dances, and a lantern lecture on Palestine in the local chapel—in Welsh.

My father's old academic friends who were now and then invited to stay, were amiable enough, but so ancient as to seem to a small boy almost of another species. He himself had been born in the reign of King William IV and his own tutor, then aged ninety-eight, who was one of his guests, was a survivor from a yet earlier time.

I found such grave and reverend seniors sadly disappointing as I had vaguely Quixotic visions of dons and the Cambridge sort seemed sadly inferior to the Spanish.

Earls I felt quite sure would be better value, for did they not wear brilliant robes and shining coronets and were they not haughty, handsome and imperious and probably lavishly generous to admiring little boys? Not so however our kinsman who had some to stay with us—a mild mousey little man—the best of do-gooders with a heart of gold, as I later discovered, but not at all my romanticised idea of nobility. On beholding five foot two of meagre diffidence clad in crumpled tweeds, a straggly beard failing to conceal a too loosely knotted tie below an ill-fitting flannel collar my disappointment was bitter. Oh stars and garters! Oh velvets, tassels and ermine! How grossly my great-aunt's scrap-books of pasted-in historic notables with their robes of real fabric and tinsel had deceived me! It was too bitter a let-down, and I instantly reacted to the shock with 'I don't think I want to walk him round the lake after all'—a chilling retraction unfortunately overheard by our guest. Yet another failure in tact but covered up by some plausible parental excuse that camouflaged open rudeness.

The fact was—and still is—that appearances are very important to me, no doubt unduly so, whether of persons or places, and actuality falling short of my usually sanguine preconception, I am always proportionately disappointed. Unquestionably, too, I was born with a strange hankering, no less, for the spectacular, the showy and the grand—strange because my parents and immediate forebears at least had all been for prudent plain-living and against any kind of worldly display at all. I have had consciously to fight down my innate and inordinate craving for gorgeous elaboration, regal splendour and even mere opulent display lest vulgar profusion should overwhelm my basic sense of fitness and propriety.

I was quite early aware of my weakness for pomp and circumstance but soon realized that fanciful exuberance was proper only to special occasions and by no means to everyday living. So, whenever designing, my unusual approach has been first to doodle unrestrainedly, working in all the exciting and jolly quirks that occurred to me and then gradually but ruthlessly (and a little regretfully) to cut all or nearly all of them out again and shave the thing down to what seemed to me its essentials, leaving it as it were, a bare tree pruned and shorn of its blossoms but remaining none the less manifestly a tree *capable* of flowering.

Then, thus reduced and disciplined, I might finally allow it an almost grudging little flower here or there, or at least a cautious bud—a potential rather than a factual richness, ornamentation implied rather than actually applied.

But this was a later prudence for, as a child, I just lamented that my lot was cast in Victorian nonconformist Wales instead of in some such sparkling setting as decadent eighteenth-century Venice, where I would of course have had my father a dilettante prince with a Baroque palace, a state barge, gorgeous mistresses, negro pages with monkeys, painted ceilings, glittering chandeliers, banquets, masked balls, processions, fireworks—the lot.

All of which would have seemed utter hell to my actual father, staid, studious and withdrawn, who seemed perfectly content in our rather bleak isolation with his Greek and Latin reading, his mathematical and chess problems, his farming and his shooting.

There were however less unworldly uncles and also other neighbours who, though all at some distance, did afford occasional glimpses of a more glittering world. Some of them drove four-in-hands and my romantic and snobbish little heart would swell within me when, after melodious tootling, one of these splendid coaches drew up with a clatter and jingle at our door.

Though the houses they came from were certainly big enough, none quite met my strict ideas of formal stateliness, even a town hall-like stucco house, Glynllifon, in debased Palladian, where a really impressive pillared and pedimented portico had failed to impose its discipline on lumpish additions. But you did drive crunchingly round a great formal fountain to alight at a shallow flight of steps beneath a wide glass canopy where white-painted stoneware goddesses upheld the clustered globes of gas lamps. Outside there was a fine park with noble trees, but within, the entrance hall alone lived up to my exacting standard of aloof dignity—a wide branching grand staircase at the end of a perspective of marbled columns, elegant footmen in blue and silver liveries seeming the only fit figures for such a theatrically contrived background.

But the rest of the house was all pretty null and vacuous, its pictures trivial, its furniture an unselected hotch-potch of the good and gimcrack, its large unused library a morgue these many years, and no stray book at large anywhere except Debrett, Ruff's *Guide to the Turf* and suchlike in the smoking-room, and the albums in the drawing-room.

Indeed all our country house neighbours were thus philistine—three ran their own packs of hounds, two had yachts, all took their shooting with earnest seriousness, few had travelled at all; only one was politically active, though others took some part in local affairs as Lords Lieutenant or on the Bench, and none was really literate though the only two who could speak Welsh may have picked up a little culture from their far more cerebral tenants and humbler neighbours. All jolly and friendly enough, though I now understand that it was not the miles of bad roads alone that accounted for our infrequent meetings. Both my parents and they must have found each other's company pretty unrewarding. . . .

But one of my mother's sisters, my aunt Hilda Greaves, and one house, were a shining exception to this disappointing rule. Of only moderate size and not grand at all, yet with an appealing air of quietly assured good breeding and of friendly welcome, Tanrallt was a long low white Regency house spread along a high hillside terrace backed by cliffs and hanging beech woods, with its deep verandah facing the sun and the sea. It had been built by William Madocks (of the Embankment) up above his little new town of Tremadoc, and he had there entertained much enlightened company including Sheridan and Peacock and where for a spell Shelley was his embarrassed and embarrassing tenant. My mother was born and died there, but my sharpest memory of it was while it was the home of this remarkably astringent and lovable maiden aunt. She read the latest books, she had friends who were writers. Unlike my mother, she did not draw or paint, but with impeccable taste and rare discretion, born of wide reading and her own alert intelligence, she rescued the house from careless neglect and so lovingly restored and furnished it that any Jane Austen character walking into any one of its rooms would have felt as entirely at home as did my entrancing aunt.

Many years later, I found for her a clever Belgian to restore the defaced chiaroscuro murals in the dining-room and I recall her own search for just the right shade of watered silk for the panels in the drawing-room. For years she collected books and prints bearing on the house and on its earlier inmates, and I watched with sympathy and delight her gradual perfecting of the always charming garden her erection of the Shelley memorial therein and, most of all, I was aware of how she herself was the vitalizing centre of the whole enchanting ensemble.

Though there was plenty of family building going on in my boyhood—three big houses for uncles, and my father busily enlarging his—this aunt was the only accessible relative with any real knowledge of architecture, even though my mother had a genuine feeling for it and a considerable sense of period. My father's architectural interests were confined to construction and equipment—his chief contribution to our rebuilding in about 1890 being the planning and carrying out of a reservoir with a long mill-race to a distant overshot water wheel that worked saws and planers for the contractors' joiners, pumped water, produced electricity for the house, and ran the farm machinery a quarter of a mile away by means of a patented system of wires and levers that were the wonder of the whole neighbourhood. So too of course was the electric light and there cannot have been many within a five-mile radius who did not sooner or later turn up to marvel at it, begging to be given the 'shock' which, it was believed, was a sovereign cure for rheumatism.

But much more daring innovations were being introduced by my Uncle Dick Greaves in his far more ambitious house Wern—

he being a skilled engineer and one of the leading gadgeteers of his day.

He had his own fully equipped machine shop where he and a little band of devoted craftsmen made every sort of contrivance first for his own house and estate and then for his neighbours'—a turret clock for the stables, a hydraulic railway (that children could ride on and did) from kitchen to dining-room, a chemical refrigerator in the cellars (that exploded), chimes of bells on every landing and in every corridor rung by remote control from the butler's pantry to ensure punctuality at meals—the tunes on Sunday being those of hymns. The gates at the drive-end were operated by levers within the lodge, closets could be flushed by hot water in winter, there was a telephone from the garden tea loggia to the pantry, a private railway siding for the delivery of coal and a 'hot man' made of copper in my uncle's own image on which his wet clothes were hung and buttoned for shapely drying.

Inevitably there came a day when his spanking team of chestnuts and the elegant coach were seen no more, replaced by a monstrous high-slung steam carriage with fat twin funnels at the back, usually belching black smoke but sometimes flames. In the beginning it was—despite its reputed power—a far less reliable vehicle than its predecessor, but love conquereth all, and my uncle's devotion and endless ingenious alterations and improvements gradually transformed it into a really serviceable though still rather chancy and very smelly conveyance.

One oddity was that sometimes at the bottom of a particularly steep hill the machine would be deliberately halted for a panting minute or two to get up a head of steam sufficient for the effort of climbing. But nursed by him, it managed the same extended driving tours that he had previously made by coach, and he loyally stuck to steam cars until long after they in turn had become a curiosity. He had really been bred to steam, for as a young man he had helped to build the engines of a small steamer at Caernarvon and then sailed out in her as engineer and, despite fire and other misadventures, finally reached Japan, which from his accounts he found, in 1870, utterly enchanting.

Back home, his job was to help run the family Blaenau-Ffestiniog slate quarries, which he did up to his death at over ninety with great technical ability. He could be extremely amusing in his brisk and rather cynical way and was much admired and liked by his men—and by me.

His elder brother, my Uncle Jack, was a rather remoter figure —tall, like all the Greaves', with a fine full beard—and splendid indeed when wearing his full dress Lord Lieutenant's uniform, scarlet tail-coat, epaulettes, sword and white-feathered cocked hat for all the world like a Crimean general. He lived to be ninety-eight, and held this and other offices until he was well over eighty when he was also still hunting his own pack of beagles. Both he himself and we, his nephews, would have had far more fun had he not unfortunately married a dragon of the very strictest rectitude.

My jolly Uncle Dick on the other hand, who declared that his 'big brother had enough worthiness for two' was extravagantly hospitable and ultra-modern and more than up-to-date in most things though he had a weakness for puns. I remember one extremely elaborate one: being president of the Royal Agricultural Society whose show that year (only) was at Park Royal on the edge of London, he was also judge of the root section. My aunt, fearful of growing fat was meantime undergoing a course of massage at their hotel—Browns—and when my uncle was asked about their trip to London he said, 'Oh, all right, though I did feel it a bit hard to return from a whole day quizzing turnips to find my wife being mangled by a Swede.'

I had seven uncles and aunts on my mother's side, and all of them had strong though greatly different individualities. I also greatly liked and admired another of my mother's sisters, my godmother Aunt Connie, Lady Smyth. Very handsome, downright, outspoken, merry, impatient of formality and protocol. I gathered as I began to understand more about my elders, that she had been something of a problem to her adored little general, Sir Henry, when he held various governorships including that of Malta, whence by the time I went to school, she used to send me cases of splendid oranges. Also she would send me occasional copies of the 'Mafeking News' or whatever it was that the ever-newsworthy Robert Baden Powell published during the siege—he being also her nephew by marriage—so adding further to my prestige and popularity.

I had another much admired but seldom seen uncle—very handsome, jolly, generous and six foot seven tall. He had inherited a fine Scottish estate from an uncle of his and with it a famous cellar which last, most unhappily, proved his undoing and led to his ultimate downfall and disappearance.

His would-be benefactor had himself been the tallest member of Parliament of his day, a banker and an art connoisseur and had sought to bless his favourite nephew by leaving him all he had and making it quite unnecessary for him ever to do a stroke of work or bother his head about anything or anybody. This so happily remembered uncle was finally shut away incommunicado with his loyal valet as sole confidant. The moral of this sad ending of a career that had promised brilliance was not allowed to be lost upon us boys who were anyhow thoroughly indoctrinated with the virtues of sobriety and steady work.

Now and again I would be taken to see neighbouring squires who were not members of the family, and pretty eccentric some of them were. I suppose it was as a middle-aged schoolboy that my father took me to stay with our gaily unpredictable bachelor neighbour Fred Wynne, whose grandfather had himself dreamed up, built and garrisoned Fort Belan on the Menai Straits to repel Napoleon's threatened invasion. For this patriotic gesture (though I cannot but feel that it was largely for the fun of it all as the 'threat' at that part of the coast must have been pretty minimal) he was created Baron Newborough. When he died he was buried at the foot of the ruined tower of St. Mary's Abbey on Bardsey Island which he owned besides the fort and a couple of big houses on the mainland and, so it seemed, a large part of Caernarvonshire. This Fred had inherited everything as his father left it away from the title through some quarrel with his firstborn, sourly remarking that he disapproved of 'the worship of the rising son', an impish quirkiness that was certainly transmitted intact to our entertaining but incalculable host. The Fort was everything my young imagination could possibly have asked of it with its deep moat and drawbridge, its ramparts bristling with cannon, neat pyramids of balls alongside, a dock and warehouses full of nautical gear and machines, ample living quarters surrounding the square within the ramparts and a caretaker 'Governor' whose impressive duty it was to hoist and lower the flag that floated high above the arched gateway from dawn to sunset whenever the owner was in residence.

The occasion for our visit was to accompany our host on the maiden trip of his brand new steam yacht *Firefly* to Bardsey Island, there to inspect and arrange for repairs to the family monument.

After breakfast we set off in Fred's steam pinnace up the Straits to Caernarvon, there to collect 'Mr. Jones the tombstone' as the monumental expert—a gleaming little launch with a tall polished brass funnel—about which, however, there had just been an 'incident'.

Though not really much of a sailor, Fred Wynne was none the less a member of the Royal Yacht Squadron whose rules, etiquette and protocol are all notoriously terrific—or were. Further along the Straits, on the Anglesey side, dwelt another member, Sir Richard Williams-Bulkeley of Baron Hill, Beaumaris who, as Commodore, wielded almost godlike power—which, indeed, he delighted to exercise. One unlucky day he chanced to see through his binoculars this elegant little pinnace steaming along with the all-but-holy White Ensign flying from its stern staff. Now there is (or was) an inflexible rule that the yachts of members to which the right to fly the said ensign has been granted, may also display it on such tenders as are capable of being hoisted aboard *only*, provided that they themselves are on board.

The launch in question was far too large, or its mother-yacht not large enough, for this condition to be complied with, as the Commodore well knew, whence a stern rebuke for our crestfallen host. The *Firefly* herself was, I would guess, of some hundred tons Thames measurement and, of all things, paddle-wheeled, because our host liked the sound of its flip-flap on the water. It must have been the last steam yacht to be so propelled for I should think at least a generation.

Apart from the monument ploy, as overlord of the island, our host was paying an overdue ceremonial visit to his viceroy 'the King' of the island with whom we took tea.

The tea itself was memorable, as Bardsey teas were apt to be, and lobsters of unusual splendour are—or used to be—no more remarkable on a tea-table than are shrimps elsewhere. But what caught and held my boyish interest was the regalia displayed on the dresser—including a somewhat cracker-like crown which our host duly put on before delivering a short Welsh speech of welcome, to which Fred graciously responded (in English).

But it is to the fabled burial of 20,000 'saints' on Bardsey that it owes its chief celebrity. The journey, first to this furthest tip of Caernarvonshire and then across the boiling strait to the Blessed Isle, must, in the age of faith, have been hazardous indeed, especially for a corpse, and the saintly rank that a Bardsey burial seemed to bestow must have been dearly paid for in hardship and fatigue—not by the principal, certainly, but by his patient bearers. So difficult indeed was the journey that three pilgrimages to the island's abbey of St. Mary counted as being equal in merit to one to Rome. It was commonly said that his lordship chose his burial place in the hope that such a mass uprush of saints all around him at the Resurrection must ensure his own inconspicuous arrival in their midst.

Unlike Belau, Brynkir Hall had no eccentric resident owner—or none that I ever saw. One of the largest houses, only just within our visiting radius, it had stood forlornly empty for many years, its traditional family represented only by a clutch of unmemorable memorials in its little church. There were of course all sorts of titillating rumours about the place and its mysteriously absentee owner, and one day in my teens we drove over with a picnic lunch to reconnoitre and to confirm or dispel them. What we found was a vast and sprawling pile of sombre early Victorian masonry that had monstrously overwhelmed the demure Regency villa which had itself replaced the original seventeenth-century manor house—the former still surviving incongruously as part of the great house, the latter but a ruin in its garden.

What was most surprising was to find this already intimidating muddle being still further added to—a building gang being engaged in throwing out yet another wing in the forlorn hope, apparently, that it might somehow unsnarl the impossible tangle that successive additions had produced—one new wing crazily blocking out daylight from the last and obstructing access. Had there ever been an architect of any sort involved he must have been mad, whilst the latest addition could only have been designed, if designed at all, by one who had failed as a chapel architect, so unhappy were its feeble attempts at ornamentation in lugubrious cement. Wandering off through the dim and dusty interior to the far end of the house, the pleasant fragrance from the formidable pitch-pine staircase being erected in the new hall gradually gave way to the doomful smell of active dry rot of which too there were visible signs in plenty.

'Oh yes,' agreed the foreman, 'pretty bad and of course getting worse all the time—but we have no orders about that—our job is to get this here new bit finished.' But it never was finished—and itself fell into semi-ruin—as it deserved to do—unused. I later gathered that the ill-starred place had been bedevilled by some eccentric clause in a will that made further additions, no matter what, a condition of inheritance. My Uncle Dick told me how as a boy, alerted by rumour, he had gone up to Brynkir, which he found completely deserted both by family and staff. Prowling round and pressing his nose against the dining-room windows he saw a large table all laid for breakfast, obviously hurriedly abandoned with eggs half-eaten, teacups half-full and chairs all anyhow. The explanation of this *Marie Celeste* drama seems to have been that one of the sons of the house had been found to have run away with the governess and that the whole household had rushed off hither and thither in pursuit.

My uncle later bought the Brynkir estate for the sake of the shooting and many were the lunches I attended in that vast and echoing dining-room—the only room still reasonably useable. During the First World War it billeted German prisoners, and great was my uncle's distress when these enterprising captives discovered an unsuspected cellar still full of excellent wines—which they generously—and wisely—shared with their guards. It was only the discovery of a monumental pile of obviously distinguished wine bottles that—too late—gave the game away. Before my time there had been at Brynkir a Russian-type vehicle drawn by three horses, troika-wise. A man being tried for his life for murder and on the verge of conviction for lack of an alibi, suddenly remembered that, when in Pwllheli market on the relevant day as he claimed, he had been startled to see this outlandish turn-out. It was proved that the troika had indeed been in Pwllheli that day—his claim was accepted and he was *not* hanged as had been confidently expected.

Chapter Three

School and Holidays

Both Frederick Sanderson and Oundle, though still obscure, were just beginning to be heard of, and some Cambridge friend of my father recommended him to go and see them. With a scientific or engineering career in view for me, it was to Oundle that he ultimately sent me, and thither I went, straight from home, for the 1897 summer term—the only new boy in the whole school.

Off I went wearing a bowler hat, black jacket and tie, and pin-striped trousers instead of the tweeds of home. Everything was new and strange to me including even my own reflection in the looking-glass.

From the point of view of happiness, it was not a very good plan and I can remember the mixture of incredulity and dismay that I felt when assured from the chapel pulpit that I was then and there experiencing the happiest days of my whole life. Why? I think it must be that all the jolly schoolboys become school-masters in due course, and it is thus that this monstrously untrue generalization is handed out to generation after generation of bewildered children.

Probably the happiest sort of schoolboy is the 'early ripening' sort—precocious and athletic, quick at book-learning, and fully matured in the early twenties into the active, social, limited, unimaginative kind of young man with a college cap or two and a middling degree that used to staff our public schools.

To us Oundle boys of the 'nineties, Sanderson, who was to become famous as an educational pioneer, did not do himself justice. He did not explain himself—perhaps he could not explain himself—and uninterpreted to the censorious young, many of his acts and pronouncements seemed fantastically wrong-headed. Looking back, one wonders whether he was so sure of himself and his ultimate ends as to feel no need for present justification, or whether, doubting the issue of his experiment or his own abilities or methods, he hesitated to declare his aims and disclose his hand until the system had been proved by results.

No doubt, too, he had to go warily and be guarded in his speech and keep an eye on the school governors and the parents, for the premature scaring or scandalising of either might well mean his being deprived of his real medium of self-expression, the school itself.

And what was it that he had to express, this iron-willed soft-spoken headmaster? A belief in equal opportunities for all, in the discipline, satisfaction and usefulness of hard work, in cooperation as against competition, in education as against examination successes, the brotherhood of man as against a narrow patriotism, the service of mankind as against self-advancement; of a school of good citizens as against a small aristocracy of scholarship and a ruck of mediocrities.

He hated caste and privilege with their hollow pretensions and that inequality of wealth that gave them support and countenance. He mistrusted athleticism, deprecated bloodsports, was more interested in the present than the past and in the future than in either, and in pure science more than in anything else save the general progress of the human race.

Altogether a very surprising, modern-minded radical—this comfortable-looking, middle-aged man—surprisingly at any rate as the new headmaster of an ancient and rather moribund school.

Yet had he been able to reveal himself more clearly and definitely he would, I am certain, have found a group of us boys ready and ardent to put his quickening ideas into active practice. But the highly conventional and matter-of-fact schoolboy intelligence was incapable of bridging the non-conducting vacuum that the Head's inarticulateness left between his apparently unrelated acts and any apprehended standard of life and conduct. Without a specific 'Sanderson's Revised Standard of Values' and a 'Sanderson's Chart of Life and Service' we young voyagers were often sadly at sea and out of our reckoning as to what was the meaning of this or that enactment or of this or that dark saying.

He could get angry, tremendously angry. On the whole I think that made for respect. His dramatic explosions of anger—those sudden unaccountable thunderbursts from out an apparently clear sky were occasions not soon to be forgotten by those present, especially by those conscious of ill-doing—which meant most of us. When the bolt fell, and the victims had been told to present themselves at the Head's school study for retribution, we who had suffered the ordeal in person knew the awful uncertainties of their situation. He exercised his punitive functions at a white heat of passion, perhaps because then and only then could he trust himself to operate at all. I discovered later that his wrath was painfully pumped up for the occasion. To the malefactors, however, this explanation did not occur, and we merely knew that, having sown the wind in some form or another, we were fated to reap the whirlwind—almost literally—a hail of swishing cane strokes that seemed almost to envelop one, as the attack usually had more of *élan* than of definite objective. The expiatory strokes were liable to fall on one's back or legs, one's hands or forearms —departures from the orthodox practice much canvassed by the school as breaches of the unwritten charter of schoolboy rights and liberties—as possibly illegal and even actionable. The matter, however, never got further than academic discussion. We were discussing a question of style rather than of principle. Corporal punishment, so far as I was concerned, brought with it its own consolations of martyrdom—an almost comfortable glow of exultation, pride in one's fortitude, a consciousness of being the object of general sympathy and interest, and a feeling that one had expiated one's crime, that bygones were bygones, and that one could forthwith and honourably prepare for some new misdeed. It was not until after my day that Sanderson finally abolished all punishment, as he also abolished all prizes and rewards, as part of his gradual policy of substituting co-operation for competition and of merging the individual in the group or team.

When he was in form, his science lessons were a pure joy. He would whimsically put himself on the level of his class and join in the pursuit of some (to us) new piece of knowledge with a humour and ingenuity that made the demonstration an intoxicating adventure, a raid into new and unknown territory that ultimately brought our morning's objective into sight as a blazing revelation. One longed that he might guide one further and more often, but with the constant growth of the school, the headmaster inevitably rather ate up the teacher. I think he particularly liked teaching divinity, but if we were using the instruments of scientific research, as we did, I was impatient that they should be employed on anything so academic and remote as biblical history. I wanted to go on making the thrilling and illuminating 'discoveries' that natural science yielded so miraculously under the headmaster's guidance. Who could really care about Assurbanipal or the Syrian succession when Boyle and Dalton were waiting for us in the laboratory? No doubt the divinity lessons were reckoned as providing the literary factor in our education for, though the system was later changed, in my day boys on the science and engineering sides were shown no other path to Parnassus. . . . No, I am wrong! Once and once only we were given an essay to write. I remember the subject yet, and I vividly recall my thrill of delight at this rare opportunity for written self-expression, and even something of what I wrote.

The many rare qualities and the greatheartedness of Sanderson are remembered by many people who interest themselves in education, thanks largely to the piety of two books by H. G. Wells, with one of which I helped him.

With advancing years, with the triumph of his ideals and the realization of so many of his aims, Sanderson mellowed and softened in a delightful way, his power of expression increased, his vision ranging far beyond his own or any other school into the distant future of the human race.

He displayed latterly, perhaps above all things, an amazing sense of proportion; a realization indeed of what were the great things and what the small; what stood for true human progress and what was reactionary and anti-social. He became a disturbing though amiable exposer of all shams and pretensions, possessing, as he himself asserted, a 'secret touchstone' by which he tried the worth of all actions and professions. His own set of values he continued to keep steadfastly inviolate and constant, untouched by any taint of opportunism, unwarped by any concessions to expediency. Certainly F. W. Sanderson is one of the friends I find myself especially wishing were still alive.

As a schoolboy I do not think I could have been considered 'a success'. Athletically, though I did everything, I did nothing really well and little with much zest, though I did rather enjoy football and played in the school fifteen, and won, from time to time, quite an array of nasty little electro-plated sports and rowing cups. Organized games were compulsory, and on the whole, disliking both games and compulsion, I spent most of my time on the playing field wishing I were doing something quite different somewhere else.

I trace an abiding detachment from unpleasant duties to my forced and perfunctory performances on the cricket field. I would be bitterly conscious of yet another golden afternoon wasted in tedious lounging or meaningless running about, when, if the world were not mad, I reflected, I might have been revelling in the same sunshine miles away in exploring some fresh part of that enchanted countryside. School, meals, games, chapel, roll-call, lock-up and bounds on the one hand; on the other, finger posts with enticing and melodious names upon them—Fotheringhay, Barnwell, Lilford, Kings Cliffe, Rockingham, Stoke Doyle, Warmington, Polebrook, Warton Waterville and the rest—the meandering yet navigable river, maps and guides, and most poignant of all, woods, villages, and church steeples to be seen in the blue distance and on the horizons of that softly rolling country—but never, never to be visited.

Though I chafed bitterly at the day's routine, so obviously devised to make a satisfactory reconnaissance impossible, I am ashamed to confess I only once broke out of the little circuit to which the time limits confined us. It was the desire to explore a very notable Elizabethan ruin, Lyveden New Bild, that drove me to this one breakaway from obedient docility. I remember it all vividly to this day, but not the punishment, whatever it was, so that I cannot well plead ferocious reprisals as an excuse for my subsequent lack of enterprise. I never defied authority again, and it is one of my abiding regrets that I tamely suffered it, thus to waste a very large part of my school life.

Still the little market-town of Oundle itself was, and yet is, a delight—Tudor, Georgian and early Victorian all good-naturedly and neatly packed together in their demure grey habits of that favoured stone country, dominated by the up-rushing silver-coloured spire of the great parish church in their midst. To walk through its friendly streets or around its grave little market-place was a privilege and a delight of which I never tired. Just because they promised annual 'outings', I joined the photographic society and—by a series of discreditable shifts—the choir.

My great reward was Kirby Hall. For as long as I live I shall remember my first sight of that lovely shell, its long grey flank catching the golden light of a July evening, the diamonds of its leaded casements flashing and glowing, the great mullioned windows in the court shadowed and blank where the glass had fallen away. Ivy and nettles, elder and briar, roofless galleries and grass-grown parapets—yet there were those still alive who had dined and slept there, who remembered the tapestries, who had trod the marble stairs since burned for lime, who had heard the great clock chime in the gatehouse tower.

Nothing, certainly could have been more stickily romantic—this slow decline of a great house into ruinous decay through the negligence of its noble owners—midsummer evening glamour—the exhilaration of 'the year's outing', and, on top of all, what I still hold to be the most gracious example of Elizabethan building in the whole of England.

No wonder it 'got' me. I dreamed about it, I wrote about it and tried to draw it. It should certainly be counted as one of the nails in my architectural coffin. How tremendously I should have enjoyed trying to record my impressions of that visit in an essay! 'On seeing Kirby Hall for the first time.' Why were we never asked to do anything of the sort? Why, in five years, was I only once invited to express myself at all in English prose? Because, I suppose, no school can be everything and at that time Oundle was

School and Holidays

very militantly 'modern' and seemed to have no time for the arts and little for the humanities.

I loved science and geometry and excelled in both; at French, which I abominated, I was almost feeble-minded, on one occasion getting only one per cent in an examination that then was and I dare say still remains, the public-school record.

'Art' was represented by a few plaster casts that I dimly remember on an upper shelf somewhere, and by the headmaster's collection of coloured lantern slides of Italian Primitives, which were, however, chiefly displayed as illustrations to Scripture.

To both of these manifestations I reacted violently and save in the matter of architecture and scenery, which were not spoilt for me by official patronage of any sort, I finished my schooldays as a rather bigoted Philistine. Passionately as I should have drunk in any humanistic and sympathetic instruction in architecture or building, had there been such, I am at least thankful that my love was not weakened and cheapened by any perfunctory exposition.

Going home for the holidays I was of course struck by the many differences between midland England and the north Wales of the 'nineties. Some of the primitive arrangements still surviving around us were in complete contrast, both with what I saw in England and to the ingenious modern innovations of my Uncle Dick and even of my father. I remember the installation of a great new dog-wheel (now illegal, despite the dog's obvious enjoyment) to do the churning at one of our farms. At some, candles were still made by the successive dipping of rows of wicks tied to sticks into crocks of melted tallow—a fascinating though smelly process.

Most farm churns and chaff-cutters and such were worked by horse-mills if not by hand, though wherever any sort of stream favoured, little overshot water-wheels were being installed. Local farm transport was by two-wheeled carts, very small in the hilly parts, and for really rough going, by heavy wooden sledges. I never saw a four-wheeled wagon until I got to England, nor a steam-roller, for we were left to consolidate our Welsh roads with our own crunching wheels. At intervals, heaps of smallish rocks would be dumped at the roadside to be broken down to potato size by some weather-beaten elder with a wire-gauze eye-shield, an old sack over his shoulders. He, equipped with his long-handled hammer, shovel and wheelbarrow, would keep his allotted section of the highway in such passable shape as he could. And passable enough they were for the slight, slow, traffic of the time and I recall no complaints save of winter mud and summer dust which were accepted as being just as inevitable as the weather.

The first motor car that I ever saw was when out on a Sunday walk from school in the spring of 1895. A splendid 'C' sprung open landau swayed round a bend in a cloud of white dust, with a liveried and cockaded footman perched high up on the box alongside the similarly dressed driver—'horseless carriage' indeed! I can give the exact date, 15 May, because I had just been glorying in the spring loveliness of the beech avenue at Lilford Park and have somehow remembered it every year ever since as about the time to repeat—somewhere—this spring appointment with my favourite of all trees.

No doubt partly because of its very rarity, machinery of any sort held then and for some time thereafter a great fascination for me—the annual visit of the old steam thrashing-machine being more looked forward to and relished than any other sort of party. Mines and quarries provided other exhibits of what Lewis Mumford calls 'Eo Technics'.

Great beam engines were still majestically pumping up and down at the Pen Kilen lead-mines near Abersoch, mines that had originally been worked by the Romans. I liked to watch too the horses and carts carrying the ore to the little schooners beached on the sands below and returning with the coal which had been swung out in baskets from the ship's hold.

Often there would be a score or so of these little vessels awaiting a fair wind in the Abersoch roadstead sheltered by the St. Tudwal Islands, mostly not carrying lead ore, but outward bound from Portmadoc with slates, some for as far away as Newfoundland whence they would return with dried cod. If, once in a while, there was a little steamer, it was much quizzed as a most laudable rarity.

There was an oar-propelled lifeboat then at Abersoch that

could only be launched at high tide and I remember one great storm with distress rockets going up from vessels in the roadstead dragging their anchors shorewards, when the lifeboat could do nothing about it and three of them were driven ashore and wrecked. A little later I contrived to get taken out on a lifeboat exercise and later still to persuade the skipper of a minute little steamer—a primitive 'puffer' of about a hundred tons, to take me on an actual voyage. We were only four, the indulgent master, the engineer, a deck-hand and myself, bound with a cargo of granite paving setts from Trevor in Caernarvon Bay to Manchester, up the newly opened Ship Canal. Thence we sailed for the Solway Firth for more granite to discharge at Preston, whence homeward bound in ballast. But not without incident, for my revered captain was thrown across his bridge and got his leg cut wide open—my first real first-aid bandaging opportunity and a fine one—spectacular but quite easy. Then, when we had almost made port, the head of one of our two cylinders blew off and we had to signal the lifeboat to come out and tow us in.

Surviving the rigours of this, my first steamer voyage, and much enjoyed—in retrospect—I leapt at the offer of another and more adventurous trip, this time right round the coast to London—across the Bristol Channel and round Land's End up the English Channel and so into London River. As a rule I tend to forget unpleasant or frightening experiences all too easily, but this passage of, I suppose, about a week of continued buffeting and non-stop seasickness certainly left me stripped bare of all my romantic seafaring notions until they did gradually return again in full force, though it took them some twenty years to do so.

With the strong head-winds and heavy seas that tormented us, it would have been an unpleasant enough trip for any vessel, but in our wretched ill-found little tub it was bleak and unrelieved misery all the way and what with sickness and bruises and lack of sleep or proper food, I reached London, still alive certainly, but too weak and giddy to feel at all triumphant. Also Barking Creek, where we tied up to discharge our cargo of granite, was in itself about as disenchanting a landfall as one could well imagine—then a lonely jumble of grubby industrial squalor where London's East End petered out in a marshy waste.

The slow journey into the City by a dirty train between the dismal backyards of seemingly unending slums still further depressed me and is my last memory of what was altogether a pretty disillusioning expedition and not at all the felicitous voyage to the world's greatest port that I had so hopefully planned.

I had rashly persuaded my father, once a keen yachtsman (but at that time without a boat of his own) to come along on this unfortunate voyage, which he gallantly did. He was a far better sailor than I, though then at some four times my own age, but he must have still had a pretty ghastly time too. Fortunately he was interested in astronomy and knew quite a lot about navigation and was so able to mitigate some of the misery by talking sailorly shop with our skipper.

My father indeed, not content with being the Third Wrangler of his year, was also a considerable all-round scientist, and was bequeathed a fascinating collection of scientific instruments and strange machines by an old professor, who, far older than himself, might well have been using them back in the eighteenth century and probably consulting with Faraday. Anyway there they were, entirely filling a long low attic over the porch at Glasfryn where, unaware of their purpose I would none the less (and illegally) sneak in and caress them from sheer admiration for their superb workmanship—beautifully turned little brass columns of the Doric order, handles like snakes, shining mahogany bases and pillars, sparkling glass globes and cylinders, magnets, curious things wound round with wire, a Wimshurst Machine, and I know not what besides.

Yes, one other thing, and really the gem of the whole collection so far as I was concerned—the air pump—so elegant simply as a piece of furniture that I later on insisted on its being given a place of honour on the main landing in place of a 'mere' armchair—for all its antique prestige. And the air pump still *worked* and had an attachment at the top of its tall glass cylinder whereby you could simultaneously release a penny and a feather to demonstrate that, in a vacuum, all things fall with the same acceleration under the attraction of gravity. As to that, my father told me that though this was so, getting a true vacuum was the difficulty and that when he had gone to see the old professor on his death bed, he had whispered to him, 'When you do that penny and feather demonstration, never, my dear John, forget to stick a nail in the feather.' I take that advice to be a good example of 'the higher truth'.

My father had persuaded himself early that I showed some of those signs of that mathematical and scientific bent for which he looked somewhat groundlessly yet always hopefully in each of us as we successively swam into his vision from the obscurity of the nursery.

As for myself, although ready enough to agree with him, ready enough indeed to agree with anyone professing to discover any potentialities whatever in a not very successful little boy, I was rather appalled at the prospect of having to grow up and somehow cope with a world in which the 'important' and the 'useful' things generally seemed so laboriously dreary and the really interesting things no more than mere play. Still, as I have said, like most fundamentally healthy small boys I loved engines. I rode on the locomotives of our local line and made quite logical but impracticable designs for steam engines and other machines with the naïve ingenuity of a young Heath Robinson. I even constructed water-wheels that actually worked and churned undeniable butter.

My earliest London memories include tattered crossing-sweepers and sandwich-men, muffin-men with bells such as are depicted in the back volumes of *Punch*, as well as organ grinders with monkeys, dancing bears and the sulphurous steam locomotives of the grubby old underground railway. I remember too the hot-water railway foot-warmers—covered in carpeting for first-class only, plain iron for second and third—and oil lamps for all. Finally and most wonderfully—the first-class corridor coaches and then *lavatories*!

Once I stayed in a country house where smoking was still only allowed in a special room separated from the house proper and only entered from without, and where, too, I last encountered full-liveried velvet knee-breeched footmen complete with shoulder knots and powdered hair.

My Uncle Dick's house-carpenter always wore a paper hat exactly like that of Mr. Chips in *Happy Families* or the Carpenter in *Alice*. I have had leeches applied to me for bleeding, and a mixture of cow-dung and cobwebs to *stop* bleeding. I have drunk negus at a Merridan Archery meeting of the 'Woodmen of Arden' and hot buttermilk in Welsh farmouses, and as a young dancing man, have had white epaulettes formed on the shoulders of my dress coat by the dropping wax from the candles of ballroom chandeliers.

Even in those days you would still sometimes see heraldic hatchments hung above the portlas of important London houses signifying that the armigerous owner had died and I remember a venerable dowager saying, 'To *me* hatchments always suggested gaiety, as such stricken houses were not occupied by their families during the proper period of mourning and were commonly lent or let to others for balls.'

I have seen oxen ploughing, and flails being used—also ploughs dragged along by wire cables between two great stationary steamengines. A very few old rustics still wore wide-awake hats and smock-frocks and all navvies had their corduroy trousers tied in by string below the knees.

I remember spending my only shilling at a bazaar to listen through a tube with an earpiece to an Edison-Bell phonograph on the wax cylinder of which had been recorded a string of deplorable American jokes. I was so astonished and impressed that after seventy-five years they are alas! with me yet—word for word.

Just to establish my claim thus to remember things long past I might cite the fact that I once stayed on the isle of Tresco with old Admiral Smith-Dorrien who had joined the Navy when that meant *sail*; that I knew General Sir George Higginson (father of the Brigade of Guards who lived to be over a hundred) whose soldier servant had served under Sir John Moore at Corruna. Also, for good measure, that, as a schoolboy I shook hands with 'The Doctor'—W. G. Grace, no less, who today's teenager has probably never even heard of, nor needs to. Yet, for his information—a quite considerable cricketer.

But my poor links with the past are pitiful as compared with those of Lord Russell who told me for example, that he well remembered his grandmother (who brought him up) keeping her Sunday afternoons free to take tea with the widow of the Young

Pretender and how his grandfather, Lord John Russell the Prime Minister, had recounted to him the conversations he had held with Napoleon on St. Helena.

But even these memories of mine may acquire patina and interest with the passage of time, and time I find has an odd way of accelerating. For example, I joined the Athanaeum in 1918 as my third club and now, quite suddenly as it seems, I find myself the senior member of that venerable institution; whilst looking yet further back, I can see myself as clearly as though it had happened yesterday, being thrown out of the United Services Club opposite, half way through a muffin, because my kind host had forgotten that a small boy was *persona non grata* there.

Chapter Four

Cambridge and a Career

Cambridge in my family was as axiomatic as porridge for breakfast, eaten with salt, and any idea of Oxford would have seemed as perversely heretical as sweetened bread-and-milk. The choice of college, granted Cambridge, was surprisingly left to me, and because I had already seen and been conquered by the Great Court and Neville's, and no doubt also because it seemed generally rather big and grand, and because one's gown would be blue instead of black, I voted for Trinity.

It was understood that I would read for the Natural Science Tripos. By some backstairs device—probably Higher Certificates obtained at school—I had somehow dodged the first part of my 'little-go' examination, but ahead of me still loomed the second part, Latin and Greek. I had done neither at school, and my leaving was darkened by the black prospect of spending my very last school holidays in mugging them up for this one examination.

My father was only too unflagging and conscientious a tutor, and for that whole summer holiday put aside his beloved chess problems and astronomical mathematics to become my classical master.

I am ashamed to say I recall no feelings of gratitude, I merely thought—and still think—this ordeal by Caesar and Xenophon not only mad but diabolical. Yet I did manage to grind at an uncongenial and seemingly useless task, and was rewarded at the beginning of my first Cambridge vacation by a wire from my tailor, whose shop faced the Senate House doors on which the lists were posted, 'Passed "little-go" fourth class congratulations'.

The blessed release! And the sheer efficiency of it! An hour's less work and I might have failed—a few days more, and I might have found myself uselessly in the third class and those days needlessly wasted! Today I am floored by the nursery Latin of armorial mottoes. Alpha and Omega, Beta, Gamma and Pi are the only Greek letters I can recognize with any confidence. So much the worse for me, no doubt, but so much the worse too for those pointless 'little-go' classics.

About the only surviving link with the Cambridge of my father's day was an old Mr. (I think) Huddleston of Madingley Hall, of whose church he had been rector—adding that job to all his others, college tutor, mathematics coach and so on. I had been told to call and pay my respects which I did one Sunday morning of my first term. The little old gentleman in black velvet coat and skull-cap who received me was in better shape than I had expected—much better than his rather ruinous Elizabethan manor house. He plied me with seed cake and madeira and recalled his memories of my father; how he had been awarded the Royal Humane Society's gold medal for a particularly gallant life-saving effort, by diving into the flooded river on a dark and snowy winter's night, to rescue a drowning man. My father had never told me of this exploit himself, but he did leave me the gold half-hunter presented to him by his college with a wreath surrounding the citation designed for it by John Ruskin, now lost, as also Ruskin's drawing and his covering letter.

The first really full-dress dinner party that I can recall was at the Master's Lodge at Trinity, at the beginning of my first term, I suppose about 1900.

We assembled in the famous long drawing-room to be greeted by our host, Dr. Montague Butler, splendidly habited in what I imagined was the gala dress of some high ecclesiastic, purplish frock-coat and apron, breeches, silk stockings and buckled shoes, looking a little like a bland and benign version of Henry VIII (whose statue dominates the college's main gateway) with perhaps a dash of Santa Claus to account for his halo of curling white hair and generous beard. Anyway, whether declaiming before the blazing logs in the monumental fireplace or showing us shy freshmen round the softly-lit Tudor portraits, he seemed to me then quite startlingly one with his historic setting and most skilful at the difficult task of preprandial social ice-breaking. For this was at least a generation before the introduction of before-dinner sherry or cocktails, as lubricants—or substitutes—for conversation.

I think there was a seasoning of dons at this dinner to leaven our youthful lumpishness, but no women, except the master's wife. I found myself seated at table next to a strikingly handsome and well-turned-out young man whom it was difficult to place. He appeared too old and far too sophisticated to be one of *us*, yet too young and apparently too reckless to be in any position of authority. He turned out to be Horace de Vere (Moler) Cole, who had seen service in the Boer War between Eton and coming up to Cambridge and had, through gun-blast or exposure, become rather deaf. This sometimes made conversation at a dinner table embarrassing as, except when excited or genuinely angry or feigning to be so, he always spoke in a noticeably low voice, whereas your responses to his often outrageous or scandalous leads, had to be loud and clear. He gained a good deal of dubious celebrity in London when he went (or was sent) down and though our meetings there were infrequent they were seldom free from embarrassment, as I shall tell.

My next two terms I spent in celebrating this classical *tour de force* of mine of just passing 'little-go' by what I considered a well-earned spell of idleness that in my case included no sort of dissipation or extravagance but merely less work and more social contacts and enjoyment. That involved none but the most civilized minimum of drinking and I have in fact never been drunk in my life, though I did once during the long vac do my best to achieve that state—unsuccessfully. It was at a gala regimental occasion at a coastal camp when I was the sole civilian guest, and the deafening performance of the full band in a small marquee and the loud but unmemorable conversation of my dazzlingly-uniformed hosts prompted me to try to make use of this otherwise rather meaningless occasion by following the examples of some of the company, that is, by getting uproariously drunk.

I duly swallowed all that was offered me by the mess waiters, from repeated sherries to begin with through innumerable refills of champagne (which I don't much like) to end with uncountable successive glasses of port in honour of an interminable series of toasts. As 'an evening out' I probably made the best I could of it, but as a piece of research into the strength of my head the results were negative.

It appeared that (as I had suspected) I was very nearly alcohol-proof, which is in many ways regrettable as most people are not, and one usually wishes more or less to conform to the mood of one's company. I did my best to do so on this occasion as we at last broke up and wandered hilariously down to the nearby beach and along the promenade to the deserted pier. It was a lovely night with a full moon reflected in an almost unbroken ribbon of light on the perfectly calm sea. I really was moved by the serene beauty of the whole scene and felt like paying it a personal tribute of some kind. So I took off my dress shoes and flung them as far as I could into the path of the moon's reflection—not only to enjoy the sparkle of their splashes but out of courtesy to my hosts, who would, I hoped, take my action as proof that I was at least a little tipsy and that their most generous hospitality had not been entirely in vain.

But in fact I knew exactly what I was doing, that my shoes were my best ones, that I should have to hobble back to camp in my socks and that though my gesture had indeed produced a moment of beauty—it was not for that that I had made the sacrifice, but in order to *seem* drunk. Or was I perhaps just a little genuinely so? After all, I am not in the habit of casting my shoes upon the waters—even when moonstruck.

Motoring was just beginning to be indulged in by a few of the more dashing undergraduates and even I possessed a little car of sorts whilst still at Cambridge, though I never became an addict, perhaps because this first car of mine was too primitive and temperamental to be relied on for more than a mile or so, the rest being all vexation. It had a belt drive from the single (horizontal) cylinder and you steered with a little handle on a vertical pillar as though it were a toy tram.

Yet really practical cars had begun to appear at Cambridge. One was owned by Charles Rolls (later to found Rolls-Royce) who was only slightly my senior, and who had hung up in his rooms a summons he had been served with for failing to have a man with a red flag walking in front of his car as the law then required.

Years later, in 1912, I would guess, I found myself staying in the same country house with him, when he took me for a drive in some prototype model that he was running in, the first Rolls-Royce I had encountered, and a revelation. When, after a halt, he got down to crank the engine, I asked him, 'Why don't you have one of those self-starters that I hear are now being made?' He replied, 'When, if ever, they make one good enough for a car of mine, I daresay I shall try one.'

Even my next car was very unlike Charles Rolls's, but its unreliability sometimes brought me agreeable adventures.

Incredible as that may now seem, I once sat for some two hours in my little car that had run out of petrol on the Holyhead Road (now the A5) waiting for another car to come along from which I might beg a pint or so to carry me on to Shrewsbury. It was on the Tern bridge from which I had a fine view of Attingham Park's splendid façade and I had a rewarding book to read, so I was happy enough until dusk began to fall and still no car in either direction. Then I asked a passing waggoner if by any chance he knew of anyone short of Shrewsbury who had a motor car.

'Why, yes,' he replied, 'the gentleman at Atcham House not half a mile ahead has just got one.' So thither I walked and, gentleman he certainly was, for he ran me back to my stranded absurdity and gave me half a gallon. I think it was this civility as well as the sedate charm of Atcham House itself on the bank of the Severn that caused me long afterwards to buy it from Lord Berwick (of Attingham Park opposite) and turn it into the Mytton and Mermaid Hotel, as a staging post between London and Portmeirion. So small a cause—so large an effect.

Then I remember sharing a very welcome lunch with a tramp

when my wretched machine had broken down, deep in the Welsh mountains. Ragged and dirty, from his battered billy-cock hat and tangled beard down to his gaping boots, he was none the less the soul of gaiety and hospitality and insisted on my sharing a most delicious great dumpling tied up in a bandana handkerchief that he called 'Savoury Duck'. He seemed entirely contented with his vagabond way of life, entertained me with funny stories about his life on the road, thanked me for my company and refused to accept any money for feeding me. I couldn't even offer him a lift as my car was still sulking and anyhow we were heading in opposite directions.

I was supposed to be reading science but the fact was that my earlier interest in the subject was becoming a little perfunctory—the old architectural itch was back again in an aggravated form. When I should have been attending lectures or been busy in the laboratory, it became increasingly likely that I would be found prowling around the abounding nooks and corners of old Cambridge, or copying engravings from the rather poor lot of architectural books I unearthed in the University or College libraries.

But even so, it was heady stuff for one in my condition, and from mild beginnings, spasmodic dissipations passed on to a state of dangerous debauchery. My lecture note-books began to reflect my divided attention. Notes about the inside of a dogfish, or whatever it might be, would be surprisingly interspersed with plans and sections of no biological import: the admirable lectures of Professor J. J. Thompson would cause pillared façades or designs for triumphal archways to materialise upon my otherwise blank sheets, possibly a subtle interpretation of his discourse on the structure of matter, but not the kind of thing that would get me through my tripos.

In short, I came to see that I was wasting my time, so far as that was concerned, and what was more, since it was indeed my time, it was the objective that I would change and not my direction. So, and only so, should I get where I wanted, which was—where? To architecture!

There followed family conclaves, heart-searching, proposals and counter-proposals. Architecture, it would appear, was either a hobby for the affluent leisured or a poorish sort of trade for poorish people, somewhere between local art-school teachers and country auctioneers—at any rate, as then practised in our locality. As a hobby, admirable: as a career, no.

Well, then, what would they suggest as a profession for me? Preferably, of course, something that was reasonably congenial and within my capabilities, yet likely to put me amongst the 'affluent leisured' (so different from the 'idle rich') in the not-too-distant future, when I might properly indulge my apparently uneconomic architectural impulses. In view of what I had learned at Oundle and in my short time at Cambridge, there seemed no very obvious alternative to the profession of engineering, and indeed my eldest brother was at this time most conveniently the director of a small new electrical manufacturing company.

Certainly to become an electrical engineer seemed to be the line of least resistance: 'prospects' (in the money sense) at that time looked rosy for such concerns, so thither I went as a laboratory assistant, with the idea at the back of my head that before too long I might find faithful service to commercial science duly rewarded by an income sufficient to support me while I practised architecture.

This step, like the voluntary cutting short of my Cambridge career, was deliberately taken with a view to one day—and as soon as might be—attaining to my heart's desire—that is, to becoming an architect. The direct approach being discouraged with so much plausible and reasonable-sounding argument, there was nothing for it but secretly to approach my objective by whatever course might offer, however indirect and devious.

To be sure, I had disquieting dreams about succeeding so remarkably in engineering as to risk seduction from my true vocation by its dazzling prizes. Might I not find myself, indeed, involved in great electrification schemes or in high commercial or public responsibilities from which it would be difficult to extricate myself without a great wrench, both to me and the interests that I served? One had heard of people being thus gradually deflected from their inner destinies, of people made rich and even famous by treachery to themselves, but nothing very reassuring about their being happy. Yet happiness—as is common though not universal—was what I chiefly demanded of life, not through wisdom or virtue or love, still less through riches or amusements, but through work—the work that I felt it was in me to do. I take that to be the normal, healthy, middle choice, neither the altruistic service of humanity nor yet, at the other extreme, selfish pleasure-seeking. Still, if the celestial train to immortality is found not to carry second-class passengers, I should certainly claim to travel comfortably first amongst the saints, and should be genuinely surprised to find myself slammed into a crowded third amongst the sinners!

I know this sounds complacent, but I may not on that account bear false witness against myself either here or elsewhere.

I was soon to realize, however, that the engineering path I had elected to tread was likely to prove no less steep and narrow than most others, and by no means a certain short cut to affluence and architecture. There was soon a lull in that first electrification boom, bringing difficulties to my brother's fledgling enterprise and misgivings to me. Had I perhaps sold my soul for an I.O.U. that was not after all going to be honoured?

There were even rumours that my brother's works might have to close down. Thus it was that when I was offered the job of research experimentalist to an electrical inventor, I was encouraged to take it. This meant, for the most part, hours of finicking manipulation of very delicate electrical instruments mostly in the stale darkness of a Westminster attic, where the minute deflections of suspended mirrors were made manifest and measurable by long beam sof reflected light thrown upon a screen.

It was some new and very sensitive form of ammeter that my inventor and I were striving to calibrate and perfect, very ingenious and theoretically unimpeachable, but which proved in practice a mass of nerves and inhibitions that it took all my time and patience to control. After hours of nursing I would at last get it behaving in a properly balanced way and reading with absolute accuracy, and I would tip-toe out of the darkened cabinet to report 'all-ready' to my chief. He would lumber in and switch on the testing current, and lo! the little band of light that had been drilling up and down the scale so primly and obediently a minute ago, would leap into a wild and undisciplined dance hither and thither and up and down like a crazy firefly—a tale told by an idiot and not at all what was required of it, which was a plain, immediate and accurate statement that a current of precisely so many amperes had passed its way. The thing indeed proved unpredictably and maddeningly hypersensitive, and as hysterical and wayward as a leading lady. Anyway, as I had been engaged for research and not as an attendant for a sort of inanimate though acute mental case, I soon began to feel depressed at being so much shut up with so very *exigent* a patient in this darkened cell, and was visited by carnal visions of great buildings glowing amber and ochre in the glare of an Italian sun.

To this phase an attack of influenza was perhaps a not unnatural corollary. Darkness, dust and depression, a nostalgia for architecture such as Victoria Street could scarcely satisfy—together they laid me low, together they worked my everlasting release. For from that sick-leave I never returned to my inventor. On the crest of my returning morale, following the trough of influenza depression, I screwed up sufficient courage to write and tell him that I had changed my mind—or rather, that I found after all I had *not* changed my mind—and that I was resolved to be an architect come what might.

This brought a letter of protest from my abandoned chief, a nice, indeed rather a clinging sort of letter. It made me feel that if I returned even to collect my few possessions, I should be in danger of having my newborn determination argued, reasoned, or coaxed out of me. For all I know, my note-books, overalls and Aquascutum still moulder in the dark of that Victoria Street attic, for I never dared to go back to retrieve them.

So far as I can recall, I seem to have taken this momentous step without consulting my parents, which would have been in line with my policy as to the avoidance of 'persuasion'. I do recollect, however, very soon afterwards sitting on the grass under a plane tree near the Marble Arch, and composing a letter home in which I myself argued, reasoned and coaxed as well as I knew how and at immense length—and the more forcibly because I had just deliberately burnt the last of my engineering boats. I remember the phrase, 'And, anyhow, I would far, far sooner be poor as an architect than rich as anything else—I would sooner fail as an architect than succeed as an engineer; and after all, if that's how I feel—why should I fail?'

The die was cast, the ultimatum delivered, I was ready to do battle and fight for my career like a hero and as melodramatically as might be, when, to my amazement, the home front immediately capitulated, agreed I was probably right, wished me luck, and arranged for me to have a modest allowance.

Certainly I was taken aback, possibly disappointed even, for one feels a little foolish after striking an heroic attitude to discover that it has been uncalled-for. Anyway, there I was, free to become an architect as fast as I liked, so far as my parents were concerned, and indeed urged to get on with it without further delay.

For this unforeseen success I had no exploitation plan ready. I knew no architects at all, either good or bad, and very little indeed about how one entered the profession—whether indeed it might have an official front-door opening only to successful examinees. There was just one thing that both depressed and encouraged me. From the look of things generally it seemed clear that either very moderate ability was sufficient to qualify one for practice, or that there must be such a shortage of properly trained architects that commissions were being handed out to just anybody with assurance enough to take them on. Whichever were the truth it certainly seemed that the architectural position, whichever it might be, should by no means prove impregnable.

By looking up Architecture in the London telephone book, I came upon a subscriber called the *Architectural Association* with an address in Tufton Street, Westminster, and that same evening I resolved to go straight round there to discover what manner of institution it might be.

Chapter Five

Flight to Architecture

No. 18 Tufton Street turned out to be a rather grim brick edifice in the Gothic taste, originally the Royal Architectural Museum but recently expanded to house the small but even then vigorous school run by the Architectural Association. Boldly I entered, boldly I sent up my card and demanded audience with the principal, which (my name being utterly unknown and therefore just possibly important) I was immediately granted.

I think I was very fortunate, in this my first architectural encounter to have happened on someone with real enthusiasm and sympathy, and in a few minutes I found myself perched up on a high stool, debating excitedly with the head of the institution who lay at full stretch along a drawing-desk in the most disarmingly unofficial manner and positively exuding encouragement. His unknown visitor proving to be no more than a stray youth vaguely and ignorantly inquisitive about how one became an architect, he none the less treated me as a perfectly reasonable being worth talking to at length, with the result that when at last I left the building it was in a state of high elation. So much so, that I could scarcely forbear to skip down the steps and whoop through the grey propriety of the adjoining Dean's Yard—a man (just) who had at length found what he had been seeking.

The encouragement of the head, the sight of all those drawing-boards and T-squares, to say nothing of dozens of other young men already cheerfully launched on the course I longed to take—the whole thing had been intoxicating, irresistible, and I had come away more or less formally enrolled as a student for the following term.

Meanwhile there was the fag end of the current term to run and the intervening vacation, and the question immediately arose as to how best I might employ this interval in preparing myself for my initiation. Fortunately (it is undoubtedly a wise provision for young architects, as indeed for young anythings), I had a large and varied assortment of relatives and connections, a number of them quite rich enough to be helpful, some of them well enough disposed quite probably to prove so.

Amongst these a sort of second cousin—A. H. Clough—was most laudably conspicuous; and it was off his friendly shoulders that I took my first rather wild little leap into actual practice. He had considerable properties in various southern counties, and what is more, an active interest in them, an interest, moreover, that had lately turned to experiments in ordered development, both residential and in the way of smallholdings.

With no technical training either in architecture or construction, he had none the less a real flair for commonsense traditional building, an eye for proportion and a quite acute sense of money values. It so happened that he was just then busily developing some of his Sussex property, in friendly alliance with a country builder who had developed a cheap and effective technique for the execution of my cousin's designs. It was his suggestion that I should attach myself to this builder as a sort of A.D.C. and through his good offices I did so.

By this time I had begun to have my share of what is generally considered 'fun'—of shooting-parties, hunt-balls, country weekends and the like—as well as a pretty good time dining out and dancing in London on the not-too-dazzling scale that befitted an obscure and quite poor young man. But for sheer pleasure and enjoyment, I had up till then tasted nothing to compare with the summer month I now spent in a little Sussex village, bottle-washing for my country builder and sleeping on a very short and unyielding truckle bed over the tap-room of the little inn. For the first time since I had left school I found myself learning what I was thirsting to learn, and therefore learning just as fast as I could be shown how.

How did one 'set out' the foundations of a house? How mix, deposit, and ram the concrete in the trenches? How lay and bond the bricks—lay the floor joists—set the window frames—bed the wall plates, and in short, accomplish the whole intricate and entrancing business of translating eighth-inch scale plans, elevations and sections into a full-sized, three-dimensional, ponderable actual *house*?

My first meeting with the builder was a considerable surprise, a shock even, though a pleasant one. I knew (so I thought) that a country contractor was a person with a slow and husky voice, rigid rule-of-thumb ideas, business methods that were shrewd to the verge of being sharp, and with about as much aesthetic yearning as the bowler hat that fittingly crowned his square and rather sportingly-dressed person. If that were the rule, here certainly was the exception.

A large head with a mass of waving black hair, a wide high forehead over deep-set and very large blue eyes that looked like a girl's, a small sensitive mouth that a drooping moustache was being sedulously trained to hide, a slight, rather frail-looking body, always neatly clad in blue serge or sober black—that was my contractor. Appropriate enough as a musician, a teacher or even as a minister, it took a little time to believe that he was indeed a builder, and that shrewd judgements about construction, materials, and design could actually be delivered by that soft hesitating voice.

But it did not take long to realize that here was a man who really loved his craft, whose pleasure it was—not merely his trade—to set brick upon brick and see his building rise from the ground solid and true in obedience to his will. There being nothing in the world like a shared enthusiasm for the foundation of friendship, we were very soon on the warmest master and disciple terms—I questioning and suggesting, he patiently answering and criticising my often impracticable proposals for altering this or that.

I kept a note-book—a book of building lore that I very much wish I had not lost. I was allowed to design and supervise the building of a tile and rough-cast porch which we both thought lent great dignity to the little house it distinguished, but which (by my fourth week) I, at least, felt was quite out of scale with and altogether too assertive for the mild little countenance that looked past and over it as over a defiantly jaunty false nose.

My cousin, kind man, said he thought the porch a good idea, and that it was a very nice porch as porches went, but that he too was doubtful whether it quite suited the house to which it was attached—it was perhaps just a little too architectural and interesting, but would no doubt be much liked by whoever lived there, and anyway it didn't matter. I was thus allowed to sow quite a little crop of architectural wild oats, mild quaker-oats that really harmed nobody yet taught me a certain discretion that I could scarcely have acquired so quickly in any other way.

There abides with me one other landmark, or rather time-mark of this phase—the surveying and drawing out of a fine old building that my cousin proposed to restore. The making of such measured drawings as I then undertook for a specific purpose is very properly held to be an important part of the young architect's training, and certainly when exercised on a subject of any distinction, this enforced intimacy with its every secret of proportion, detail, and construction, is a fine lesson in all the arts of building.

Indeed, I guessed that it must be so even as I scrambled and crept about that old manor-farm with my measuring rod and note-book—guessed that I was learning vital things in a vivid and unforgettable fashion just because I found myself so exhilarated and so happy. To this day, the smell of mouldering apples, of cheese and of ill-aired bedrooms in any sort of combination is still romantic and delicious to me, because so inextricably a part of those glowing days of my architectural springtime.

Architecture seems very largely to have taken the place of sex in the complex of my adolescence—it was, I suppose, 'sublimated' into that less alarming and far more manageable channel; and perhaps my almost violent satisfaction was due in part at least to finding an outlet that was not merely alluring but also relatively calculable. That, at any rate, was my own 'escape' from what I rather timorously felt was (or might become) a disturbing, not to say disrupting power, if I gave it half a chance.

The result was, of course, that it was given practically no chance at all, and though I think I was accounted sociable enough and duly became a regular and not unaccomplished 'dancing man', my non-architectural emotional life was as near as need be *nil*.

In retrospect, I cannot say that I see any advantage gained from so monkish a devotion to the muse, for all I can tell, something may have been lost besides much of that warming human companionship without which it is not easy to keep truly alive and supple-hearted.

Given my architectural life to live over again, there was, as I have said, much that I would do differently; but this apprenticeship to a practical working builder would be a feature I should by no means leave out. Rather would I expand it to at least a year spent perhaps under different men on several different jobs, possibly in the intervals of ordinary architectural schooling.

The old traditional process of professional instruction by articled pupilship is now replaced by the more effective one of five years' study at a recognized architectural school, leading up to three successive examinations and then a couple of years of experience in an architect's office—seven years in all before admittance by examination into the Royal Institute of British Architects, and being given the right to call oneself an architect and legally to practice as such.

The correct accepted approach to professional practice is now a straight, broad, gently graded smooth incline up the inevitable long hill. Still, by the time one has traversed this architectural processional way and reached its end and been admitted through the successive examination gateways, and rubbed shoulders and exchanged ideas with other pilgrims, one is bound to know quite a bit about architecture and building and be generally pretty well technically equipped.

Not, as I hold, that the highly finished product of this elaborate process will by any means be an architect, as I would have the term understood, unless he had the root of the matter in him already as part of his original make-up, like his love of cats or his detestation of tomatoes. Granted that our architect has been born, this is doubtless the surest way of then making him—of bringing him to flower. Indeed, so efficient is the modern machine for the production of architects that there is the obvious danger that we may (and indeed do) get a certain proportion of architects turned out who are purely or mostly synthetic—young men who were born to be stockbrokers, soldiers or dentists, and who have been somehow deflected from their proper destinies.

Yet that is no great or peculiar reflection on the machine itself, which after all only undertakes a process and can clearly only reject unsuitable material in a rough and general sort of way, and that does do its appointed job in a remarkably thorough fashion.

Even the congenital stockbroker must be the better for this processing; he could not possibly thereafter tolerate the house of his stockbroker father, if that father were of the true Victorian breed and had at all a suitable home. The architecturally educated son might well help to make a good public opinion, even if he would never make a good architect, and that is something.

To the congenital architect, with his arms wide open to receive whatever may be going in the way of enlightenment, the machine is a chariot of destiny, a celestial omnibus of which he will have little to complain, save that it travels too slowly for his ardent spirit. But in that chariot or omnibus I myself never travelled beyond the first twopenny stage, when, as I shall tell, the conscientious conductor pushed me off into the roadway, firmly but not unkindly.

My second term at the Association school had run but a week or two when, through family jobbery, I was offered a small architectural commission. As the fee proposed (and eagerly accepted) was to be ten guineas including all expenses, that description is doubly appropriate. What I was required to build was a country home for a charitable institution near Oxford, to house some twenty inmates, that had to be as cheap as plainness and ingenuity could make it, yet as attractive, granted that, as I could contrive.

An actual job! I was going right now to direct the laying of actual bricks in veritable mortar for the due mixing of which I should be solely and even legally responsible as *architect*. There would be a real working plan with my name upon it, pinned to a board and getting stained with mud and washed by the rain on a real building site, the builder and the foreman and the workmen all believing in it and obeying it. I too should be believed in and accepted, by this small circle at any rate, as an architect. Should I by any means be able to justify or maintain this faith, the very existence of which might somehow, magically, endow me with the wisdom and power that seemed properly to belong to my high calling?

True, I was very young, ignorant, and utterly inexperienced, yet probably I already knew enough to manage this affair without disaster, perhaps even with credit. Where knowledge failed I could no doubt temporarily bridge the gap by an airily constructed bluff until inspiration or information feverishly acquired, were ready to take its place.

Assuredly I would take it on, and somehow I would get away with it. After all, if I failed, my failure would, to my clients, be only relative—though to me absolute, disastrous. By employing an obscure young man as their architect at a purely nominal fee they clearly, and perhaps properly, risked the wasting of part of their small funds and the erection of a building less excellent than it might have been. To me at the time it seemed that the great risk was really mine. If things went seriously wrong, could my career ever recover from a false start at once premature and disastrous? Perhaps not, but then why envisage disaster? Why should one fail? After all, one had common sense, zeal, and a flaming determination to triumph, so why shouldn't one?

It was in this state of but slightly hesitant elation that I accepted my first commission, though realization of what the almost instant repercussions would be upon my life might well have given me pause. As I might have foreseen, the planning and carrying out of even one small building soon began to demand a large part of my time and attention, and the fact that its site was far away in the country, and that I was taking each and every step hesitatingly and for the first time, added to the laboriousness of the affair and to my absences from the school. Furthermore, the builder and the providers of this and of that would seek me out during school hours, sometimes penetrating to my very desk, to the grave prejudice of all good order and discipline.

Added to that I would take them actually to sit in with me at lectures that I did not want to miss—so that I might with true economy both absorb and emit wisdom at one and the same time.

Yet it was scarcely to be wondered at, that after a perfectly friendly interview with the principal, I received a formal letter requesting that either I should cease to use the school as my office, or resign forthwith, in the interests of the other students to whom my highly irregular behaviour could not but prove upsetting. This demand seemed to me entirely just and proper, and whilst I expressed my genuinely felt regret at leaving a friendly nest in so unfledged a condition, I added that I felt just *having* to fly would somehow produce the requisite wings and that, anyhow, as I had always understood that a 'first job' was generally hard to come by, I proposed to cling on to what had so unexpectedly come my way—and chance it.

So, with no more than a ten-guinea fee in prospect at the end of some five or six months of further labour I cheerfully cut myself adrift from the training ship, trimmed my tiny sail to this little favouring puff, and just hoped that heavy weather might providentially hold off until I had somehow picked up enough sea-sense to navigate my cockle-shell into port, there to refit for larger and more dazzling adventures. When, years later, I told Ned Lutyens of my so brief professional education he exclaimed, 'What, you took three months! Why, I was through with it all in three weeks!'

I recall that at this time my elder brother and I were sharing chambers in Cork Street, Burlington Gardens, which, complete as they were with private bathroom and a valet, strike me in retrospect as quite improbably fashionable and extravagant. Yet there we undoubtedly were, running mildly into debt and wondering, also quite mildly, where we should each be and what doing half a year on.

Now that I had a building job to carry out and was therefore presumably an architect, it seemed necessary that I should have an 'office' in which to pursue my profession on however miniature a scale. A week or so later, therefore, I installed myself in a little cupboard of a room approached grandly enough from the sedate precincts of Gray's Inn. To open the window was to be deafened by the clanging of trams and the thunder of drays and lorries from the Gray's Inn Road, and to admit little eddies of dust and straw that would quickly form a grey deposit upon my desk and drawings. Still, it could be called an office; it had my first visiting card—addressless and clubless—pinned to its door, some deal boards fixed below the window gave me a drawing-desk, whilst a drawing-board, my instruments, half a dozen books and a few shillings' worth of paper completed my professional equipment.

I was realist enough to discount the possibility of any 'client' seeking me out in this obscure retreat, and I therefore sternly repressed any carnal longings I might have for such superfluous elegances.as a chair or stool, a carpet, or even a waste-paper basket.

I paid five pounds a quarter for this office of mine to a grown-up architect who had it to spare, and from whom I understood occasional if monosyllabic advice might be sought, though that heartening expectation was scarcely realized. In the first place, he was no doubt preoccupied with his own affairs when not actually away on some job or other, and in the second place I think he deeply disapproved of me, as any orthodox and properly qualified architect very well might.

Who, pray, was this ignorant yet apparently assured young man to go setting up thus precociously as an architect? Did he think to vault thus easily into practice over the heads of his elders and betters, with no more than his amateur enthusiasms to set against their long and laborious apprenticeships? Would it not, after all, have been wiser to have foregone the five pounds a quarter and to have left the store-room empty, rather than seem to be countenancing or encouraging so unprofessional and therefore so undesirable an adventurer?

Yes, it was a mistake, and if the discreditable tenant could not actually be evicted, one could at any rate seem not to be aware of him, and make it clear to all that no responsibility was accepted for his deplorable escapade by consistently discouraging his approaches and by snubbing him whenever he dared to seek advice.

So snubbed I was, well and truly, but never seriously discouraged. Yet I do not think my landlord wished me ill; austere, taciturn and architecturally hard-bitten himself, my rather glib and debonnaire assumptions would have been well enough calculated to exasperate him, and he no doubt thought that cubbish superficiality should be met and cured by disapproving contempt. Even so, I did get occasional crumbs of help from him by sheer importunity.

On my third visit to my one and only job there took place this dialogue:

>   BUILDER (nervously jocular): What about a little sugar for the canary? Can't sing without sugar, you know!
>   MYSELF (anxiously): Canaries—sugar—what do you mean?
>   BUILDER: Well, Sir, what about a draw—a little on account—could you send me a certificate, say, for a hundred or so?
>   MYSELF: A certificate? Why of course—certainly, I will see about it.

Then on my return to London, this sequel:

>   MYSELF: My builder has asked me for a thing he calls a certificate—something to do with his being paid—what does he mean?
>   MY LANDLORD: Don't even know that? Was there nothing about it in the contract—if yer had one—or likely you didn't get that far in yer three months' schooling? See here . . .

And so it was that I became initiated into the mystery of 'The Architect's Certificate Book', with its counterfoils and serial numbering, and so it was that I contrived, by hook or by crook, to solve or get solved such other professional or technical problems as were too high for my little learning or my mother-wit—and luckily for me, always just in time, or rather, just not too late.

One hundred and sixty pounds a year, paid monthly, was scarcely a luxurious allowance for a young man in London, even sixty-five years ago, and I had had to pay my own architectural school fees out of it and now my office rent and expenses, as well as my board and lodging and all the rest. It was therefore not surprising or I think profitless that I quite often found myself exceedingly short of money and sometimes entirely without it.

At this period my only two readily negotiable assets—my watch and signet ring—would occasionally find themselves in pawn or left at a railway booking-office in pledge for a ticket. Sometimes I would miss my train through not being able to afford a hansom, and the resulting complications would perhaps be aggravated by my not having the money for an explanatory telegram or for one of sufficient length to be clear.

There was no doubt a streak of native vagueness that partly accounted for such occasional straits, but it did require some rather agile egg-dancing to maintain oneself and at the same time to launch one's little professional barque on so very slender an income. For one thing, whilst I had certainly not been brought up luxuriously, we had all lived very well and comfortably at home and in a certain style, and I was quite without the technique that seemed to enable people to be relatively quite poor and yet live a life not merely decent but obviously jolly.

However, it was not very long before I discovered that theatres had pits and even galleries, that there were places in Soho where you could dine amusingly enough, if not very well, for as little as fifteen pence, that a starched shirt might often attend more than one dance or dinner-party without discredit (given a little care and luck), that there was nothing inherently shameful in travelling third-class, and that the servants in even rather grand country houses would accept quite meagre tips with cheerfulness if one added friendliness to the silver. Mercifully for me, at some of the nobler houses one was led aside by a secretary or house-chamberlain or groom-of-the-chambers or whoever, and told that tips were not expected and were indeed against the rules of the house, which rules, however, sometimes included early attendance in a private chapel served by a private chaplain which yet had its own historic and often architectural charm. Anyway, one way and another, I 'contrived' running my little one-man show, and going out and about quite a lot.

And now, by the sort of sheer good luck that I had had no right to count upon (yet had, I suppose, in fact counted upon when I so imprudently set up in practice), along came a nice trickle, small to begin with but rapidly growing, of useful little jobs. Within a few months I had three or four more small houses going on in the immediate neighbourhood of the first, and soon afterwards a new wing to an old house in the next parish. Small as these commissions actually were, the mere fact of having some half-dozen on at once, meant to me a dazzling expansion of business as well as a fourteen-hour day and a perpetual and not really efficient scurry. Clearly I must get properly established and equipped with a telephone and perhaps even an assistant—one should crowd one's luck while it lasted!

I therefore removed myself and all my gear very cheerfully from Gray's Inn to Arundel House on the Embankment near the Temple, all in a four-wheeled cab, and was at work again within the hour in my fifth-floor attic flat. Those five flights of steep stone stairs up and down which I never passed except at top speed for the whole eight years I was there, were really great time-savers, for I needed to look no further for my exercise. There were three enchanting attic rooms with sloping ceilings and dormer casements looking to the sun and the tides and traffic of the Thames, a little hall, a bathroom, and an indulgent housekeeping couple on the same floor.

I thought myself (and indeed was) very happily placed and at an astonishingly low rent (£80 p.a.) thanks, I suppose, to the hundred-odd steps of the stairway. Clients I did not consider. If they wanted to see me they could climb as I did. A few—quite enough—did, but usually I met them on the site or on the job, or at their own houses, and on the whole I still think that is generally the more efficient plan.

Just to plug any gaps in my working time not filled by architecture, I rather absurdly set up as 'an inventor' and actually patented several contrivances as disparate as an electric starting switch, an automatic air-lock serving-hatch, and a novel sort of chair. Only the last was commercially successful, thanks to the friendly interest of Sir Ambrose Heal, who of course made a fine craftsman's job of it, and advertised it handsomely with posters on the underground as the 'Elysian Floor Lounge'. It paid my taxi fares and washing bills—no more—until the patent expired.

Chapter Six

Edwardian Glitter

One of my Cambridge contemporaries that I found in London was Horace Cole whom I had met at that first Trinity dinner party. He was gradually winning a dubious celebrity as the arch practical joker of his own or perhaps of any age. It was he who roped off and dug up part of Piccadilly under the pretext of official road repairs, leaving the police to sort out the resultant traffic tangle and to remove his obstructions. It was Cole again who chased a Member of Parliament down St. James's Street shouting 'Stop thief!' accusing the pursued of having stolen his watch. I knew the victim and there was a quite considerable to-do about it.

He was also one of the chief movers in the famous 'Dreadnought' hoax in which Virginia Woolf, Duncan Grant, and Adrian Stephen were also involved. I confess I found him fascinating and indeed got unwillingly involved in some of his lesser exploits. The last I ever saw of him was in the early dawn of a summer's morning solemnly and accurately smashing the windows of the Russian Embassy that stood next door to his own large house in Chesham Place. His missiles were pelota balls, slung from their proper Basque scoop.

It was the finale so far as I was concerned (for I fled the scene before any police or diplomatic reactions could materialize) of a large and uproarious bachelor dinner party to celebrate his eviction for general rowdyism, a trait that assorted oddly with his fine collection of modern paintings, particularly Johns and Innes's which were mostly un-hung, and stacked around his drawing-room walls very much at hazard from the horse-play of the boisterous celebrants.

Meeting him on and off generally meant embarrassment sooner or later through his exhibitionism, lack of consideration, and sheer bad manners as when he emptied a horrified ballroom by snatching a sword from a pair that had caught his eye on the wall and challenging a perfectly harmless stranger to defend his life with the other—claiming, in simulated rage, that he had been mortally insulted. I recall the hullabaloo, but not how the affair ended. I think he may have seen himself as a sort of latter-day Byron—'bad, mad and dangerous to know'.

Though nearly all my time and thoughts were concerned with architecture, I was by no means a hermit and had sense enough to enjoy myself and relax in what are more generally reckoned as 'pleasures'—dining out, dancing, theatres, country-house visits and indeed social occasions of all sorts.

I must have been lucky in my very first London introductions and contacts, a raw, unknown and utterly unsophisticated young man as I was without any prospects, most emphatically not a 'parti' and nothing particular to look at. But as an indefatigable dancing man, an appreciative and generally amiable dinner or house-party guest ready to make himself agreeable, I found myself handed on from hostess to hostess—often as just a plug to fill a sudden hole left by the last-minute failure of some more prestigious guest.

I remember being thus suddenly bidden rather frighteningly to dinner with Mrs. Humphrey Ward to find that I was there to understudy Edwin Lutyens who—even absent—was more awesome to me as 'representing the arts' than my then celebrated hostess or the rest of the company, all apparently representing, and far more plausibly than I, this or that.

Actually I always reacted cordially and hopefully, to telephone messages that began 'I know its awfully sudden and I do apologize, but are you by any chance free for dinner on Thursday night?' I would accept if I possibly could—hoping that my gradually widening contacts might include at least a proportion of interesting and congenial people even, perhaps, potential clients.

Then, through some sort of social grape-vine network, one found oneself apparently on various 'dance lists' that circulated amongst ball-giving hostesses, and if you sometimes wondered how or why, perhaps knowing little or nothing of the hostess in question, you would at least know plenty of her other guests and maybe wonder which of your partners had procured your invitation. Old Mr. Gillet who had founded the Bachelors' Club was reputed to have the most exclusive list of eligible young men, only available to 'Grade A' hostesses and the *Morning Post*'s recitals of notables attending a ball commonly ended with 'and Mr. William Gillet'. Surprisingly he was a rather crumpled little old man with a meagre white beard and not at all the sort of latter-day Beau Brummell that one might have reasonably expected.

By hindsight, I can appreciate (what indeed I gathered by indirect report in later life) that I was not, from a hostesss's point of view, an entirely satisfactory or reliable young man, though my intentions were never other than to be dependable, punctual, polite and altogether amenable.

The trouble was that I tended to be vague about dates and optimistic about time so that I too often failed to turn up when and where expected through missing trains or clean forgetting or whatever, not fully appreciating how this could upset a hostess's arrangements, though two or three rather formidable ones did say just what they thought of my manners, to my genuine distress. Such confusions were partly due to my trying to be civil to more people than I could really remember or cope with, or just to getting mixed up.

Add to which I could not always resist following up odd trails that *might* prove amusing instead of sticking to my known but not always remembered engagements. Quite often such trails did thus lead on as when one day bounding up the great staircase of my then newly-joined club, I met a stately figure, slowly descending, well known to me by sight as being constantly around the place and memorable for the old-fashioned formality of his dress, always a frock-coat and top hat, a high Gladstonian collar and a stock-like black silk cravat.

For some reason it had come to me that he must be the club secretary whom I had reason to see about something and I addressed him on that assumption. In a voice and manner absurdly appropriate to his majestic yet Micawber-like presence he answered me with, 'Alas! No, my dear Sir, I have no claim to such eminence! I am merely an ordinary member of the club—a very ordinary member I may say. Not at all, not at all—and good day to you.' I guessed that he must be an old retired actor and probably a widower, which would account for his almost constant presence at the club. Some weeks later, feeling restless one lovely spring evening, I thought to have an airing up the river, and with that in mind mounted to the upper deck of a passing bus and sat down on the one vacant seat right in front, to find myself next to my Mr. Micawber. Our recognition being mutual we fell into amiable conversation and must have amused each other as, just as we turned into the King's Road out of Sloane Square he said, 'I live close to here in Wellington Square—how pleasant it would be if you would come in and join me in a glass of sherry.'

Having no set programme for the evening I willingly agreed, and we had not long been seated before in walked a quite startlingly attractive girl of, I would guess, some eighteen years.

After introductions and a few minutes' conversation both my host and his daughter (as she proved to be) left me alone for a moment, and when he returned he said, 'You may well think me excessively unconventional, but my daughter is going to a ball tonight given by an old friend of ours, and the young man who was to have partnered her has just failed her—would you I wonder, by any chance—should you be free—care to take his place?'

Particularly relishing sudden and unexpected happenings I of course accepted delightedly, returned to my Embankment flat to dress and go on to the dance at the address I had been given. There, introduced to my hostess as my partner's sudden pick-up, I felt it proper to pay this unknown hostess some attention which turned out to be easy enough, as besides being most cordial to me, a quasi gatecrasher, she was both amusing and amused.

Saying good-bye and thank you at the end of what had been a

really gay party she said, 'Would you, if free, care to come down to us in the country for next weekend—it would be so nice if you could, we live near Windsor.' Free again, again I said, 'Yes, delighted', and down I duly went to find myself one of a large house-party not one of whose members I knew. In addition, several neighbours came in to dinner, including the officer commanding the Coldstream Guards then stationed at Windsor, who suggested that I might care to see their barracks which he thought might interest and perhaps horrify me as an architect. They did, both—and we got on together about architecture and indeed things in general extremely well.

I never saw him again for some six or seven years—when, after he had returned from the war as a General and quit the service, he somehow got into touch with me and asked me to build him and his large family a country house, an adventure that we both enjoyed immensely. That was the long-term ultimate consequence of my encounter on the club staircase.

But there were other short-term results, for amongst my co-guests at Windsor was an amusing middle-aged bachelor who asked me to another weekend party at his own country house. Being all for such 'mystery cruises', I accepted, and when the time came, found that I had arrived at an enormous place with a party of twenty or so—mostly unknown—already assembled. Standing on a terrace overlooking a lake, the house itself, though well-mannered and dignified enough was undeniably dull, though its contents were splendid.

Our host, so it seemed, had a routine for the entertainment of his house-parties—the women were let loose in the house to rearrange the furniture and pictures to whatever they might jointly decide was the best advantage, this being done with such help from the household staff as might be needed, whilst the men engaged in clay-pigeon shooting competitions from the terrace. Inexplicably and surprisingly I ended up as the champion, just possibly as a result of my relatively temperate indulgence at our host's by no means abstemious table.

One of my fellow guests was an agreeable old bachelor who, on leaving said, 'I am celebrating my birthday (or something or other) by giving a dinner at the Berkeley, day after tomorrow, it should be a pleasant party anyhow and pleasanter still if you were free and could by any chance join us.' I was and I did, and most memorably enjoyable it indeed was, largely because I sat next to and thereafter assiduously cultivated a most delightful girl. Everything went swimmingly—we exchanged addresses and actually made a definite plan to meet again, but something sabotaged our project (I think she was unexpectedly summoned back to her home in Scotland) and I never saw or even heard of her again. I have long since entirely forgotten her name, but should this by some unlikely chance ever meet her eye, and she should recall our brief encounter, I should like her to know how immediate and deep an admiration she could rouse in 1913 or thereabouts.

As to my pigeon-shoot host—I never saw him again either. I heard later that he had committed suicide, from sheer boredom. With no need to work and with no particular aims or interests in life, political, cultural or other, he had I gathered just found his luxurious existence too tedious to be borne.

This sort of dinner-party 'enthusiasm-at-first-sight' was an abiding hazard too often the prelude to ultimate embarrassment, since my attitude to any admired girl would become panic-stricken and frozen on the instant, if any sort of real intimacy seemed to threaten. It was almost certainly fortunate that fate intervened to abort this particular attack.

A light-hearted flirtation conducted more or less in public, that was fine, but if a tête-à-tête showed the slightest signs of becoming at all personal I would take fright and do all I could to bring things back to cool normality. I was just plain terrified of finding myself somehow 'compromised', thinking that even the mildest sort of 'love-making' must be assumed to be the prelude to a proposal of marriage.

As that was quite out of the question for years to come, I being then entirely engrossed in my work on which too I depended for my bachelor living, and as I did not want a breach-of-promise action either—I became as discouraging as a convent novice directly my companion showed any signs of a contrary inclination. By today's standards (and possibly by any) I fear my behaviour was unacceptable—though at the time I believed I was being most gentlemanly and considerate.

I recall travelling all the way down to stay in Somerset at the invitation of a currently admired Junoesque young lady, whose family I barely knew. There was a wooded knoll on the edge of the park to which I was conducted soon after arrival where I was invited to seat myself on the trunk of a fallen tree to admire the splendid prospect, which indeed I did. My companion sat down alongside and expatiated on her interest in architecture, her present aimlessness, her frustrations and her family's thwarting of her artistic ambitions, all the while moving closer and closer to me whilst I courteously made way for her until, when I had reached my end of the log and another retreat would have dismounted me entirely, I got up and sat down at what had been her end with the whole length of our seat between us. I, of course, covered up my uncooperative poltroonery as best I might by talking away about the landscape or whatever and how much the slight change in viewpoint had improved it, so that I was let off with nothing worse than a sort of puzzled sulkiness instead of the all-out onslaught I had half expected. However, I had been so shaken by my experience and so dreaded its repetition in some even more compromising form that I invented a fairly plausible excuse for having to catch the very first available train back to London—which I thankfully did.

On another occasion where the propriety of my behaviour might I suppose well be hotly debated pro and con between the over eighties and today's youth, is what might be called 'the case of the private brougham'.

I was invited to dine with friends in Belgrave Square and go on to a dance in Cheyne Walk as sole escort of their only daughter. I had stayed with them in the country and genuinely liked the daughter who was lovely, artistic, good-natured, modest and unwarrantably diffident about herself and her excellent qualities, which tended to make her overrate those of others—including mine. We both knew plenty of people at the ball, but mostly danced together and towards its end I said I thought it about time I took her home, lest her parents should be anxious. 'Oh no,' said she, 'I have kept the brougham and I should like to drive *you* home, it's a lovely moonlight night and it will be along the Embankment all the way with the shining river for company.'

I protested that it was miles and miles to the Temple and my flat, far far away from her own home where she would be late indeed, but no, she would not listen and I eventually agreed to the expedition, not without misgiving.

Certainly it was beautiful, dawn was breaking as we reached our journey's end. I talked as entertainingly as I could in my corner of the carriage whilst she sat mostly silent in hers. It was an unforgettable drive, the most memorable of my life, compounded of beauty and panic. As I alighted at my door after what seemed like a night-long drive, I shook her hand, thanked her for the lift, said goodnight to her and to her coachman and bolted for cover.

Gentleman or cad? I have reluctantly come to think the latter, through cowardice, inexperience and lack of *savoir faire*. Surely I could at least have kissed her hand at parting without being compromised or added 'My dear' to my abrupt 'Good-night'? But no, my own selfish 'safety first' obsession held me firm in thrall. Yet it was that, I suppose, that kept me as it were 'intact' and free until the day when a cautious courtship ended in absolute certainty and all my doubts and fears were swept away.

I freely confess that my architectural ambitions considerably influenced my social contacts. Artists, writers and actors or Bohemians of any sort might indeed be more interesting and often much more fun than the county families and city magnates with elegant town houses in Mayfair or Belgravia, but it was the latter and never the former who had jobs to hand out. Unless I could pull in my share of such jobs I should soon end up high and dry as an architect in name only, and a bitterly frustrated one, for want of opportunity to exercise the talent that I then firmly believed that I possessed.

So, like any other sort of 'social climber' I freely accepted the invitations of the prominent and affluent to luncheons, dinners, theatres, balls, and weekends in their country houses, without any prospect or pretence of being able in any way to return such hospitality. Indeed far from attempting to entertain others, however frugally, I could only just afford pretty spartan living for myself alone, though I seemed to thrive well enough on a mixed and irregular diet of alternating quails and kippers. I marvelled indeed how anyone could possibly survive the habitual eating of the long and elaborate meals to which I was bidden—perhaps four or five courses for luncheon and up to eight for dinner with the various wines judged appropriate.

Country house breakfasts too were quite something. On reaching the dining-room perhaps an hour after having been called with tea and cream, thin rolled-up brown and white bread and butter, you would find a range of covered silver dishes keeping hot on a sideboard over little methylated flames, cherishing porridge, and a selection of omelettes, kippers, eggs, bacon, grilled kidneys, or kedgeree flanked by a cold table offering ham, tongue, brawn and such game as might be in season. In support would be hot scones and racks of toast, as well as trophies of hot-house and other fruit. Coffee, China and Indian tea would be ranged and kept hot on a side table and one just roamed around and helped oneself as fancy and appetite might dictate.

Within reasonable limits of say, up to an hour (unless there was some fixture to be kept) one came down when one chose, sat down where one liked and wandered off at will, knowing that there would be an unbroken fast of some three or four hours until luncheon was announced. In case the set menu of that meal failed to satisfy, there were always cheese and biscuits, 'luncheon cake' and port followed by coffee to make good any deficiency. Of course one normally only encountered such displays of 'conspicuous consumption' as one of a house-party.

Dinner parties were extremely formal and you processed to the dining-room with your lady on your arm, and you both sat down at table where your name card told you to and discovered (to your pleasure or dismay) who your left-hand lady might be.

A menu card would be within reach and personally I always clutched and scanned it with unconcealed interest at once, as I reckoned that my hostess would appreciate serious notice being taken of her cook's efforts and it enabled me to chart my course through the meal and to decide where to skip or go easy and where to indulge.

When the several contributing factors to 'an evening out' were all one hoped, that is, your host and hostess, your neighbours at table, the food, the wine and the whole setting—it could all be most enjoyable—but it was always a bit of a gamble. There is no easy escape from a long and dreary dinner and its desolating drawing-room aftermath save through downright implausible lying—or a bleeding nose, and mine never would oblige.

In my innocence it was years before I realized that such 'set pieces' were not necessarily a fair sample of a family's habitual meals, though by our present standards even the every-day eating of the period was certainly formidable. For instance, if you were asked to dinner, preparatory to being taken on to a play, the invitation often included supper at the Savoy afterwards, the idea I suppose being that, dinner having been a little earlier and not quite as heavy as usual, one would suffer night starvation unless thus sustained. I even recall one country house where the fear of that fate befalling a guest was so acute, that, on retiring, after a monumental dinner, a dance and a generous supper, I found laid out in my bedroom all the materials and utensils for a sort of self-service barbecue.

On a steel trivet beside the still glowing fire stood a covered dish containing raw chops, kidneys, bacon and sausages, a long-handled grill for their cooking, leaning in readiness against the mantelpiece. On an adjoining table were decanters of two sorts of whisky and all the equipment for a solo late supper or very early breakfast. I do not claim that this was common country house form, even in my far-away youth, for my host was, in general, pretty eccentric.

Having extravagant tastes, this enterprising landowner sought to supplement his rent-roll by establishing all sorts of local industries—a game farm, a brush factory, a mineral-water works, a distillery and I don't know what besides. If my memory fails here it is not for want of reminders for, on leaving, I found my suitcase gay with pasted-on advertisements proclaiming the unique virtues of all my host's wares.

The parties to which I went fade generally, in retrospect, into an agreeable dreamlike blur, from which emerge odd little vignettes that I can still see as vividly as in a sharply focused photograph: Pavlova and Lopokova dancing round the fountain in the garden of Lady Kennet (widow of Captain Scott, and Peter Scott's mother). Then there was a supper party with Mrs. Patrick Campbell; a commemorative dinner after which Geoffrey

Scott and I had to carry Augustus John to safety; a gay evening at Dick and Naomi Mitchison's, at their Chiswick house, River Court, where, having jumped over a bonfire, I said I could beat that by clearing their garden wall—not knowing there was a high drop to a road on the other side. I recall a splendid pineapple amongst the fruit they sent to my bedside. . . .

Edwardian dress seems strange in the 1970s. When (about 1905) I became more or less a Londoner, my elder brother thought I might just get by without bothering about a frock-coat such as he himself wore on more formal occasions and that an ordinary morning-coat would suffice.

With this morning-coat of course went a top hat, a stick-up collar, a tie or maybe a cravat with (sometimes) a white 'slip' between it and the waistcoat which was either black or grey.

Trousers were either in stripes or small (sponge-bag) check, patent leather boots with boxcloth tops *or* spats—generally white or buff; fawn or pale yellow gloves and of course a cane of some sort, as elegant as might be, if not a slim umbrella; for dinner parties and dances and the 'dress' parts of a theatre, tails, white tie and waistcoat, even white kid gloves, as well as a collapsible opera hat.

At large country house parties it would be tails and white ties again for dinner, but after the ladies had retired (picking up their silver candlesticks and lighting them in the hall in the less technologically advanced houses) the men would be apt to change into dinner jackets before settling down to their cigars and whisky in smoking or billiard room. I suppose the idea was to preserve the rest of the house and our dress-coats from smelling too vulgarly like a pub. In such circles very few women yet smoked.

I submitted meekly to all this ritual of dress and so on partly I think because I was at heart too timorous a nonconformist to defy convention where it seemed overwhelmingly against me and where the issue was less than vital. I did for a short spell dare to wear a deep blue waistcoat with pearl buttons as part of my otherwise correctly sombre day dress but it attracted so much shocked attention and even roundabout kindly-meant advice 'not to dress so theatrically' that I sadly abandoned it.

The same fate overtook a meek and tentative little pair of mini sideburns, only a fraction of an inch below the standard ear level short haircut of the day—but again, public opinion made it perfectly clear that such defiance of accepted fashion was entirely unacceptable, if no worse. Anyhow my feeble little one-man revolt fizzled out as it did not seem worth pursuing and I became, so far as clothes were concerned, the completely standardized young man that seemed then to be required.

I lately found a faded but still perfectly revolting photograph of myself—sitting on a log eating a picnic lunch with a woman client—old Miss Thackeray—on an open hillside, her half-finished house in the background. I am wearing a frogged fur-lined overcoat with an astrakhan collar, stick-up white collar with generous black silk bow-tie, spats and bowler hat. I no doubt had a cloth cap folded in my pocket as was customary for wear in the train, as no one ever then went bare-headed except indoors.

For certain occasions of course one had no choice *but* to conform, as for instance for a levée or a palace 'Drawing Room', which entailed full court dress—knee-breeches, buckled shoes, cocked hat, dress sword and all, which I partly borrowed and partly hired—the whole turnout being officially inspected.

I have lately and reluctantly come to the conclusion that why I so deprecate the unorthodox extravagance of the youth of the 1970s in their dress, hair styles and decor generally, may be nothing but plain old-fashioned jealousy of their uninhibited freedom to follow their own individual fancies.

A dance at Kent House stands out sharply in my memory for a particular and very good reason. The ballroom design and decor were by Paul Sert, and the black and gold walls crowded by apparently full-sized elephants and apes, made as exciting and dazzling a background as you could well have to a party that was in itself anyhow pretty gay. Indeed I found myself so unusually exhilarated that I all but proposed to my chief partner of the evening as we sat out between dances: I wish I had! Many months later and in very different circumstances I did so propose with the happiest results that have now lasted well over half a century. But on that occasion terror won and even the influence of the spectacular party was (just) not quite enough to break down my habitual caution. Most of the girls with whom I had always been so afraid of getting entangled, were dancing partners, met only on social occasions. But I had had my first sight of this one in quite another way.

It all began with a printed postcard from a Housing Association to which I belonged inviting members to attend a meeting on Merrow Downs, near Guildford, where St. Loe Strachey, High Sheriff of Surrey and editor-proprietor of *The Spectator* was showing his own amateur effort towards solving the rural housing shortage by means of cheap cottages. He was, it seemed, challenging the professionals or anyone else to better it.

I had propped this scruffy little card on my desk, thinking that if the Saturday afternoon in question chanced to be fine and I free, it might be fun to run down and see what was doing. It *was* fine, I *was* free, and I just happened to remember the fixture in time to catch the appropriate train. In due course I found myself sitting in a marquee listening to a gay and provocative speech by our host, St. Loe Strachey, to the effect that it was urgently necessary to do something about the provision of cheap country cottages and surely, if proper architects gave their minds to it, they ought to cook up something far better than he had contrived to do, a mere journalist and only part-time countryman.

Anyway, there was his own bid for what it was worth and he wanted to see it well and truly beaten. To that end he would he said, offer a plot of land to anyone who cared to take up his challenge and build a cottage on it, which done, he would buy the cottage if he liked it or, if he did not, he would give its builder the land on which it stood.

I liked this sporting offer and the engaging way in which it was made, but it was all getting only part of my attention because I liked even better the looks of a young lady whom I had seen earlier, moving about amongst the audience.

I had mistakenly assumed her to be one of the party brought by the Surrey Lord Lieutenant—Lord Midleton—to whom I had seen her talking, to whom I too therefore somehow attached myself during the tea interval, only to discover that she was actually Amabel Strachey, our host's own daughter, and that my ingratiating efforts had therefore been misdirected.

Because I had immediately resolved that I must somehow contrive to meet and see more of this girl at whatever cost, I stood up and accepted her father's challenge directly it was formally announced. The stratagem succeeded, and having thus established contact, I contrived to see quite a lot, though never enough, of Miss Strachey (for she was that, and I Mr. Williams-Ellis until our actual engagement) partly at her country home, Newlands Corner, partly in Queen Anne's Gate (No. 14, once the stately setting of the Townley Collection) and of course at all possible dinners, dances and other parties to which we could both contrive to get asked. Almost at once we had discovered that on top of all else, we shared various architectural amusements and enthusiasms—Strawberry Hill Gothick, for instance, and the rustic absurdities of Papworth, 'Author of the celebrated treatise on the dry rot', and the other romantics.

Incidentally I beat the field with a four-roomed cottage that cost precisely £101, complete.

We managed to get asked to a good many parties to which we discovered (usually in our cautious roundabout way) that the other one was likely to be invited. So, what with the necessary visits to my 'cheap cottage' site (nice informal occasions), we did contrive all through the next London season, to see each other pretty often.

Chapter Seven

My Own Home

It had been at about my twenty-fifth birthday, that is to say around 1908, that my father unexpectedly handed over to me the control of the old (Williams) family property of Plâs Brondanw in Merionethshire which I had gradually gathered I would ultimately inherit as second surviving son, but this decisive moment marked an epoch. Nothing could have appeared more casually informal than my father's offer, nothing, just then, could possibly have been more ecstatically welcomed by me. I expect he knew this, and believed that he was providing me with an anchor and something definite to work for. He was right.

At that time I fully shared my mother's piously dynastic views and regarded everything ancestral with a reverence almost superstitious, if not indeed religious. Also, I was in the antiquarian phase, and the guardianship of a rambling old Carolean Plas, a 'Capital Mansions House' set in a wildly romantic little estate amongst the Welsh mountains that had been held by my family for over four centuries, was well calculated to inflame me.

This house, abandoned for our Caernarvonshire home on my grandfather's death, had never been deflowered by restoration or improvement. It had, however, suffered a good deal by being divided up into tenements when the local slate quarries were booming, as also from neglect.

Amongst the seven families that I found installed in the place was that of a rather celebrated salmon poacher who had found the great chimney of the brew-house admirable for the smoking and curing of his fish. It was his precipitate disappearance that gave me my first foothold within the walls of the old house, and I instantly set about contriving a little flat from which I might gradually expand, as tenants left or died or could be suitably transplanted to cottages on the estate.

I had found two carpenter brothers and a stone-mason who would jointly contract to do what was immediately necessary, and the work began. It has been going on, save for the interruptions of war, fairly continuously ever since, to my great embarrassment and delight, one thing leading insidiously and appropriately to another.

One begins staidly with a new kitchen range and a bathroom, and yet, in a little while, one finds oneself building terraces, orangeries, triumphal arches, and planning further works of almost equal urgency. I have known few things in my life so intoxicatingly delightful as arriving in the star-lit dawn of a winter's morning after an all-night train journey from London and driving with my mother through the frosty air to inspect progress.

The smell of the deal shavings and the fresh distemper as I scrambled round with a candle before the men arrived—smells soon to be gloriously blended with that of frying bacon on a brazier in the old brew-house, beautiful and unforgettable. Gradually, yet surely, the old house and its rehabilitation became my chief absorbing interest outside my profession—a passion, an obsession if you like. Yet it was really part of my profession, it was for Brondanw's sake that I worked and stinted, for its sake that I chiefly hoped to prosper. A cheque of ten pounds would come in and I would order yew hedging to that extent, a cheque for twenty and I would pave a further piece of terrace. I had indeed come to reckon all my small earnings in terms of forestry catalogue prices, masons' wages and painters' estimates, and with so many thrilling things waiting to be done how could I find the heart to spend anything but a minimum on mere food and clothing?

Still I had to contrive even for the sake of the practice, to appear sufficiently presentable, and, if I dined frugally off poached eggs or kippers whenever I was left to myself, I had been all the more appreciative as a guest at the hospitable tables to which I was invited quite as often as was good for me.

My devotion was really that of a much-in-love young husband and a devoted father, though the object of my solicitude was that far simpler, more calculable and more limited liability than a fellow creature—a house and garden.

To me, the enchantment of the place was strangely reinforced on the very day I took possession and on which partial restoration had made a small bit of the old house my own. It was a cold wet day and I was just turning in off the high road when I met an old harpist and a boy fiddler trudging along, so asked them in for a bite and a warm-up in the hope that they might play to me, which they most cheerfully did whilst I lunched.

I had never before happened across such wandering minstrels, nor have I since, and I could not judge their real quality, but I still vividly recall the delight with which I heard (for the first time) their spirited rendering of 'Codiad-Yr-Ehedydd' (the 'Rising of the Lark') and 'Gwenith Gwyn' that to this day remain my favourites of all the lovely Welsh folk tunes to which I was then so memorably introduced. To my great happiness 'Codiad-Yr-Ehedydd' was, years later, adopted as the quick march of what became my regiment, the Welsh Guards.

It has been indeed only gradually that this intense local loyalty has come into any sort of perspective and to some extent been overlaid and obscured by other ties and interests.

It is warming indeed to see the avenues that I then planted growing so flourishingly and the whole place maturing in ever-increasing beauty, but I can still vividly recall the pangs of pleasure that the mere fact of *possession* of a dilapidated house and garden once gave me. It is still there and it is beautiful, and that is enough. If it is movingly beautiful also to my descendants I hope that they or one of them may be able to live there. If it is not wonderful to them, then I hope it may be enjoyed by someone else who will yet think kindly of those forerunners who spent four hundred years, off and on, in making what they admire.

I find that in 1929 I had written this:

> If it were not for the haunting fear that the amenities of the house, the little village, and the mountainous estate might suffer through ill-advised building or otherwise, I would most gladly see the whole property dismembered into freeholds. Possibly these feelings reflect my present political convictions and quite possibly these convictions are not my final ones, and indeed I find myself in an oddly provisional frame of mind about most things—my views dissolving views.

But later, as very gradually I was able to make improvements, to add to the amenities of village and farms and to extend my tree-planting, I seemed to become ever more securely attached to my setting to which indeed I added a couple of adjoining and very beautiful properties that include the twin mountain summits of Moelwyn and Cynict and the seventeenth-century manor house of Parc, since they had been widely advertised as promising areas for mineral prospecting and development.

Some day, it is to be hoped, really informed and sympathetic State protection may make natural beauty less precariously dependent on private piety.

I had long been envious of those other countries that had National Parks and most gladly served on the original Government Committee that was appointed to consider the establishment of such in England and Wales.

Even before that I had given the National Trust a mountain ridge that looked to Snowdon across the Gwynant Valley with the expressed hope that it might one day form part of a Snowdonian National Park, as it now does. Being as it were Member for Wales, I had some say as to how the Park boundaries should be drawn, and I was concerned that they should include *me* as they happily do. After all, as I pointed out, I was part of the local fauna that it was part of the Park's mission to protect. To avoid 'leaks' and premature controversy these boundaries were 'top secret' until our Report was published and the official Government announcement made.

However, in the meantime I had to meet King George and Queen Elizabeth up at Pen-y-gwryd and explain just what was intended. I told the King he was being given 'classified' information, but did not quite tell him to keep it under his Crown. The Queen's comment was characteristically shrewd. 'It's fine your preparing this splendid countryside for the people, but are you doing anything about preparing the people to make proper use of it?'

My slowly evolving architectural development at Brondanw and its surroundings and indeed wherever I have built is inexorably recorded phase by phase in abiding materials. I can turn back and I can see that this is good, this other indifferent—I progressed, I fell away, I recovered.

Piety for Brondanw and its surroundings was clearly not enough, nor were the rather wider responsibilities to the general surroundings of my fellow citizens that I felt as my practice grew. Over the siting of each new building that I was called upon to add to existing landscapes or town-scapes, as well as over its actual design I felt an increasing responsibility. I was in fact growing a social as well as an aesthetic conscience.

This new growth was fostered by various influences, among them, that of two friends, Peter Thorp and Lawrence Weaver. I can still recall how immediately and completely I was won over and not a little dazzled by Peter's eager talk and charm of manner. He was an acknowledged authority on printing and book layout, dandified, exquisite and rather mysteriously affluent.

His top hat, collars and cravats, his boots and spats, even his ivory-topped malacca cane were all specially made for him by the most celebrated tradesmen—the whole charade of being a sort of Edwardian Beau Brummell however having—so it emerged—a serious purpose. He wanted the best possible, not just for himself, but for *everybody*. His over-simple prescription for achieving this was to soak the conspicuously rich by disguising himself as one of themselves, and pleading his cause from within their own glittering ranks. This he most eloquently did, not infrequently with some success. He opened one of his campaigns with a grand banquet to mark the founding of his *Agenda Club*, supported not only by Cabinet Ministers, editors, and other assorted V.I.P.s, but by professional persons of all sorts, the idea being that members should pledge themselves to use their influence or give their professional services free to any cause or person that the committee reported as in need of such, but where there was no money for fees.

However, for all its initial publicity the thing never really got properly off the ground. As a sort of premature, one-man, do-it-yourself Welfare State it was a flop, but it certainly turned the minds of some of us—mine was one of them—to spheres of social usefulness that were only in part professional.

His next ploy was more productive. He got successions of carefully selected and exceedingly rich and reasonably benevolent persons to give really dazzling dinner parties in their own grand houses to guests—up to a dozen or so—all men—selected as appropriate to the particular theme of the after-dinner discussion. This would be chosen to fit in with the known interests of our host. As building or design was generally involved, I was often one of the company though I recall parties where topics were as remote from my specific profession as the care of the blind, typography, advertising, and urban traffic regulations.

Lawrence Weaver was another friend whose influence helped me to see where what I did fitted into a wider context (I later wrote his biography). He was at this time working on *Country Life* and it was over a *Country Life* competition that I first met him. It was for suburban houses at Gidea Park, where the competing architects had actually to submit their entries in solid bricks and mortar and at their own cost, on sites purchased from the estate concerned.

Altogether it was a pretty sporting event. I considered myself to have a rather ingenious plan that I felt inclined to back, and the chance thus offered for a little perfectly 'professional' speculation was irresistible.

Recklessly enough I entered my fancy and built my house, furnished it with all the affectionate pride of a young bride, laid out and planted the garden, and awaited the day of judgement.

A voice on the telephone. 'Is that Mr. Williams-Ellis? Good. Weaver here, speaking from *Country Life*. I'm just back from Gidea Park. That's a jolly little house of yours—could you let me have the plans? No, not a winner, I'm afraid; the judges felt you had tried to do rather too much for the money, but it's a great lark, and I like it. Yes, I've got a photograph, but I want a few notes—would you send me some? Or perhaps look in here? Tomorrow 2.30? Splendid. Goodbye.'

Well, if I'd lost the prize and possibly the five or six hundred pounds I had staked in land and building too, I had at any rate established contact with 'L.W.' whom I had heard was a delightful person.

I certainly found him so from the very first. He was interested in all architects, but especially in young ones showing the least animation, doing his utmost to get talent recognized wherever he found it, and giving criticism and advice in the most friendly and helpful fashion. He influenced me in many ways and like Peter Thorp, bubbled with all sorts of exciting ideas and projects.

But though these were the two who first strengthened my feeling that to put up buildings that pleased me and the client was not enough, I had already begun to try to put such ideas on paper other than what I pinned to a drawing board.

Quite certainly my first attempt to *write* about planning and amenity was made on a little steamer crossing over to Islay from Glasgow, where I had arrived by way of Edinburgh, sometime about 1905. I wrote when still under the spell of my first meeting the previous day with old Sir Patrick Geddes, a senior prophet of social and architectural planning, on an intoxicating crystal-clear morning spent in his famous Outlook Tower. All Edinburgh and its superb setting of Firth and mountains had been set before me by his *camera obscura*. The consequence was that my reaction to Glasgow's congested squalor was so immediate and so violent that I had to record it.

Having thus suddenly burst into writing, I soon found such expression generally soothing to my temper and to my young indignation at current planning follies. The discovery resulted in a good deal of railing against the Establishment and the status quo, generally in letters to *The Times* and other papers and in bits and pieces in the weeklies. Certainly there was no lack of material for an Edwardian Angry Young Man's scorn and indignation—especially if he had any concern for civics, housing, and town planning or for the face of the land. A question had of course already arisen. Was Britain doing worse or better than her continental neighbours? I didn't know. Gradually I managed to accumulate a small travel fund and through fourth-class on the railways, fifth-class lodgings and minimal meals of extreme austerity I somehow contrived to stretch five pounds into covering a whole week of intensive, *too* intensive foreign sight-seeing, which began in Holland.

The outcome of my study was not always as intended. One day I was quizzing the street sky-line of a huddle of excitingly variegated Dutch gables when they disappeared, to be surprisingly replaced by the kindly wrinkled face of an old woman who was holding a glass of water to my lips, as I lay supine on the cobbled street.

What had happened, it seemed, was that whilst absorbed in my architectural comparisons I had stepped backwards in front of an oncoming tram which on the old lady's assurance that I was only stunned, had clattered off on its way. But I think I must have had mild concussion as, on coming to, I felt that I absolutely *must* escape from Holland immediately. For no particular reason I took the first available night train for Berlin. I think I may really have been in flight from the extreme frugality of the last few days and that I must have recklessly travelled first-class, otherwise my chance companion could scarcely have recommended the Adlon Hotel as undoubtedly *the* place to stay. So, knowing of no other, thither I innocently went and, despite my grubbiness and tattered rucksack was courteously allotted a very grand bedroom with a private bath of which, after a week's abstinence, I stood in real need. My concussion euphoria must have been with me yet, as having done all I could in the way of toilet not to disgrace my sumptious surrounding I went down to order and gobble up a really gala breakfast, beginning with a delicious iced quarter of a cantaloupe melon, my first introduction to that admirable appetizer.

But after a reconnaissance of the public rooms, including the famous hall presided over by a large marble bust of the Kaiser, it suddenly occurred to me that such imperial pomp must be pretty expensive. This suspicion born of returning sanity—was amply confirmed by enquiry at the reception desk. After settling my hotel bill for one night, I would I found, only be left with just enough to scrape home on, granted maximum austerity. I managed it, and, as the Adlon Hotel came to play a quite prominent part in the history of the Third Reich before both were pulverised, I was glad this once to have savoured its Germanic swagger.

Foreign travel then didn't add very greatly to my expenses, though Brondanw did. The rooms that I was gradually reclaiming there had somehow to be furnished, and not, repeat not, just with necessities. My rooms and office in London too needed more than I had taken there in that cab. So every Friday morning at this time, whenever I could decently slip away, I would go off very early to the old Caledonian Market. It was a place of intoxication to a young man in my situation, for there were then for sale all sorts of agreeable antique objects at prices so trifling as now to seem entirely ridiculous. These wares were spread out on the cobblestones of the great open and exposed market-place on hundreds of scruffy little pitches, their proprietors crying their oddly assorted wares with the refrain 'Sort 'em out! Any price yer like!' A haggle was expected, with offer and counter-offer bandied to and fro until a bargain was struck by clasped hands.

Porcelain, pictures, bronzes, silver, carvings, furniture, there was something of everything from deplorable junk to the fine and the valuable. Whence the fine and valuable had come or how it had sunk so low, one could only wonder, though the place's reputation as a thieves' market was not I think generally deserved, for the police were little in evidence.

So I largely furnished Brondanw and embellished my Victoria Embankment flat from this source with shillings-worths that would today be pounds and though I was no connoisseur in anything, I did gradually pick up a certain expertise from friends and rivals at the market so that occasionally I would buy something that I knew was really good even if it had no appeal for me and I would then pass it on to a West End dealer at perhaps ten times what it had cost me. That certainly added a certain spice to the weekly early morning treasure-hunt. I would rush round the market as soon as the gates were opened, haggle, buy, and then off again to the underground station with my catch and so back to my drawing-board only a little behind normal office opening-time. On the whole the market vendors were a reasonably honest lot, except for their strange descriptions of their wares, erroneous mostly because of optimism and an ignorance even greater than my own. Only once was I bilked and that was over a charming inlaid Regency table for which I agreed to pay fifty shillings, delivered by its owner's own donkey cart, one pound down and the rest when I got it. It never arrived. Perhaps he lost my address or perhaps got a better offer and meant to return my deposit. But we never met again—or if we did, I failed to recognize him. I think I should still recognize that loved-and-lost table. Maybe I shall see it one day in a Christie's sale, being knocked down for around a hundred guineas. The great days of the old Caledonian Market, as I knew it, ended with the coming of the First World War and none of its would-be successors have ever approached it as a worthwhile hunting ground.

Odder and less accountable than this addiction, was my simultaneous enrolment in a long and highly organized course of supposedly strength-giving exercises at the 'Sandow Institute', St. James's. I suppose I imagined that my largely sedentary life was making me 'soft'. Pictures of the magnificent Eugene Sandow draped in a leopard skin, bulging and rippling with muscles, constantly appeared as advertisements in almost every paper with persuasive quasi-medical commendations. So I went to see the great man at his impressive gymnasium, and, mesmerized by his vice-like handshake, sparkling eye and bristling upturned moustaches conceded that my daily running up and down five flights of stairs and almost nightly dancing might indeed be inadequate exercise 'for a man of my build and potentialities' as he put it, and I signed on for a long and expensive course of body-building, progress being recorded by regular measurings and weighings on a most encouraging chart. But at last, with less than half the course completed, I could bear the tedium of the exercises no longer and finally slunk away, one of the Institute's gutless failures. My folly was at least harmless—as harmless as my elder brother Rupert's current study of Chinese, which he had as little possible use for as I had for a Sandow torso. We should all be allowed, I think, a certain ration of futility.

My quite groundless concern about exercise persisted for years. I joined the Princes Skating Club in a vain effort to become an accomplished ice-dancer. Much later, after the Second World War, a friendly General at the War Office who hated horses, but who was obliged, officially, to have a couple of chargers and a groom, put them at my disposal if only I would give them a certain minimum of exercise. For weeks beautifully turned-out groom and horses duly paraded prestigiously outside our London house to carry me off to Rotten Row for my early morning ride. I felt both virtuous and rather grand, but I dislike early rising and was never really horsy so, after a few weeks, I found some polite pretext for ending the arrangement.

My own chosen off-time diversions were and indeed still are a good deal less decorous if not indeed a little dubious for I was, and still am, a compulsive trespasser.

Strictly speaking, I have never actually 'burgled' a house—but 'breaking and entering' is a lesser crime of which I have often been guilty. My most rewarding ploy in this line was my illegal entry into a particularly fine Inigo Jones house in Norfolk, Raynham Hall, near King's Lynn, and to King's Lynn I had gone on a sketching weekend. The Sunday being fine and Raynham within reach, I hired a bicycle and set off determined at any rate to see the outside of the house even if, as was probable, I was not invited in. What I in fact found was that the whole great house was entirely shut up and deserted with not a soul about to question me or discourage my inquisitive prowling. In the course of this prowling I discovered that a basement window in the back premises was insecurely latched. So, after prudently hiding my bicycle in a shrubbery, I prised the window open and there I was safely inside and with a whole Sunday afternoon wherein to study and record some of the Master's interior detailing—or so I hoped.

It was immediately apparent *why* the house was uninhabited, indeed uninhabitable, as all the main rooms were full of scaffolding, ladders, and builders' gear of all sorts, being in fact obviously in the middle of very thorough restoration and redecoration.

This was unlooked for good luck as it allowed me to get close up to cornices and other architectural features otherwise quite out of reach and I was able actually thus to measure and accurately record them.

I was so engaged high up on a ladder in one of the great state rooms when I heard footsteps still a room or so away but audibly approaching. I habitually just slid down ladders anyway, without using the rungs, just to save time, and so, within seconds, I was not only down at floor level, but out of the room and into the next, away from the direction of those threatening footsteps. Luckily all these state rooms led one into another in the fashion of their period, so that I was able to keep at least one ahead of the unknown until I reached the end of the suite. Fortunately this last room had a lesser side door leading into a lobby and then on to the back parts where I found a staircase up which I quietly padded. Alas! I couldn't give all the attention they deserved to the splendid bedrooms as I had to listen out all the time for (as I supposed) the watchman or caretaker. However, I dodged about until I heard him mounting the lesser staircase when I felt safe to descend the main stair to the ground floor and continue my architectural cribbing—still alert, of course, to any sound of footsteps. In due course I heard them descending the way I had come down and then die away and finally a slammed door—and silence. By this time dusk was falling and it suddenly occurred to me that my follower might have been alerted by the discovery of my bicycle and that he might well have taken possession of it as a clue to the suspected trespasser. If so, how was I to get back to King's Lynn and explain the loss of my hired machine? So I pocketed my notes, scrambled out of the window by which I had entered, leaving it exactly as I had found it—and dived into the shrubbery where I had left my bicycle. It had not been moved—there was no one about—and I was soon pedalling back to my inn much fulfilled and exhilarated by my architectural spree.

I felt that I really ought to write to the owner, Lord Townshend, at least some sort of a roofer or an apology and to warn him of the faulty window catch or perhaps tell him how conscientiously his house was patrolled—but I didn't know him or how he might react, so I thought silence would be wiser—until now.

But this was only one of many such agreeable architectural misdemeanours. Any empty house of architectural interest that I happened on was an incitement and I seldom had much difficulty in quickly getting in and out again of dozens without ever being challenged. Of course an empty house is no temptation to the ordinary professional burglar who is after portable valuables, but in my experience, almost any house can be so very easily entered with a little ingenuity that I can only conclude we must be an extraordinarily law-abiding people or thefts would be incessant instead of being still newsworthy.

One of my forced entries was more than architecturally rewarding, for apart from the interest of the old manor house itself, part seventeenth century, part Regency, I found a musty lumber-room tucked away at the top which had clearly been overlooked when the rest of the rooms had been cleared. It looked as though no one had entered it for a century and indeed it seemed to contain nothing of much later date than the Regency —a brass-buttoned blue tail-coat of that period, breeches, buckled shoes and a sort of 'John Bull' low-crowned top-hat still in its leather case, an old-fashioned muzzle-loading shot gun and a miscellaneous collection of obsolete sporting gear of all sorts still partly wrapped in odd sheets of early nineteenth-century newspaper.

I then knew nothing of the history of the place or of its owner, but quite apart from the charm of the old house itself and its marvellous setting, I felt I must do all I possibly could to give life back to anything so appealing and so clearly and poignantly near its end.

Remembering that a fancy-free cousin of mine was at that moment vaguely house-hunting and ready to settle almost anywhere that was really and truly remote and countrified I thought I had found him the very thing—and so did he.

But it emerged that the owner was a dipsomaniac living abroad who never answered letters, even those from his own solicitor and was in effect completely incommunicado.

No doubt, we were told, that when in the fullness of time Mr. X had duly drunk himself to death, as we were assured he surely would, the property would automatically come on to the market and we could then negotiate.

But he lingered on unduly, my cousin suited himself elsewhere, and I feared that Mr. X might well outlive his cruelly neglected old home where ivy was growing in through cracks and broken windows and where the once lovely garden was already a wilderness with sapling trees pushing up the slabs of its terrace.

Some years later, however, there was a happy ending, when an indomitable family rediscovered my sleeping beauty and somehow contrived to negotiate its purchase. Knowing of my former interest in their prize, they invoked my help as architect for its restoration—a shared labour of love that in the end yielded a reward in beauty that would have been worth many times our joint efforts. Eventually presented to the National Trust by its devoted owners, it is now assured of the care and attention it so well deserves, one may hope, in perpetuity.

Once I wormed my way through an iron fence to get a closer view of an obviously distinguished classical building that I had glimpsed through a straggling shrubbery and a grove of neglected trees. It was in a tatty London suburb to which rumours of bygone splendour had directed me and if flagrant trespass was ever justified and generously rewarded it was there and it was then. For, standing there behind its dismal screen of sooty evergreens, was the little domed and porticoed palace that I had long known of but never seen—Chiswick House. Slighted, weather-stained and in obvious disrepair it was none the less still magnificent and in a daze of admiration I mounted the sweeping flight of steps to the main door which opened to my push and there I was, within, my footfalls on the dusty marble floor echoing from the vault above. But soon, standing agape beneath the dome, I heard other footsteps, the creak and flap of a swing door, nearer footsteps, and there was a man eyeing me strangely from a dozen feet away.

'Who are you? Where do you belong and what do you want?'

'Oh,' I said, 'I wanted to see the house which I thought was empty and as the gates were locked I got through the fence and I'm sorry if I'm trespassing but I am an architect particularly interested in buildings of this period and especially those of Lord Burlington. As I *am* here, may I please have a look round?'

His reply was a firm, 'No, quite out of the question, it would disturb the inmates.'

It transpired that the place was a private lunatic asylum and that, knowing the gates to be locked and believing the perimeter fence secure, he had at first supposed me to be a new patient somehow at large.

However, my identity and harmlessness established, I was courteously allowed to have my look round *outside*, in return for showing him where his fence needed reinforcing.

Revisiting the scene of this half-exhilarating half-depressing adventure over half a century later, it was wholly delightful to find how beautifully the whole place had been purged of irrelevances and restored to all its original elegance by the Ministry of Works. Now, open to the public, it has once more taken its place as one of the brightest gems of Palladian architecture that we possess.

The year 1912 is a notable one in my career, for it brought me my first big job, and the building remains to testify to my then architectural outlook and orientation. I have recently revisited this work and can recall all my bubbling excitement over every detail of what I still think a pretty good job. But what was I like then as a person? I have no such clear conception. I have so little evidence to help me and I find myself a barren and hesitating witness. Perhaps most of me that mattered then was built into that great house, perhaps the rest is dim because for the time this building *was* my life. I don't know. If it was so, it is scarcely to be wondered at, for rarely indeed can a young architect's dream have been realized so soon and so completely.

It all began, as did my finding a wife, with an encounter that was so much of a coincidence that few novelists would dare to use it in the framework of their story. I was travelling back to London by train from a hunt-ball in the far west and, feeling uncomfortable within, I stumbled out at Swindon to see if a tot of brandy might not steady me—a refreshment-room remedy never sought before or since.

As I was creeping back into my compartment I was hailed by a friend who presently came along to tell me that the man he found himself travelling with was going to London to find an architect to build him a new house on the site of his dilapidated old castle and hadn't I better come along and be introduced.

And so it was that, long before I could have expected a commission on so grand a scale, I found myself launched on a job that stretched all my faculties to their limit, but wherever knowledge failed me I quickly found out what I needed to know before committing myself irretrievably. For luckily I was not hurried, there was no deadline, and anyhow, being at the beginning almost single-handed, the plans themselves took some time to get into final working shape.

Ultimately all was approved and settled and there I was, responsible for the building of a really fine country house with all its appropriate outworks—gardens, stables, garages, powerhouse, cottages and the rest, all worthily in the same manner as the great house itself—a job that with an appreciative client was sheer delight. Indeed it suddenly made my tentative and cautious courtship and my ideas of a possible consequent marriage look almost realistic, and was not Brondanw almost fit to receive an at any rate romantically minded bride?

But the reader may well already have noticed something ominous about the date of all this. I was absorbed in the near completion of this most satisfying work when over my astonished head broke the thunderclap of war—the first of the two that fragmented my career.

Chapter Eight

War

Just to illustrate the surprise and confusion in the public mind at the actual declaration of war in August 1914, I offer my own bewildering experiences as a sample.

I was staying on its very eve at Wroxall Abbey in Warwickshire as one of a large and long weekend party which had not been cancelled even though successive official announcements were becoming ever more menacing. On the Sunday, however, we did disperse and I was given a car lift to London by a yeomanry officer whose depot was at Buckingham. There we duly called in to learn about the mobilization arrangements and inspect the ranges of saddlery and equipment, all being hopefully furbished up for expected imminent cavalry charges. Back in London, apart from the rumble of heavy transport all night, there was little sign of anything out of the ordinary apart from the long queues at recruiting stations.

Having become a practising architect within six months of the word 'go', I seem to have assumed that I should and must get into the army and the war at once, though at my first attempt to 'join' I had been told that no one over thirty would be even considered, and I was thirty-two. However, that nonsense must have been almost immediately dropped.

On my way to the Horse Guards for another try, I fell in with one of the Asquiths and we presented ourselves together, rather absurdly, for enlistment in the Household Cavalry which we thought might be more interesting than foot-slogging, with life just possibly made a trifle easier by my having a couple of cousins of some seniority already commissioned therein.

As chaos seemed to reign at the Horse Guards, so much so that we were not at all sure whether we had been actually signed up or not, I later boldly marched into the War Office with an introduction that I had managed to bully out of someone to the Military Secretary, no less, and I was not thrown out. Indeed he listened patiently to my silly plea for instant service and said, 'Just tell me your priorities and I will see what can be done about it.'

I chose the 9th Lancers because of a family connection—and incredibly, but sure enough, about a month later I was informed that I had indeed been gazetted to that elegant and gallant regiment.

But by the time my commission came through, I was already a lieutenant in a Kitchener's Army Infantry Battalion, so that I had to choose which of the two outfits I wished to belong to. The despondent 9th Lancers, whom I went to visit in their camp, told me that they feared that their fate might be to become a re-mount depot and riding school with the war all over before they could themselves get into it—so I decided to stay on my feet. I am not really at all horsy and should have been pretty useless and quite out of place in that *galère*. The decision, like so many of my others was a matter of pure chance. On the second Sunday of the war, travelling down by train to lunch with the Stracheys at Newlands, I had fallen into conversation with a large and handsome man sitting opposite. We exchanged platitudes about the weather and the war, when suddenly he said, 'By the way, if you haven't yet fixed yourself up, you might care to join my outfit, the Imperial Light Horse. I am the adjutant. We are parading in Hyde Park next Sunday, and if you like to join us there as a full lieutenant, that would be splendid.' Cavalry again? Well, perhaps it didn't much matter and in any case I didn't know quite what to make of such a sudden suggestion. Was he what he purported to be? Could such an unlikely sounding unit really exist? And could he (not even in uniform) hand out commissions as he pleased, and anyhow what about 'security' and discussing military matters with strangers, about which one was being so vehemently warned?

To my surprise, my adjutant turned out, on enquiry, to be genuine. So I bought a 'general service' uniform and duly paraded to be inspected and harangued by old General Sir Bindon Blood. The gist of Sir Bindon's speech was that though it was most gratifying to behold such a fine company of men with so many bemedalled old campaigners amongst them, none the less he feared he must disappoint many by a message he had just received from Lord Kitchener which in essence read, 'No more fancy cavalry *please*. I only want Infantry.'

As the Imperial Light Horse, we were it seemed, already disbanded, but if we would consent to become infantry—we could march more or less straight off to our prepared camp in Surrey, as the umpteenth battalion of the Royal Fusiliers, part of 'Kitchener's Army'. And that we did, without, I think, any resignations; and that was how I suddenly found myself a soldier.

In my own private life it was not only the completion of my one grand job that the declaration of war imperilled, but the infinitely more important matter of my, as yet, undeclared courtship.

My happening to join the bit of Kitchener's Army stationed only a dozen miles from the Stracheys' home in Surrey, was no sort of wangle, just luck, an unlooked-for gleam in an ever-darkening sky. But it was not until just short of Christmas that *we* actually became engaged. I was in camp and she a Red Cross nurse, her home having by then become a hospital. She told me that after we were married, she was determined to continue with her writing, and I thought, 'Thank goodness!' because I really didn't know what I should do with a full-time wife. A wartime engagement was apt to have its ups and downs, in no case of our own making, but her tours of duty and my military commitments constantly mis-fitted.

With my Royal Fusilier service battalion, I entrained for our Surrey camp which consisted of tents, mud and confusion, the men in blue overalls, only the officers in uniform, their swords the unit's only weaponry.

Our Colonel, as a Member of Parliament, obviously preferred Westminster (or London anyway) to our makeshift camp and he was largely an absentee, until scandal finally removed him altogether to make way for a charming old gentleman who did really try his best to turn us into an effective military unit. Certainly we were a pretty mixed lot, the senior officers largely Boer War veterans, mostly irregulars, a leavening of others from 'good' regiments a little mysteriously available to our very scratch outfit, the rest as green and untrained as myself. Inevitably I felt a fraud, first because, on the strength of a few years as a trooper in the Inns of Court Mounted Infantry, I had been made a full lieutenant over the heads of half a dozen ex-regulars; then because I really knew little if any more than the rank and file of the mysteries of infantry training which, presumably, was what they were there to be taught. Anyhow when an elementary course was offered at Chelsea barracks under Guards instructors, I leapt at the chance of learning something myself.

It was, as I had expected, a quite admirable course, and I returned to my unit all aglow with martial ardour to find myself regarded as the very fount of military wisdom to be dispensed by lectures and demonstrations to all and sundry.

To find myself thus suddenly of some actual use was certainly cheering and made my whole battalion's set-up seem less futile, but having savoured the assured professionalism of the Guards, their discipline and apparent efficiency, I found myself harbouring disloyal thoughts about a transfer.

The formation of the Welsh Guards seemed to offer me the chance, and having duly applied and been accepted, I joined them in the grandstand at Sandown Park racecourse, still providentially in Surrey and even nearer Amabel's home than had been my Fusiliers—my bull-nosed Morris Oxford two-seater providing the link.

I felt a little badly about deserting my nice old Colonel who indeed offered to promote me Captain if I stayed, but apart from the glamour of joining the Brigade of Guards, I felt that my old raggle-taggle outfit would need far better regimental officers than I should ever be to work it up into really effective fighting trim. Such officers, to judge from its ultimate good record in the field, it must have eventually got.

Now St. Loe Strachey, my father-in-law-elect, who was greatly concerned about defence and all things military—had cooperated with Lord Roberts and Lord Haldane about 'preparedness' and had himself run *The Spectator* demonstration infantry company to show how quickly men could be trained, so long as their arms and equipment were forthcoming.

Further, he had organized his own private army of country neighbours, some fifty of them—'The Surrey Guides'—all mounted on their own horses and in elegant bottle-green uniforms. Fully familiar with their county's intricate terrain, they were expected to be able to find their way about it unerringly by day or night and so guide troops from A to B by the shortest or safest routes, if need be across country, in the event of enemy invasion or other military emergency.

St. Loe was eager that I should take part in, witness and criticize an all-night exercise of his corps, for which he would mount me. So, after dinner at Newlands, off we set in the June dusk to join our section and, with the rest of the corps, carry out the set task of safely guiding an imaginary infantry unit past imaginary hazards over hill and dale, by woodland bridle-paths and downland tracks, from somewhere near Guildford to somewhere near Dorking. It was a perfect night and a lovely ride and after a bath and breakfast back at Newlands, I drove myself up to Wellington Barracks where I was due on duty as the weekend picket officer.

My first job, it being Sunday morning, was to parade the Welsh Guards and march them out of the grilling heat of the barrack square into the cool and soothing shade of the chapel. Alas! All too soothing for, standing there next the aisle at the head of my men, I was soon startled by a shattering clatter—it was my sword catching in the pew-end, as, fast asleep, I had toppled over. Horrified, I did my best to pull myself together, but a little later I was rudely awakened by someone vigorously shaking my shoulder—I had remained devoutly kneeling, fast asleep again, whilst everyone else was standing.

Monday morning of course brought a summons to the orderly room and a painful confrontation with the adjutant. It appeared that no less than five old Guards Generals had reported the Sunday's scandal and that full retribution was expected and would certainly be exacted. I agreed that it must have looked bad—indeed was bad, but that it had not arisen through all night dissipation as perhaps had been not unreasonably assumed, but from sheer military zeal, mistaken and excessive perhaps, but surely not punishable. It was no good. 'You will do four extra weekend tours of picket duty'—and that was that.

Whilst four other subalterns rejoiced at being thus let off this hated chore, I, who assumed their burden, was filled with bitterness, for I had just become engaged and here were four eagerly anticipated golden weekends suddenly snatched away from me by unfeeling and obviously vindictive authority. Was I still a schoolboy, I raged, to be thus lectured on deportment and 'kept in' at the whim of a petty tyrant, a jack-in-office, my junior in everything but his absurd service rank—and so on and so forth in a black fury. My fuming was, I eventually realized, utterly unfair, for what had become of my avowed admiration for the Brigade's inflexible discipline? I cooled down of course, and served my sentence, though had I been offered a flogging as an alternative to the privation of those four lost weekends, I would have opted for it gleefully.

Later on, as soon as my forthcoming marriage had been officially announced, I was sent for by my commanding officer at Wellington Barracks whose sanction I of course had had to get, when the following dialogue took place:

- C.O.: Ah! I have been asked by your brother officers of the Welsh Guards to present you with this cheque on their behalf and my own as our wedding present. I don't want you just to blue it on nightclubs or any such nonsense, but to have some lasting memento of our regard. I suggest it should take the form of a silver salver, engraved with our signatures, which would be the usual thing and in order.
- ME: Thank you very much, Sir. That would indeed be delightful. But it so happens that we already have a certain amount of family silver that just lies at the bank or stored away as we have small hope of using it. So might we perhaps choose something else?
- C.O.: Why, yes, of course, but what—because I should like to know.
- ME: Well, Sir, what I should really like would be a ruin.
- C.O.: A . . . WHAT?
- ME: A ruin—as an outlook tower. You see, Sir, there happens to be a rocky eminence close above my home on which I have always felt

there should be a tower of some sort as a fitting crown and as a superb view-point commanding wonderful panoramas from the summit of Snowdon to the sea.

c.o.: Well, if you want a ruin, I suppose you had better have a ruin—though it's an odd sort of wedding present, I must say.

Amabel and I were married in the little St. Martha's chapel perched on a hill-top on the Pilgrims' Way above Merrow, and inaccessible except on foot. For we had aimed at a quiet wedding and for that reason and also in order that we might get down by train to Wales the same day, it was timed for the early hour of eight. Being thus doubly out of the ordinary, our rustic wedding apparently qualified as 'news' so that, what with reporters and photographers, it wasn't quite as quietly intimate as intended. There even arose rumours that ours was a runaway match, disapproved by the families on both sides, despite the actual facts, the bride's parents and brother, and my mother and my own three serving brothers, all being present.

Nor was our arrival at Brondanw unmarked. Loyal and friendly tenants had decorated the lodge arch with an enormous wreath surrounding the legend, 'Welcome to Lt. Clough Williams-Ellis and his grateful bride.' That exhausted the locally available English, the rest of the welcome by speeches and song from those who packed the house's forecourt, being of course in Welsh, both eloquent and melodious—to all of which, illiterates as we are, we could only respond in English.

How quickly can a fortnight's leave come to an end? I can tell you: I *know*. Part of it was spent in visits to various old friends en route as we meandered back to London in the car my soldier-servant had driven down for me—all the way in second gear only, because unluckily for both of them he had failed to discover the others. But neither seemed any the worse. We had been married only a month or two when unofficial rumours of the heavy casualties suffered by our 1st Battalion in the bitter battle of Loos gradually made it clear that a reinforcement draft would very soon be sent out to it. In anticipation I was granted four days' leave in Wales, which really only amounted to two—the rest being eaten up in travelling down and back again. Amabel and I were planting the little trees that now form the wood up by the Tower, when a telegram was brought up to me on the second day, ordering me back for immediate embarkation. Thus suddenly, by the week's end, I had exchanged the serene peace of Brondanw for the front line of the ill-famed Hohenzollern Redoubt, shying bombs at undoubted visible Germans and dodging theirs. I say 'front line', but in that shattered corpse-strewn labyrinth, still mostly held by the enemy, it was most difficult to tell just where you were, which way you were facing or which saps, craters or trench fragments we were supposed to be holding.

Such then was my first real taste of the war—a slow crawl up to this ambiguous and sinister fortress from our shell-harassed billets in the cellars of what had lately been Vermelles—a warning that a counter-attack was expected at any moment, that the position must be held at all costs, and that, my company commander having suddenly gone sick, his command devolved upon *me*. But the battle of Loos, which had just been bloodily yet fruitlessly fought over this terrain, had left both sides exhausted, and our spell in this sector came to its appointed end without providing any item of interest for the newspapers.

With me there remains a remote yet nightmare memory of blear-eyed watchfulness, of a strange feeling of serene inadequacy in a setting of explosions, stench, death and ugliness which, grotesquely macabre, seemed to belong to some quite other world than mine. I seem all through, to have contrived to take a curiously detached view of the whole war so far as my part in it went and—in my own mind—to have disclaimed responsibility for it or its conduct or its conclusion, and generally to have reserved the right to remain fatalistically critical.

It was not the heroic attitude: I merely found myself being conventionally dutiful in a rather resentful fashion, yet making myself as useful and efficient as I could because one clearly owed that much to one's side as well as to oneself, and because the awful abyss of unfathomable boredom so clearly yawned ready to engulf me the moment I relaxed my zeal (morbid, if you like) for my new and strange profession.

I have known no tedium so utterly blistering as that of routine trench warfare in a relatively quiet sector, with its interminable sequences of 'front line', 'support' and 'rest billets', the monastic isolation from the real world, the interminable days and nights for regretful yearning dreams of home and of life as it had been, as it might be now save only for this bloody war, as some day it might yet even be again—if . . . . Always and for ever that provisional, day-to-day, unsettling 'if'. Increasingly it had to be accepted that a little wooden cross was what one could look forward to with more likelihood than anything else; but there was not much planning to be done with regard to that. So one planned with what conviction one might for pleasanter if remoter eventualities. Meanwhile, we were supposed to be killing Germans. Actually that winter we were mostly just eating our heads off and our hearts out killing time.

I sent home for my water-colours and did sketches of trench and billet scenes and of such architectural fragments as were within reach, until it grew too cold and the colours froze upon the paper. Then I distracted myself by getting an ex-schoolmaster stretcher-bearer in my company to come round to my dug-out or billet and give me lessons in Welsh with his Bible as our reading book. Any off-time, when we were back in rest, I would borrow a horse and go off exploring the back areas with a Baedeker, a sketchbook and a map. Once I got into trouble through tying up my borrowed mount in the fascinating little hill town of Casell, and then, forgetting all about it, getting back by car and lorry lifts. I had to return next day to fetch this horse and then found I could not find nor identify the creature, not having remarked its colour, size, sex or anything else about my means of conveyance on this, one of my greatest sprees of the war. I never pretended to be able to remember a man's face, so why should I be expected to recognize that of a horse I had barely met, on a day too when I had eyes and thoughts for nothing other than the healing architectural intimacies of this little market-town, its merrily spinning windmills and its First Empire château?

Ultimately the horse was somehow recovered, and I prolonged the rare and grateful savour of this short escape from the war by the writing of two articles, duly published, on what I had seen and thought.

Despite this un-horsemanlike lapse which went the rounds as a good story against me—it did not end my riding, whether on duty or for pleasure, as the then Prince of Wales, attached to Guards Division H.Q., lent me one of his own two horses when not needing it himself, which was often enough as he preferred, of all things, *bicycling*.

My father-in-law sent me occasional books for review, I made plans for all manner of buildings, possible and impossible, I snooped around on horseback and on foot, and generally eked out a meagre little spare-time peace-life within the imprisoning framework of the war.

Yet it was these peculiar employments of my off-duty days that were to shape my wartime destiny. My activities came to the knowledge of Divisional Headquarters, which, needing a sort of trench ferret assistant to the Operations department, 'borrowed' me from my battalion as Guards Division Intelligence Officer. In that capacity my map-reading, sketching, reconnoitring and reporting propensities could all be employed, and with few routine duties and a general roving commission I contrived to lead a more useful and less devastated existence.

The production of panorama pictures of the enemy's works as seen from our own front line now became a recognized part of my military duties, survey plans of our own trenches and redoubts were in constant demand, with notes on their condition and also confirmation or otherwise of doings on the Germans' side as reported by battalion observers. One spied from Artillery Observation Posts or from a tree, scaled with climbing irons, and occasionally from an aeroplane or observation balloon, and once in a while one got arrested and detained by zealous commanders in neighbouring sectors suspicious of the pryings of a perhaps not very convincing Guards officer.

The first time I was airborne on one of these reconnaissances was in the basket of an observation balloon for the study and sketching of the enemies' defences.

I was allowed up for half an hour only, as it generally took the Germans about that time to decide that the target was worth shooting down and to get its range. I was told, however, that if their shrapnel was bursting pretty accurately I was to telephone at once and I would be hauled down as fast as might be. My further instruction was that if the shooting got *really* close I must quit the basket with my parachute instantly, as, if the balloon were hit, it would be too late to jump, as it would come down in flames on top of my parachute and burn up both it and me.

Not terribly encouraging, but, as I had begged for this ascent as a special favour, up I went and sketched away busily for a quarter of an hour or so before being interfered with in any way. Then bang, bang, came a couple of ranging shrapnel shots that straddled me nicely—then more—quite near enough, I guessed, to justify my telephoning to the ground control to be hauled down, so I took up the instrument.

'Those last ones pretty good shooting, and I've got what I wanted so I think I had best come down.' No response. More shrapnel and still no response. I had never done a parachute jump, and I didn't want to do one unless I absolutely had to. However, having adjusted my harness, I perched myself on the edge of the basket cursing ground control and ready to launch myself into space just ahead (I hoped) of the burning balloon above me.

Five minutes, ten minutes, fifteen minutes, whilst the shooting continued off and on, but now less well aimed, and then, at the end of a lifetime as it seemed (and might have been) the balloon was majestically hauled down to earth.

OFFICER-IN-CHARGE: Jolly good show!
ME: What do you mean—good show?
O.I.C.: Oh, sticking it out like that.
ME: Sticking it out! Why I tried to signal I was through a quarter of an hour ago but you left me to it!

Any hard feelings on either side were happily dispersed by an N.C.O. coming up to report that the telephone line had been cut—presumably by a shrapnel splinter. I wondered where I might have landed (if at all) had the wire hawser tethering the balloon been severed instead.

I was still at that time the Guards Division Intelligence Officer (or 'Trench Rat') and I had boldly asked the General commanding, Lord Cavan, whether, if he thought it a good idea, he would give me a chit to the neighbouring air unit (it was the Royal Flying Corps then) asking them to take me up. He did. I had as yet never flown in an aeroplane, but off I went to the flying field with my official authorization.

After some discussion out of my hearing, a young airman in full flying kit appeared and I followed him out on to the otherwise deserted aerodrome across to his little machine tethered in a corner. As I fitted myself into the spare seat beside him he handed me a Lewis gun—a weapon that I, of course, knew about but had never fired.

'What am I supposed to do with this?' I asked. 'Try and shoot down the other fellow before he gets us,' he replied. I explained that I was no great marksman at the best of times and that he had better not rely on my shooting with a strange weapon fired from a wobbling 'plane my first time up.

He clearly didn't think much of me as a protector and how rightly, but he did none the less take me back and forth over the area I wanted to study, until he shouted, 'Had enough?' and I shouted back, 'Yes.' We had been shot at all right but only with shrapnel from the ground and, in the absence of any German plane, I was spared the humiliating likelihood of missing an enemy target—and so perhaps getting my pilot killed, if indeed I didn't incompetently shoot him myself.

Safely landed, I told him I had simply no idea that flying was so exceedingly uncomfortable and that one got so violently flung about. He looked at me darkly and said, 'Well, what do you expect on a day like this, don't you realize that we are all grounded—the Hun as well—and it was only that straight order from the G.O.C. that sent me up at all.'

I felt apologetic but thought it best to let him believe that the information I had gathered was vitally important and urgently needed—so that he would at least feel that our flight had been really necessary. In fact it would have been far more productive on a better flying day, but then the enemy would have been airborne too when my incompetence with that Lewis gun might have been fatally exposed.

Afterwards I was sent for by the then relevant top airman (later Lord Brabazon of Tara) who was sick in bed. I found to my relief and surprise that it was to hear how useful my air lift had been and not, as I had rather expected, to get a wigging.

Brigade or Divisional Headquarters would usually now be my official home and that quite often meant *architecture*; once the fairytale towered and moated castle of Esquilbec whilst we were out of the line, and then vaults in the great ramparts of Ypres, whence I could unofficially yet conveniently explore the tragic though still beautiful ruins of the town I had known and loved whilst it was still serenely obscure and before war had made it famous and a rubbish-heap. Amongst its shell-eroded buildings which day and night the enemy's guns were further pulverizing, little architectural fragments could still be found, and my Brigadier and I had begun to make quite a notable collection in our headquarters cellar, especially of wrought ironwork when our pleasant partnership was dissolved by his being shot through the head.

He had begun by saying, 'You are looting, you know—I can't allow that.' I replied, 'Of course you can't—but this is salvage and that is officially encouraged.'

That was accepted on the understanding that we shared the proceeds fifty-fifty and I duly sent his half home to his widow.

But I had a certain amount of desk work as well as field work and whilst acting as G.O.3 at Corps H.Q. I was responsible for instance for compiling the daily intelligence summary that went out to all units in the corps giving military information, particularly such as affected their own sectors of the front.

It was just after the bloody opening Somme offensive had ground to a temporary halt and everyone was worn out and down-hearted and, to my mind, badly in need of cheering up.

My previous General having encouraged my putting in little tail-pieces of nonsense, I had rather enlarged these when the new General took over and the exhausted surviving troops had been withdrawn to rest and boredom. There had then come along and through my hands an unusually long-winded and pompously worded instruction from G.H.Q. as to the correct official names to be henceforth used for certain military stores and equipment. In the middle of what we were going through this piece of niggling bureaucratic fuss about anything so trivial seemed to me so grotesque as to be really comic, and I let myself go in making fun of G.H.Q. as I thought to great effect—describing an imaginary scene where those in charge of our destinies were met in solemn conclave to decide by a show of hands exactly what should be called what.

Through a glass partition between my office and that of the General, I saw him pick up his copy of my current issue that had just come off the duplicator. I did rather wonder how he would take my definitely disrespectful little digs. He had his back to me and when I saw his neck flush purple, I knew.

He turned round to face me, to glare at me and finally to beckon me in to his presence. Standing stiffly to attention I received the most ferocious telling-off of my life, and it was so expertly done that I really felt I deserved it and was certainly shaken when a court-martial was mentioned.

Reading my well-intentioned satire over in very cold blood indeed after my trouncing, I did come to see what my General meant and that to troops whose belief in the High Command was anyway already low, owing to their recent apparently fruitless suffering and losses, my derision might not be the best possible morale-builder after all.

My General had said that the appropriate punishment for my insubordinate behaviour would have to be considered, but in fact nothing whatever came of it all, except some weeks of nagging apprehension and regret for my impulsive folly in blaspheming the most high. Perhaps I was reported to G.H.Q. via the Army Command—and just possibly they saw the communiqué that I had satirized as I had, that is, as a piece of Mandarin pomposity that deserved a bit of fun-poking. Maybe they even told whoever had drafted the silly thing not to dress up a plain directive in fancy prose. Both my General and I were spared the embarrassment of further contact during this, to me, menacing period, through his being suddenly wafted off elsewhere never to be seen again—by me. I bore him no grudge as I saw that he, as a General and a Guardsman at that, was bound to react as he had done in defence of discipline.

My second spell in the Salient was after the battle of the Somme, when the corps to which I had been attached as acting

G.S.O.3 withdrew there to recover from that offensive and repair its appalling losses. It was just then by way of being a quiet bit of the line, yet it was always disagreeable enough, with wretched waterlogged trenches and the everlasting shelling.

Some day someone would have to storm the High Command Redoubt that so insolently dominated our front line, and, if successful, to pass beyond it down into the Steenbeke valley, and with luck, up and over the next rise and away beyond. So a 'Book of the Beyond' must be compiled, from observation, from the depositions of refugees, from maps and photographs and every other imaginable source, and thus might the Intelligence department justify its tedious hibernation in a static warfare sector, and so perhaps be kept usefully amused and out of mischief.

Had I known that a year later I should myself be intimately and responsibly involved in this battle that now seemed so remote and problematical, should find myself indeed, creeping furtively up the Steenbeke itself reconnoitring for likely crossing places, my interest in this mostly invisible enemy hinterland might have been less perfunctory.

As some relief I attempted to start a light supplement to the official daily Intelligence Summary for which I was again responsible, to be called 'The Ypres Gazette and Salient Advertiser', but the proposal did not please Authority. Then I turned my attention to the invention of various offensive devices including man-traps for catching Germans alive for identification. I actually got a series of such man-traps made. They were to be buried in No-Man's Land and to be baited with dummy British corpses. The enemy had only to step on to one of my machines to be (fairly) painlessly yet firmly secured by one or both legs when a flare would automatically illuminate him and give warning to our sentries, who would then haul him in on his sledge-mounted trap by a wire hawser.

Though having high official blessing after being demonstrated before an approving gaggle of Generals and though I offered to set my 'catch-'em-alive-oh!' traps myself, no front-line commander would allow the experiment to be made on his particular sector, at present blessedly quiet, and, like that stirrer-up of trouble the Trench Mortar man, I was always passed along with cordial recommendations to a neighbour. It was generally held that my unconventional methods of warfare would provoke the enemy to vindictive reprisals.

As it was, I almost became ill with the black, despairing boredom of it all, and applied to return to my battalion.

Then, suddenly and most blessedly, I was granted leave!

Leaves were golden intermissions that made the otherwise desolate war years worth living through.

For me they were above all that strange and hectic wartime thing, a honeymoon by half-yearly instalments, with, at the end of each, a railway station parting, the pattern of which was each time more or less a repetition of my first departure. Quite lately, more than forty years later, a letter from my father-in-law, St. Loe Strachey, to his old friend the President of the United States, Theodore Roosevelt, has come to hand. It gives a stoical glimpse of what Amabel and I too felt:

> My daughter's husband went to the front last Wednesday. . . . I am glad to say that my daughter has a really stout heart and though she is only twenty-one and has been married a bare three months, she is facing the music splendidly. I was with her at the station to see her husband and a small group of officers off and I was really proud of her. Of course she did not break down.

Leaves meant Brondanw and Wales with possibly a day or two in London at each end, wartime trains making this inevitable. I remember one such London evening at the beginning of a leave, the mood being heightened, as all leave days were till the last, by a sort of exultation. We were staying with the St. Loe Stracheys at Queen Anne's Gate and I had invited my admired friend Lawrence Weaver, who was also on leave from the Navy to join us, for I wanted to show him off to Amabel and her parents. After dinner I remember we were all a good deal excited by the events of the moment and we declared ourselves a cabinet of all the talents, my father-in-law representing the Press, Sir Maurice Hankey (a fellow guest and then secretary of the Imperial Defence Committee) politics and the High Command, Mrs. Strachey and

Amabel (Commandant of a hospital and a V.A.D. therein respectively) were the 'Auxiliary Services'. I was the Army, and Lawrence the Navy. Severally we foretold the future and prophesied generally in that warm way that is born of such occasions, Lawrence finally giving us a finished sketch of himself as an A.B., his extravaganza including such episodes as the polishing of brasses and the zealous execution of sanitary fatigues—his improved technique for each being mock-seriously expounded.

There was so clearly a certain reckless despair beneath his gaiety that left one a little uneasy.

We had each and all I think, begun to feel that the winning side would be that which first set its house in order and best employed its available manpower, and here was Hankey no doubt in the right place, but Lawrence was still scrubbing out latrines. He and I were still fitfully corresponding on conservation and the shape of things to come, for it was the physical planning of our country itself, or rather the lack of it, that was making me so uneasy about the future. Speaking, I felt, as much for Lawrence as myself and indeed for many others, I summed up our dialogue in a *Manchester Guardian* article. Britain, I said, was, from the point of view of use of the land, a Frump and a Slattern:

> Anyone who cares for England must be interested in national planning, the provision of a comprehensive co-ordinated and compulsory development and conservation scheme for the country as a whole, urban and rural, public and private. The economic case for an orderly and far-sightedly managed national estate is so overwhelming that one really need not speak of national pride or the need for beauty.

It was on one of these precious leaves, these honeymoons by instalment, and on its second day, that I got a telegram ordering me back to France—not because of some emergency or disaster, but that I might complete my corps quota to some wretched G.H.Q. course. To do a man out of his leave for a thing like that —a leave that, as always, might be his last! I had been enraged before, but never with such dumb, impotent bitterness—there was just nothing to be done but for me to report myself immediately and for us to part—as usual.

The course turned out to be one on reconnaissance that I found interesting enough until, a day or so after its beginning I fell in a faint for the first and last time in my life and went sick with a fierce attack of 'flu. In retrospect it all looks suspiciously like a bit of dirty work by my subconscious self deeply and darkly plotting for the completion of my interrupted leave, or at any rate avenging it.

But even my subconscious self was not all-knowing—it did not guess, I imagine, that a certain convalescent drive that I took in a car impudently borrowed from the Town Major of St. Omer, where I had been 'hospitalized', was to change the whole complexion of the war for me.

I had heard fabulous whispered tales of our new hope—'the tanks'—and that their discreet and highly hush-hush headquarters were not so very far away. Determined to see and hear what might be anyway possible of this mysterious arm, I boldly called on the commanding officer, a joy-riding subaltern in a dubiously borrowed car, with no better credentials than my highly unofficial and impertinent curiosity.

Fine soldier and leader that he was, there was to me something engagingly unmilitary about the commander of the tanks, General Sir Hugh Elles who welcomed me with informal friendliness, sat me down by the fire to tea and buttered toast, and proceeded to talk of the new warfare at length, amusingly and with enthusiasm.

I came away a hot tank partisan, and when shortly afterwards a whip came round for volunteers for the new corps, I put in for the command of a tank section. It seemed, however, that I was still to be kept to my reconnaissance line, and in that capacity I went to the Third Tank Brigade for the battle of Arras.

But as usual in warfare there was a long, tedious and undramatic wait, during which I tried to work out reconnaissance methods suitable to this new arm.

'Pelmanism', a system of memory training was fashionable at the time and it occurred to me that I might apply their methods to this military problem and might indeed concoct a new Pelman 'little grey book' myself, primarily concerned with the memorizing of landscapes, buildings, trees, trenches and the rest of our battle-scarred scenery, where observation could often be but brief and furtive and immediate sketching quite impossible. So I set to work and showed how almost anyone could, by a simplified quasi-shorthand method, produce a perfectly legible and understandable record of what he had seen, and I drew lots of little pictures in simple outline to show how readily this could be done. There was a section too on 'Reports' and how to make such as short, clear, and unambiguous as possible—'like a telegram sent to a very stupid man from a very poor one'.

Rather pleased with my compilation, I tried it out as a lecture with blackboard accompaniment and then sent it off to Pelman's.

They accepted it, offering me a fee of £100 which exactly balanced a stupid bet I had lost about the ending of the war—stupid because I had been madly optimistic and also because I am quite sure that I should never have been paid had I won!

Thinking it would be pretty much in his line, I had written to Robert Baden-Powell as Chief Scout, asking him if he would contribute an introduction, which he instantly and enthusiastically did. In due course the galley proofs came along, were corrected and returned, and then—just nothing.

But one day I was sent for and told to report to G.H.Q. Conducted to the department concerned with spies and counter-espionage I at last began to guess. It must be those damned proofs—confiscated by the censors for some ridiculous reason and handed over to G.H.Q. as suspect. Luckily I knew from London days both the Colonel and Major who confronted me and this somewhat restored my confidence. Surely they knew me well enough scarcely to believe me an enemy agent?

None the less I was put through it in due form. How came it that I was in correspondence with a concern known to have foreign connections—did not some of my sketches represent actual battle area terrain and landmarks on our side of the line and did I not actually refer to some by name—and so on and on?

True I had given some of my landscapes names, but all fictitious—'Susan Copse' I recall—in honour of our first-born of whom I had only just had news.

Anyway, after conscientiously doing their stuff, they conceded that my explanations were perfectly satisfactory, that I might have back my proofs and proceed with publication in support of our war effort. But the result of this dull-witted interference from on high was that by the time the book (called *Reconography*) was out and ready for the widespread distribution that had been promised, the war was almost over and no one wanted lectures on anything except demobilization.

So there were the stacks of my poor little *Reconography* 'grey books' by the ten thousand with almost no takers—my efforts in producing it largely wasted. The publishers generously handed over their large remainder stock to the Boy Scouts organization which seemed the most fitting recipient. I now have no copy myself, but I can still recall most of my sketches and aphorisms which would seem to suggest that the Pelman system must have had something in it.

My immediate superior in Tank Corps reconnaissance and intelligence was Major (later General) 'Boots' Hotblack and, ultimately, I succeeded him.

His legendary gallantry, experience, tireless enterprise and energy made him the very pattern of the good soldier. Always good humoured and helpful however exhausted, we others could not but strive, however vainly, to live up to his example.

One thing he did for me was to make the war more interesting through his own intense absorption and keenness. The other, though it did not make me 'brave' in his own rare way, taught me at least to be fatalistically unafraid in tight places.

It was fairly early in my running-in period with him that we were reconnoitring together in unpleasantly featureless country when we were spotted by a German field battery that decided we were a worthwhile target and opened up at us with both shrapnel and H.E.

Their aim was all too accurate, and there being no other cover, we both dived headlong into a providential pond and there remained until the strafing was over, with nothing to show for all the ammunition we had caused them to waste, but a ring of muddy craters.

An escape of that sort is always strangely exhilarating, and I think it was the sight of Hotblack's beaming mud-stained face when we finally surfaced, that enabled me thenceforth cheerfully to accept that sort of happening with a Kismet equanimity and reasonably steady nerves.

After Arras so far as I and my Brigade of the Tank Corps were concerned came the chastening third battle of Ypres, the exhilarating tip-and-run affair of Cambrai, then the last great German offensive, and finally the various battles of our own victorious sweep forward. On the 29 September 1918 came the opening of the famous second battle of Cambrai. Hotblack was severely wounded in the head whilst, as usual, in the thick of the battle. On this occasion he had been himself actually driving and fighting single-handed a tank of which all the crew had been killed repelling a local counter-attack.

I met him being carried back from this exploit, his fifth time of wounding and found myself promoted to fill as best I might the place that he had invested with an almost legendary gallantry.

However, I had been well schooled by him and things were now, at last, coming our way, and before I had made any blunders that might have justified my being relegated to more becoming obscurity, the Armistice was rumoured and then finally announced.

Since I had ended the war thus accidentally as a staff officer at at Tank Corps Headquarters, I had free access to the Corps Commander. I was not slow to ask him about getting home—for good. To be kept on for an army of occupation or some such aftermath of horror had been my abiding nightmare, and I was not going to risk that last detention if lobbying or wirepulling, however flagrant, could possibly avert it.

My good friend Lawrence Weaver, now released from the menial tasks he had so well described and by now high in the Civil Service and a knight, asked for me as superintending architect at the Ministry of Agriculture. The job included the designing of smallholding settlements and such for ex-service men at that time all the mode. He managed in fact to perform the necessary operation of turning me into a 'pivotal man' urgently needed at home for reconstruction. Confronted with this carefully prepared emergency exit, my General still demurred. It seemed that a history of the Tank Corps and of its part in the war was required, and further that he desired that I, having been involved in most of its battles, should write it. Ultimately he agreed that writing this history might best be done at home, for I had urged that there I should have the great advantage of a professional author in the person of Amabel to help me. So at last, on the understanding that the book would certainly be produced and quickly, I was released and so almost miraculously was out of uniform and home for good within a fortnight of the Armistice.

Faithfully we kept our bond. Amabel in fact did almost all the writing whilst I fed her with memoranda, eye-witness accounts, official documents and raw material generally. We delivered by the date agreed, the book being duly published by *Country Life*, half the proceeds going to the Tank Corps Benevolent Fund.

Surprisingly, our book became a recognized and official military work of reference and its concluding words (as below) were reproduced on the menu card of the 'Speed the Tanks' luncheon at the Savoy at the beginning of the Second World War when the War Office was at last beginning to awake from its long sleep. We had foreseen such a sleep, a foreboding, most cruelly and bloodily fulfilled. It was not without significance that Major Clement Attlee—formerly a Tank Company commander, later Prime Minister—should have supported the appeal at this function, the only time that I ever met him:

> The creed of the present writers can be very briefly summarised. A considerable amount of evidence points to the conclusion that in the phase at which military science has arrived, and at which it will probably remain for at least a generation, a superior force of Tanks can always tip the scales of the military balance of power.
> Within the period of a generation, a time may again come when we shall have to defend our lives and our liberties. We lead the world in the design and manufacture of Tanks. Let us not abandon that lead in the production and use of a vital weapon. We know too well the tragic cost of one day of war, and it has been said that had we been visibly prepared, the Germans would not have attacked.
> Obviously we cannot be going to fall again so quickly into an old error. We certainly intend to be armed, but who can say that through sheer absence of mind it will not be with arquebuses? Surely not for the sake of Army precedent, for the sake of emphasising our pacific

intentions, for the sake of saving a little money, or even—dearest of all—for the luxury of 'not bothering' about our Army, must we lose our present unparalleled position of advantage. This advantage is not only a material one. The Tanks are accustomed to win. Do not let us throw away a fine tradition of victory. 'Of all that, in our agony of striving we gained by the way, let us lose nothing.'

But the military establishment and the Government took no heed nor of Liddell-Hart's pleadings, and all but lost us the next war.

The production of this book was more domestically dramatic than the military authorities or its readers knew, for my co-author was expecting our second child and it was a race between baby and book. Fortunately she found the race exhilarating.

Meantime the book had been serialized at full length in the *Daily Telegraph*, as newsworthy, and apparently was rated an authoritative account of the 'New Arm'—authoritative because of its Corps Commander's introduction. He knew the circumstances and stood godfather to the baby, our second daughter Charlotte, born the moment her mother had done correcting the book's last proofs. Twenty years later he attended Charlotte's wartime wedding at St. Martin-in-the-Fields to Lindsay Wallace, a biologist like herself and a New Zealander snatched back out of the Navy to continue his research work at Cambridge where they met.

The pretty wide range of Generals and Brigadiers with whom I came into contact in the 1914–18 war seemed to me a whole lot better than their generally accepted popular image so wittily fostered by our old friend David Low's cartoons of Colonel Blimp. There were real Colonel Blimps right enough but they, I would judge, were seldom if ever promoted above that rank or else had got themselves killed off or been sent home before I got into the war. The Generals I came across seemed, as seen from below, pretty competent though some were certainly oddities.

One with whom I served for a spell was brilliant, but seemed too idle and sociable to be an effective commander. Yet I dare say his easy-going friendliness may well have produced better service from those under him than would a stricter attitude, and anyhow cheerfulness and confidence followed him everywhere no matter how bleak and menacing the actual outlook.

Finding him at some critical juncture, lying back with his feet up reading a French novel with a bottle of old brandy ('My favourite food') at hand—I registered some slight surprise when all I got was, 'Just you tell me if and when I'm *really* needed, meanwhile you know what's wanted. What's the point of *my* working when I have collected a splendid and expensive staff to save me bothering?!!'

Just because I had chanced to make one or two lucky guesses about the course of current events, my General would often take me along with him to the various headquarters where he had business with his opposite numbers and where I would glean all the information I could from their underlings.

At one Corps H.Q. I was left alone with the Commander's A.D.C., Prince Arthur of Connaught, who opened with, 'I expect you want particulars of last night's raid, a nasty business.'

Asked how the enemy had managed to penetrate so well held a front he said, 'It was opposite the sector held by our Scottish Division and the Jerrys came over disguised as jokes so of course our poor Jocks never saw them.'

It was at a time when there was little enough to laugh at and one was grateful indeed for almost any such schoolboy nonsense, my own General providing plenty of it himself.

But one of our visitations produced a situation at once farcical and not a little embarrassing.

It was to some technical headquarters and I was turned over to the director, a Major, whilst my General conferred with his supreme boss. I was very much interested in what I was shown but a bit surprised at the unusual deference shown me by the Major—'Now this will interest you, Sir. Yes of course, Sir', and so on until it dawned on me that the opulent fur coat that I was wearing bore no rank badges and that my innocent Major had assumed that his unexpected visitor, inspecting his establishment, must be someone pretty grand.

All right, I thought, I am getting the very best V.I.P. treatment and being shown just everything, no harm done—let it ride.

But then came a message to say that my General was going to

stay to lunch with the establishment's overlord and would I lunch with my Major.

As we took off our greatcoats in the mess ante-room I prepared for the crunch as my so grossly deceived guide regarded the lieutenant to whom he had been saying 'Sir' for half the morning. It was quite a situation. Neither of us referred to it.

One sad little footnote, entirely personal, but so grievous at the time that I had entirely forgotten it until now, as is my self-protecting but sometimes dangerous way with things that are painful to remember. Once of their charity, the authorities granted four day Paris leave spells for those who had been long without any leave at all—allowing two days and three nights in Paris and two days for the journey thither and back.

I was granted such leave for a date far enough ahead to allow my fixing up with Amabel for her to get corresponding leave from the hospital in which she was a V.A.D. and also for us to book a room in a quiet little left-bank hotel that she knew about. Never have I been more cock-a-hoop and gleeful than when I settled into my grubby seat in the dilapidated train that began my journey Pariswards from somewhere behind the front. I found my way to our hotel. 'No, Monsieur, Madame has not yet arrived.' According to our plan she should have been just ahead of me—but what matter if it was the other way about? So, despite my lack of French I somehow discovered and noted down the arrival time of all the trains coming in from all the Channel ports we were using—and so I spent my two days, so dazzling in prospect, so desolating in realization, in running hither and thither in gradually deepening gloom between hotel and railway stations.

No Amabel, no word of explanation. At last the time came for my return to duty and back I went with anxiety now added to sore frustration. What *could* have happened? It was some little time before I got a letter which reflected my own lamentations. The explanation was the simple one that because of a sudden submarine threat, all civilian cross-Channel traffic had been temporarily suspended. We ought both of course, to have been grateful for authority's tender concern for non-combatent safety, but it was difficult to feel so.

I had not really intended the 1914–18 war, architecturally and otherwise so barren, thus to occupy so much space but I ought perhaps to justify having done so by suggesting what seem to have been its effects upon me.

In the course of it I realized that what I really cared about was not just defending my country but having a country really worth defending. I saw a fabulous destruction of life, wealth and beauty continued for years—a destruction that I not only witnessed but assisted in. It was all hateful to me, and the monstrous waste and cruelty of those years still frightens me even in retrospect.

I was confirmed in my original conviction that war is the most disastrous madness for all concerned, and my abhorrence of it inevitably led me to take an interest and even some small part in politics. Incidentally it left me greatly questioning much that in the old days I had innocently accepted as right, or at any rate inevitable.

From the purely professional point of view its most obvious results were pleasant commissions from various comrades in arms including no less than four General Officers. One was permitted, so it seemed, to express pacifist views, so long as it was generally known that one had failed to live up to one's principles.

But I persist in preaching them, and my first post-war book opened thus:

> I dedicate this book to all the beauty of my country, natural or other, in gratitude and grief. This grief is for all the destruction of lovely buildings and for the spoiling by war of beautiful places almost throughout the world. The tale of destruction is limitless, no one has yet taken full stock of it, the mind winces, a full inventory would be intolerable. But what we do know is that on every single day of the long years of war, beauty was somewhere extinguished as indiscriminatingly and as finally as the human lives to whose destruction this massacre of loveliness was merely a hideous accompaniment. Of that we were soon and poignantly aware from what we daily read in our papers—mostly between the lines. Everywhere over Europe and Asia the lights of loveliness were going out either one by one or in clusters—the legendary beauty that had nourished the hearts of men for centuries—lights, too often, that could never be relit. Bombs or bulldozers, land mines or flame throwers—destruction raged across the earth in cataclysmic fury, leaving such a train of ruin as we had never

dreamt of. One day some sleeping coral isle would become a smoking hell—on another the great Monastery of Monte Cassino would be no more.

The day after, the pastel-tinted walls and bubble domes of some provincial Kremlin would leave Russia that much the poorer, whilst some gilt and fretted temple in Mandalay would be pounded into dust. Next, a mellow little Tuscan town of touching beauty would be rent and crumbled, or a great baroque church with all its stores of treasures, a Touraine cathedral, some old fortified Norman farm, a Dutch town hall, or a whole mediaeval quarter of some famous old German city with, perhaps as well, its clean-lined new quarter with much fine modern architecture along with it.

And the wonderful harbours that have been wrecked where the beauty of old waterside buildings was always doubled by reflection— the Channel ports, the Mediterranean and Adriatic ports and those on the French Atlantic sea-board.

This was a mere fragment of a long and bitter anti-war tirade— but still I stick by every word of it.

Chapter Nine

Back in London

During the war great things had been done on a tremendous scale; individualism and private interests had to a large extent been merged in a communal effort for the sake of the State and our common need. Some of us were so sanguine as to believe that that spirit would inspire our reconstruction phase, in which, however, we were woefully mistaken. In my own little sector for example, all the jolly plans for ex-service men's smallholdings that we prepared with such enthusiasm, all the model colonies envisaged with such magnanimity, the very rules and axioms of civilized amenity that we then so hopefully enunciated—all, or nearly all, were gradually whittled down to a less heroic and 'as-you-were' standard. It became clear that departmental zeal alone was powerless to do much towards realizing 'the new civilization' in the face of soaring building prices and the rapid collapse of patriotic exaltation.

Wherefore, disillusioned after three months as a civil servant, I decided that I could no longer resist the call of private practice —almost inaudible though it then was—and I resigned from my civil service appointment.

As usual, I took this seemingly rash step out of settled employment into what was still little more than an architectural vacuum, with no more justification than a general and rather groundless optimism.

After all, if the State did not choose to take full advantage of the pent-up energy and zeal of returned architects who had an almost biological urge to build, then such architects had to find an outlet *somewhere* and the only alternative that then offered was in private practice, as of old.

'As of old'—could that possibly be, after all that had come and gone? It began to seem as though it could, and I was soon launched again with a number of interesting commissions, some of them quite large-scale 'luxury jobs', for which special permits were required.

The world, or at all events the English world, had decided, after some hopeful hesitation, to go on as near as might be, as before the war.

These were the boom years, and the great money flood of the war was still swirling impressively, and even surprisingly eddying around in strange new pockets where had formerly been the financial shoals and shallows.

Building prices, like the hopes of the rich, were high, if uncertain, and though it was exceedingly difficult to get a job carried through satisfactorily with regard to materials, workmanship, time or cost, there was plenty doing, and on the percentage basis, one was well enough paid for one's extra trouble.

It was not so bad on large and definitely 'luxury' work, when one's client had comfortable margins that he could draw on, however unwillingly; but with little houses for people of definitely limited means, the perpetual movement of prices, generally upward, and the impossibility of accurately gauging the cost or of getting a fixed-price contract, meant unending harassment for all concerned, but especially for the architect. In such cases, with ruthless ingenuity, one compressed and simplified and generally contrived to try and make the financial and architectural ends meet acceptably. How grateful one was for any early practice or acquired skill in overworking the pound to make it yield its uttermost in cubic content, in equipment and in value generally!

Cubic space was certainly expensive and hard to come by in post-war London, and I had to start work again in just such offices as offered. But with a third child we needed a home as well as an office and there seemed much to be said in the circumstances for living over the shop.

A seemly but seedy stucco-fronted Belgravian house of the middle size in South Eaton Place was ultimately bought as a likely subject for reconstruction and alteration, and drastically dealt with on a somewhat ambitious scale.

The idea was to combine every kind of labour-saving dodge with a sort of Chauve-Souris gaiety—we determined, in short, to be what was in 1919 exceedingly colourful and modern, and we were.

I was then a good deal influenced by a new and dear friend Claude Lovat Fraser, whose dresses and decor for Nigel Playfair's most memorable production of *The Beggar's Opera* at the Hammersmith Lyric had been a revelation in the sensitive use of colour, subtle shades only then procurable by his dyeing all the fabrics in his own bathtub, helped by his equally colour-conscious wife, Grace.

His little broadsheets too showed the same fastidiousness both in their typography and their decorative wood-cuts—simplicity and clarity their outstanding characteristics. He had an unerring sense of period—especially of the seventeenth and eighteenth centuries—and his influence on current design was manifest and would undoubtedly have been far greater had he not died untimely.

Enid Bagnold in her autobiography has paid warm tribute to his great charm and kindliness but no one, I think, has yet dealt with his actual work as it deserves.

Much ingenuity was expended on fitting up the ground floor as offices, while up above, plumbing, built-in fitments, telephones, radiators, electric fires and such-like were installed on an almost American scale, whilst a central dinner lift connected all five floors. A balconied nursery and pillared roof garden, complete with fountain, and a garage in rear, with a minute flat above it, rounded off our equipment for what we then considered the good life, so far as it could be lived in London by such as us. For a few years we were very well content and the practice grew.

I had already begun to concern myself, as a citizen, with the wider aspects of architecture—town and regional planning. Contact with Sir Patrick Geddes, Sir Raymond Unwin, Sir Charles Reilly, Sir Guy Dawber, Sir Lawrence Weaver, Sir Patrick Abercromby and Sir Herbert Griffin, the Seven Knights Errant of the movement, and my own brief experience with the smallholdings scheme had all made one feel increasingly that to build 'private paradises' though it was fun and brought in the necessary income, was not enough. I had already been writing propaganda pieces in this sense, that is for planning and conservation, against jerry-building and ribbon development, and I was an active member of the new-formed Council for the Preservation of Rural England, under the chairmanship of Lord Crawford. Soon, however, I began to feel increasingly that to say what I had to say in words was not enough. Ought it not to be possible to use the mode of expression that came most naturally to me, actual building, to show an example, a life-size model, which would surely be both more eloquent and more convincing than mere writing? 'To go as you please is not usually to arrive at what is pleasing' I was saying. 'Development' even of a place of great natural beauty, can and should be an enhancement and not a desecration, a belief that I still dreamed of one day trying to prove true.

Meantime, together with the pioneers of the old amenities brigade, the seven knights errant and others, I wrote, made speeches and took part in debates, and when I succeeded Lawrence Weaver as President of the Design and Industries Association I, as an architect, naturally tended to switch attention from the design of pots and pans, fabrics and furniture, to the look and disposition of the houses that contained these things, that is, to Town Planning and outdoor amenities generally.

This was a deviation from the D.I.A.'s normal activities. It was accepted with encouraging alacrity, and we quickly established a zealous little band of about a dozen to reconnoitre a few selected towns, which we aimed to shame into a livelier care of their amenities and a general pulling up of their sagging municipal socks.

I recall Oxford, St. Albans and Carlisle as amongst our targets. A 'task force' from the D.I.A. would descend thereon complete with photographers and busy-body snoopers, seeking out everything that we deemed obnoxious, uncivilized or unworthy—anything at all indeed of which the citizens *ought* to be ashamed, a series of 'Cautionary Guides' being the end product.

Having pooled and discussed our evidence and ideas, I would write the accompanying text and act as general editor—the rude captions being especially good fun—some parodying those of the several *official* guides which of course had nothing whatever in common with our own satirical, debunking 'Private Eye' productions. And the thing *worked*! The well-produced little books (one of the team was a publisher and printer) proved best-sellers, were generally quoted from in the national press as well as locally, and caused a gratifying amount of laughter as well as fury—our technique of poking fun, proving as we had hoped, more wounding than grave reproof.

Action and reform often followed our commando raids. A Civic Society would be founded to encourage general seemliness, unsightly advertisements and slatternly dumps disappeared, dilapidation was dealt with, trees were planted, shops were purged of clutter, houses were repainted and, as a sort of faint mirage of the massive Civic Trust face-lifting schemes to come but still more than a generation ahead, we did really start something. There were many indignant letters about us in the newspapers, as well as approving ones and we got by (just) without a single court action, altogether quite an exhilarating spree.

Then, as to my practice, suddenly, out of the blue, I was commissioned to turn the famous Stowe into a school. There had been a press announcement that this great house, the largest and perhaps the most celebrated in England, had been sold to a property dealer. This prompted my father-in-law to ask me, as an architect, to write an article on the place, its past, its present state, and its possible future, for *The Spectator*.

I went down to see it with the greatest enthusiasm for here, as I knew, was exemplified classical domestic architecture on the grandest scale set in a superbly contrived landscape of avenues, terraces, lakes, groves, temples and monuments. All the outcome of some two centuries of evolution under a succession of architects and landscapists of the highest distinction working for appreciative patrons who seemed ever ready to launch out on new embellishments, no matter what the cost.

It was a week or two after my article had appeared that a Mr. Percy Warrington was announced at my office as wishing to see me 'about Stowe'.

There entered a short tubby clerical figure rather reminiscent of Chesterton's Father Brown, but entirely lacking his touching humility; on the contrary indeed, exuding self-importance and bustling enterprise. He had been much interested he said, in my account of Stowe and my suggestions for its future use, but that that had in fact already been settled as he had arranged to acquire it as the latest link in a chain of schools that he himself was in process of establishing. Would I care to help the project with ideas, if not with publicity or money? I explained that I was not a columnist nor a fund-raiser, but an architect, but that *as* such I should of course be proud to follow where my illustrious predecessors had so brilliantly left their mark—Vanbrugh, Gibbs, Robert Adam, Bridgman, Capability Brown, Soane and the rest—if his colleagues so decided. It then appeared that he was already assembling a Board of Governors for his projected new public school which, though including a Bishop, a General and a couple of peers, would, he assured me, certainly accept his decision as to the appointment of an architect as in most other matters. After all, he added, the whole financing of the project depended entirely on him alone.

So almost at once there I was with this great echoing long-neglected palace of four hundred rooms to deal with (I counted them on the survey plan) *sans* water supply, *sans* drains, heating, lighting or even adequate maintenance. Somehow the huge building had to be transformed into a reasonably functioning school for—to start with—two hundred boys in four separate 'houses' within the fabric. All this was to be done in a matter of months—and the number to be accommodated was to be increased two- or threefold later on.

The first thing was to see how the vast complex of buildings could be so allocated as to yield all the accommodation needed and how to provide all the requisite services, with minimum disturbance to the architectural integrity of the historic fabric. Fascinating as a problem, it was no sooner solved (and by the deadline date for the school's opening) than further transformations were put in hand as well as a number of entirely new buildings—two classroom blocks, laboratories, a sanatorium, a boarding house, gym, squash courts and so on.

I had throughout the staunch support of J. F. Roxburgh the headmaster designate whom I had had to bully into putting in for the job. He had insisted that he was entirely happy where he was as second master at Lancing, and was anyway too young for a headship. It was lucky for me and for the school that he did apply and was appointed, for a time came when the Reverend Percy Warrington began to turn both difficult *and* unreliable as his trusting fellow members of the board were later to discover to their cost. But with Roxburgh my relations were entirely cordial though in the end both for me and the only two governors that I had come to rely on, General Sir William Robertson and Dr. David (Bishop of Liverpool), the sky began to cloud over when Mr. Warrington's over-elaborate and even dubious financial contrivances started to show alarming signs of instability. Lord Annan (an old Stoic) has dealt with these troubles in his biography of Roxburgh—for which I was able to contribute a few impressions. But my several years' work at Stowe were mostly a delight, though there was sadness too in seeing so much let go or neglected simply for lack of funds. The great monumental lions and the range of bronze vases that adorned the south terrace were all sold off at auction by the property dealer. Somehow I contrived to get plausible understudies to occupy the plinths of those noble lions cast in concrete from models made for me by the sculptor John Bickerdyke—less noble, even 'Utility Lions'—but still preserving the general feeling of the grand approach.

I bought one statue myself as a memento—a marble Freya, the Scandinavian Venus. There had been a circle of seven such deities representing the days of the week, but at a much earlier sale the then Duke of Buckingham, a most splendid bankrupt, had sold off the other six, leaving only mine—who, representing Friday, was presumably deemed unlucky and attracted no bidders.

When, some long time after buying her, I had chosen her intended site and wanted to bring her away, search as I might I entirely failed to find her; all I could recall was that, somewhere in those overgrown groves, the nymph still awaited her rescuer. So I offered a reward to the first schoolboy to discover her hiding place and we were soon reunited. She now graces the foot of a high flight of steps at Portmeirion.

What had most distressed me about these sales was the school governors' decision not even to bid for the Grand Avenue—which was some mile and a half long in a straight run from the great triumphal arch looking to the house across the lake to the twin lodges at the other end. This was being offered for sale in seven lots as it was fully wide enough for a ribbon-built row of bungalows on either side of the driveway. I pointed out the obvious dangers to the school governors—the destruction of the finest avenue in England, the befouling of the new school's main approach—but no, 'We simply can't afford to buy another square yard, whatever you say', which seemed to me so madly, so culpably short-sighted that I attended the auction and angrily bought the whole thing myself.

My one object was to preserve it intact (for the avenue's very trees were being sold along with the building plots) so there I was landed with an absurd detached strip of property in a far-away county with which I had no connection and over two hundred miles from my agent who would have to look after it. When it emerged that part of the avenue was 'copy-hold' that there were various obligations with regard to the maintenance of the roadway and fences, responsibility for tree safety and so forth, he was less than enthusiastic about my acquisition.

Coping with everything at such a distance was indeed pretty difficult and after a year or so I wrote a letter to *The Times* saying that, though I had made it safe for the time being, I could not promise to hold the avenue for ever, but that if some benefactor could be found who could better afford to guarantee its preservation in perpetuity by giving it to the National Trust or otherwise, I would most gladly pass it on 'at a reasonable loss'.

This brought an immediate response from the Vice-Provost of Eton who thought it would well become Old Etonians if they were to present the avenue as a sort of christening present to their youngest brother public school—Stowe.

So it was that this splendid avenue is now as safe as anything ever can be, under the care of a special committee, expert arboriculturists who, felling, trimming and replanting to a settled programme year by year, have in mind the state of the trees a hundred years hence as much as their look tomorrow. The actual presentation on behalf of the O.E.'s was made a ceremonial occasion, Prince Arthur of Connaught unlocking the symbolical gates that I had designed to go between the elegant twin lodges. A happy outcome.

Ashridge Park, near Berkhamsted, my next challenge, an immense castellated Gothic mansion built for the Duke of Bridgewater, 'the father of inland navigation', cannot compare either in extent or quality with Stowe, but I had only just finished Stowe's conversion when I was asked to perform a like operation at Ashridge. It was to be resurrected as the Bonar Law College, an institution to be dedicated to the study and dissemination of Conservative political principles. The whole splendid estate had been bought from Lord Brownlow by a property speculator and there was great uneasiness as to its ultimate fate until Lord Stonehaven bought and presented the actual house to the Conservative party whilst the National Trust, greatly helped by George Trevelyan and Miss Courtauld, secured a number of key areas such as beech groves and viewpoints and thus created a sort of Trust archipelago. I had known the house as a fully-going concern in the Brownlow's time when the forty or so indoor servants must have been none too many to keep such a hospitable and rambling immensity reasonably serviced. I came upon a list of the domestics and their several duties stuck up somewhere that ended with '2 lamp boys'. As the house had not long stood empty and had been pretty well maintained I was this time chiefly concerned with internal reorganization and re-allocation of function, the provision of heating, lighting and plumbing, transformed service quarters, decoration and conversion of stables and outbuildings generally to new uses. The provision of a general dining-hall offered a challenge and a chance and I proposed to adapt the chapel for this use but that was vetoed so I then switched to the exciting transformation of the enormous and pretty useless conservatory that ran along the south front in crenallated Gothic stonework. Then there was a lodge to be built and various other architectural ploys around the place, all in settings that deserved one's best endeavours. But even before I had really got going on the many pretty puzzles, it looked, for a little, as though I might already be through with it all.

One evening I, with an assistant, were rolling up our survey plans in the dusk of the great central hall preparatory to driving back to London, when who should emerge from a shadowed archway but another architect, with *his* assistant, with *his* sheaf of plans. It was an old friend, Lord Gerald Wellesley (now Duke of Wellington) and we greeted each other in equal astonishment.

It emerged that he had been commissioned by the Bonar Law Foundation's General Secretary John Buchan,[1] whilst I had been given the job by its Chairman, John Davidson.[2]

We agreed that it was all very awkward and embarrassing and that the only thing to do was to report to our respective patrons and let *them* sort out the muddle.

In the event it appeared that a Chairman trumped a General Secretary so I was told to go ahead. Any sort of quarrel or even a coolness would have been painful, but of that there was never a sign—the chief credit for which must certainly go to the loser—Gerry.

If, for an early nineteenth-century country house, you can accept a Gothic Revival abbey—'An apt mixture of Castle and Cathedral styles'—complete with cloisters, vast central tower chapel steeple and all the rest, then Ashridge is well enough.

Its transformation was completed a year or two later and it was ceremoniously opened by the then Prime Minister, Stanley Baldwin,[3] at an Ascot-like Conservative Garden Party on the great south lawn.

My next official meeting with Stanley Baldwin was also a gala gathering. This event, however, was clouded for me (and for me alone) by half an hour of the most intense anxiety I have ever known.

It was at the opening of another conversion, that of Lord Dartmouth's enormous house in Charles Street, as the new head-

---

[1] Later Lord Tweedsmuir.   [2] Later Viscount Davidson.
[3] Later Earl Baldwin of Bewdley.

quarters and club of Sir Evelyn Wrench's English Speaking Union.

On my arrival on the opening day I found to my dismay that the ceremonial arrangements had been changed so that the inaugural speeches were now to be made from the balcony at the head of the great marble flight of stairs, with the most privileged V.I.P.'s massed below on the stairs themselves—some half-a-dozen to each step with no support whatever save that of the wall into which the steps were built, at one end only.

Had I been warned of this intention I should have emphatically declined to take any responsibility for the stairs' security without a thorough testing *and* precautionary propping from underneath, but by the time I had arrived it was too late to change things back again to the admittedly less dramatic setting of the ground floor. All I could do was to thin out the load a little without causing general alarm. 'Stairs look solid enough, but they haven't been tested or specially supported and they can never have carried such a load before—it's asking rather a lot, you know—I really would thin out a bit—you would hear and see just as well from the hall below. Just in *case*—if anything *did* give way—most unlikely of course—but frankly I shall feel a lot happier when the party's over.'

Which indeed was no more than the truth, for with such a crush of Top People so (to my apprehensive eye) precariously poised high above both me and the marble pavement of the hall, I imagined the newspaper headlines that would greet the sort of catastrophe that I was nightmarishly foreseeing. With the Premier himself, half a dozen other ministers, the Viceroy of India, the American ambassador and scores of other notables all involved, how eminently newsworthy would be my imagined holocaust! Publicity for the architect (presumably responsible) would no doubt also be considerable—and not favourable.

The speeches (of which I apprehended not a word) seemed interminable, I winced at each round of applause and prayed that no one would start stamping instead of clapping, my ears were strained to catch any premonitory cracking or rumbling that might presage fracture and collapse. However, nothing happened, the assembly dispersed itself about the building, I to conduct Mr.

Baldwin round my newly designed Walter Page Memorial Library. This had given me my best chance of new designing in this complicated conversion job. He seemed to like it as much as I did, well enough anyhow to ask me to plan his own library for him when, later, he moved into Eaton Square.

Meantime, I somehow seemed to have become—unsuitably—almost the official architect of the Tory Party, for my political convictions were not theirs. I did several jobs besides Ashridge for its Chairman John Davidson. Then I was asked to alter and enlarge the Ladies' Carlton Club and to build or alter houses for Lord Carson, Bonar Law, Sir Geoffrey Fry, Lord Cushendun and other right-wing politicos from none of whom did I attempt to conceal my own mildly leftist views.

None the less there did come a time, as I was later told, when there was a certain murmuring and it was suggested that it was rather unnecessary to employ so politically dubious an architect when there were plenty of perfectly good Conservative ones better deserving any patronage that might be going.

I don't suppose in fact that it made much difference—I know of only one job that was definitely twitched away from me on this account—and I only wondered that I had been accepted for so long.

Not that this quasi-official ban affected my general practice in the least, where almost all my clients were anyway Tory if anything at all, though they would, from time to time, amuse themselves by mildly teasing me about my supposedly subversive views.

The only Labour members of Parliament I ever had as clients were Sir Oswald Mosley (when he *was* Labour), for whom I altered and extended a lovely old manor house in Buckinghamshire, and Richard Crossman, whose garden in Oxfordshire I had the pleasure of planning. And how about the Liberals? Asked to renovate for Lloyd George the old Welsh house to which he retired and in which he later died, I fell immediately under the spell of his most subtly exercised charm, as indeed did almost everyone else. Guessing that I might think he still harboured resentment against the elders of my family for their near half-century of opposition and disapproval, he began one evening over dinner at Churt, to praise my father, saying that whenever he appeared as a solicitor before the Bench in Wales on which my father sat, he could always rely on his complete impartiality, fairness and wisdom.

At breakfast next morning I happened to quote some odds and ends from *1066 And All That* that had delighted me, as I found they also did him. He had never even heard of the book—a shocking gap in his political education as I told him—a gap that I subsequently repaired by sending him a copy. Anyway, we were having such fun over cock-eyed history generally, that when his barber was announced, he insisted that I should come into his study with him and sit in on his overdue haircutting, the barber patiently poising his scissors whilst Lloyd George laughed.

Though I saw him on and off whilst altering and renovating his last home with the loving guidance of his second wife Frances whom he had lately married, and although he was keenly interested in the building of a much-needed bailiff's cottage for which I contrived to get approval in spite of all the licence restrictions by using nothing but old materials salvaged from far and near, he was by that time clearly failing.

When the end came I was asked to pin-point the exact spot for his burial within the wood on the banks of the hardby river Dwyfor that he had known and loved from boyhood and where he had always wished to lie. The setting seemed itself to dictate the form that the grave should take—a simple oval enclosure of rugged masonry with an arched entry and a surrounding stepped pavement following the natural fall of the ground—the great boulder on which he used to sit at the centre of the enclosed lawn marking the grave itself. Lewis Mumford gave a long account of it all in *The New Yorker*, from which the following is a brief extract:

> The point of the design is that the pilgrim who visits this grave can pass around it, while getting a full view of the interior of the enclosure, without being tempted to trespass. In fact, no sign is needed to warn him against intruding, since the spiral walk was contrived to keep him far enough above or below the grave to prevent access. Apart from the simple inscription and the serene enclosure, nothing

disturbs the landscape that Lloyd George saw, and only a small sign by the roadside reminds the tripper that this is consecrated ground. To the honour of the tourist there was, when I visited it, not a sign of his presence in so much as an empty cigarette pack or a scrap of paper. The restraint of this monument only emphasizes the perfect combination of pure form, delicate textural contrasts, and sensitive siting. And the whole impression is singularly in character, for this is the scene the hero's eyes beheld, this is the Wordsworthian 'old grey stone' on which he sat; and even the fact that he sat there says something about his quality as a human being. Each visitor who brings his private image of Lloyd George to the grave will find a setting ready for it, and when time or indifference effaces all the images, something that Lloyd George's life evoked in the mind of the architect will nevertheless remain visible—and valuable. This is a classic memorial not because it imitates some other work of excellence but because it has the same sense of the human scale, and the same delicacy of feeling that a Greek tombstone of the fourth century had. Would that we in America had a comparatively forthright and eloquent memorial to Lincoln.

Later, I designed the Lloyd George Museum that stands within a short distance of the grave and, last of all, his memorial for Westminster Abbey, carved by Jonah Jones and unveiled by the Prince of Wales in the presence of three Prime Ministers— Messrs. Macmillan, Wilson, and Heath, with Jeremy Thorpe gallantly representing the Liberal Party and delivering an eloquent and moving address.

But that was not until 1970, and it illustrated once again our national talent for organizing solemn yet colourful spectacles exactly matched to the occasion. As too, on this day, was the music, the band of the Welsh Guards playing as someone remarked, 'as though a symphony orchestra'—with the great organ and the processing choir all contributing together with the lighting and colours to an unforgettable ceremony.

One of Lloyd George's family remarked, 'How deeply the Old Man would have enjoyed it all.' And so he surely would, for indeed my first sight of him (in Privy Councillor uniform) was in Caernarvon Castle of which he was Constable, when, in 1911, he was the life and soul of the Investiture of Edward, Prince of

Wales—a brilliant bit of revivalist pageantry for which indeed he was himself largely responsible.

Some two generations later I duly attended Prince Charles's similar Investiture against the same historic background and set to much the same general pattern, but it seemed a little to lack the spontaneity of its predecessor through being so very elaborately and thoroughly rehearsed and organized. Inevitably, I suppose, when instead of we relatively few original spectators, the whole world was this time looking in on the show through television.

Also, although Lloyd George's grandson played a part in the proceedings as one of the Welsh peers given ceremonial duties—I think any survivors present from the 1911 occasion must have missed the Old Constable, as I did.

As I have said, most of my contacts and practically all my clients were Conservative-minded, and it was not until after the first war that I reacted with a sharp swing leftwards, partly through Amabel's influence. She herself had begun to react against the Conservatism of her father and his paper *The Spectator*. She continued however for a while to work for it as, successively, poetry and then dramatic critic and finally as literary editor, spheres in which it was wisely deemed that some political latitude could safely be allowed.

It was at her instigation that I actually joined the I.L.P. and lectured on town and country planning at their summer school at Lady Warwick's Easton Lodge. All the left-wing top brass of the time were there—Ramsay Macdonald, James Maxton, Clifford Allen,[1] Oswald and Cynthia Mosley, H. G. Wells and my late brother-in-law John Strachey, yet to make his mark with the Left Book Club, as an M.P. and then as a minister.

Of our almost incredible hostess, Daisy Warwick, we got a more intimate close-up later on when we spent a quiet weekend with her. We both fully appreciated the fascination for which she had so long been famed. Certainly she charmed me into planning her a model village which she proposed to establish in her park,

[1] Later Lord Allen of Hurtwood.

but of course it was never built. Though a congenital deviationist, I have generally voted Labour but not without flirtatious glances to the right and left.

I was quoted with approval by the Webbs for my published views on Russia's heroic reconstructive efforts in their great book on the Soviet Union, whilst on the other hand I was officially urged by the Conservative Party Central Office to stand as its candidate in an election that my understudy, when I refused the offer, easily won. I couldn't help feeling that the intelligence service of the Conservative H.Q. must at the time have been singularly ill-informed. Possibly it had heard that a tentative Liberal approach had been abortive though not, I guessed, that I had none the less been speaking on behalf of a Liberal candidate, Dame Juliet Rhys-Williams and against a Conservative away in Essex. Such then is my unedifying political posture—not at all because I think politics unimportant, but because, elect what government you will, the things you most dearly care about are so rarely effectively dealt with.

Over a generation ago I wrote bitterly, on the subject of 'Propaganda, Politics and Press', that whilst hopeful measures have now and again reached the statute book and even been to some extent implemented, the things that I really care about always seem to be sooner or later elbowed aside in favour of something else deemed to be more important or known to be backed by a more powerful lobby; whence my political disenchantment. However, *tante de mieux* I do still loyally join E. M. Forster in giving two cheers for democracy.

Chapter Ten

The Neo-Georgians

In 1920 a growing family—two girls and a boy—and a practice also fortunately increasing made it clear that our convenient 'over-the-shop' plan in our particular house, could not be indefinitely maintained, and soon the spate of work entailed by my part in the British Empire Exhibition at Wembley brought things to a head and precipitated the removal of the office.

Rather hastily, I took an unremarkable suite in Westminster, and had no sooner committed myself than I chanced to see a 'To Let' board on a stucco Doric portico in Ebury Street—a portico that had always charmed me. I investigated.

Entering under a classical inscription which said, 'The arts, sciences, and letters may the Holy Ghost prosper', I found a spacious galleried hall, high, well-proportioned and well-lit and, by that same evening, I had arranged to lease it. Though I had to pay rent for a period for the offices I had already taken yet never used, I was in no doubt but that my sudden decision was, for me, a wise one. Formerly a chapel and a school, then an antique warehouse, and then my studio, I ultimately sold it to Sir Oswald Mosley for undisclosed purposes (I had previously restored his country house) and he passed it on to Ian Fleming who there, I understand, dreamed up 'James Bond'. Who and what next? And what about that inscription?

Having experienced the contentment and indeed the positive pleasure of working in a finely proportioned great room, I could never imagine willingly going back to the normal office arrangement, though of course there must be some retiring room for such interviews as may be best held in private.

My Ebury Street studio's finest hour was when I lent it to Sir Francis Younghusband for a party to meet the lamas that he had brought over from Tibet.

There were about a dozen of them, impressive-looking old gentlemen in their flowing robes and exotic head-gear mostly bearing long horns (rather like Alphorns) with which, seated on the floor, they would now and again interrupt all conversation with booming blasts. The lamas were said to be 'philosophers' so Bertrand Russell was set to gauge their quality as such through an interpreter, only to discover that what they dealt in and were eager to discuss was neither more nor less than magic.

Perhaps we should have guessed as Sir Francis had told us that they liked to be given toys, mechanical if possible, and the more ingenious and surprising the better. We had passed this information on to the hundred or so guests who had been invited to this exotic party and they had responded generously to the lamas' obvious delight. It was as well that the poor old things had something to play with as the thickest pall of fog came down on us during the course of the evening, the densest I have ever known—so impenetrable that the taxis had apparently thought it prudent to go home, leaving us with small hopes of doing so ourselves.

Gradually, however, people did manage to melt away somehow though a few, with difficult journeys home, elected to sleep where they were as best they could. Amabel and I were all right as our house was only a short walk away, but I selfishly forgot the fate of the poor bewildered lamas. But Sir Francis, who after all was used to organizing Tibetans, contrived I am sure, to get them home with his usual efficiency.

We gave other 'parties with a purpose' at this time—one 'to meet and hear' Vatchell Lindsay declaiming his poems—another, that now seem strangely dated, to introduce our friends to the new wonder of 'wireless', a man, a machine, and a roomful of little gilt chairs, being hired from somewhere, the company spellbound at the wonder just as I had been a generation earlier when listening to the first Edison Bell phonograph. We were considerably frequented by the Georgian poets—Amabel's first book having been *An Anatomy of Poetry* and as, first poetry and then literary editor of *The Spectator*, she had most of them passing through her hands. In fact someone depicted her as the conductress of the Georgian omnibus, Eddy Marsh being shown as its driver.

With offices removed to Ebury Street, we ourselves moved to Royal Avenue where the wide-open traffic-free space seemed made for active children, with Wren's noble façade of Chelsea Hospital ending the tree-lined perspective giving abiding pleasure to ourselves.

In the 1920s ready escape westwards from Chelsea to real country by way of Putney and Kingston was still invitingly open. Anyway, when the Duke of Northumberland offered woodlands and a couple of farms for sale on the top of the North Downs up above his Surrey home, Albury Park (between Shere and Guildford) and only a couple of miles cross country from my wife's old home at Newlands Corner—I was tempted to buy the property as a weekend and holiday refuge for the family—and did so.

There being then no planning or by-law control of any sort, I designed and built a romantic and most unorthodox house entirely supported by the trunks of mighty trees that ran on upwards through the floor and thatched roof with lead collars round them where they emerged to stop the rain running down them into the house, especially when swaying in a gale—a movement however that was barely perceptible.

The walls were of rough unpainted elm weather-boarding and the great open fireplace and its round brick-and-flint chimney stack were carried on top of a big concrete cistern into which our wooden rainwater gutters delivered and into which a trap-door opened in the floor in front of the hearth through which we hauled up water as needed by rope and bucket.

There was no road to the place at all but the site was high and dry, and we had no difficulty in dodging our way through the woods over a carpet of pine-needles overlaying sand. If we needed water beyond what our roof collected, the nearest of our two farmhouses—a furiously picturesque and charming old place all tile-hanging, lattice lights and creepers—had an immensely deep well, from which by windlass, we could ultimately hoist up a bucket-full to carry up the hill. So, without piped water, or a road, or electric light or telephone, or indeed a postal delivery, we did very well—just the carefree contrast to London that we wanted, a wild though safe repository for our three children with their nurse and nursemaid whenever convenient so to leave them.

No single person came within our sight ever, though a missing writer, whose disappearance was a nine-days' wonder, was said to have hidden in the house. Indeed so secret were we (though only twenty-six miles from London) that it was several years before we were even discovered by the rating authority and required to pay our dues.

After we had been there a year or two the Duke told me he felt it had been a mistake to sell off land that almost overlooked his park, and that he hoped that if I ever thought of selling, I would let him have first refusal. Of course I agreed to do so, though having no present thought of selling what I had so lately bought. However, a few years later, I was approached by a London hospital that was seeking a site for a country convalescent home and thought my upland might very well be what they were looking for.

I immediately told the Duke, as such a development on his borders was, I imagined, just what he had come to fear, saying that he had better get the land safely back as soon as might be, or else, who knew, I might one day be so tempted by a dazzling offer as to find it irresistible.

Having bought the property from him at auction—farms, buildings, woodlands and all at a low agricultural rate, though only an easy hour's drive from the centre of London—I couldn't now decently ask him to compete against outsiders in the matter of price and anyhow I didn't want either to move out myself or be jostled by development of any sort or indeed to contemplate any change whatsoever in that lovely and withdrawn bit of downland country.

So I made this proposition. He to pay me back what I had

originally paid him, but leaving me my house and its immediately surrounding woodland, freehold, with access thereto, whilst we exchanged mutual covenants binding us each, in perpetuity, not to permit development of any kind on our respective properties. This solution, suiting us both, started a most beneficent chain-reaction amongst some half-dozen of our neighbouring land-owners, mostly large ones, whereby a long continuous stretch of the North Downs, roughly along the Pilgrims' Way, was soon protected from development of any kind by similar covenants—for ever. This neighbourly arrangement of ours set a quite important planning precedent, which is why it seems worthy of mention here.

When we left Chelsea and moved up to Hampstead, we thereby added a good many now congested miles to our Stapledown run, and anyway, being now on the edge of the Heath, our Surrey lung had become less necessary as well as less accessible. Thus, when our old friends Charles Laughton and his wife Elsa Lanchester asked if we would let the place to them, we agreed, and, somehow, they managed to live there in an odd mixture of primitive hardihood and sophisticated luxury whilst playing every night in London. However, the time came when they decided that they needed more amenities and comforts than our wooden shack could provide and I built them on lease a more orthodox but still sylvan-looking little house on the site of a garage, a 'replacement' that my restrictive covenant had allowed for.

When Charles moved to Hollywood and became an American citizen 'sophisticated luxury' had manifestly won—his house in star-spangled Beverley Hills being all of 3,000 miles from Stapledown simplicity, as I discovered when over there in connection with a Welsh Walt Disney film. Both Charles and Elsa indeed seemed endlessly adaptable to almost any way of life, a happy side of their excitingly complex characters. Elsa was an old friend whom we had first met staying with H. G. and Jane Wells in Essex, thereafter regularly patronizing her brilliant little 'Cave-of-Harmony' cabaret where Milton Rosmer, Cyril Scott and Miss Sterndale-Bennett were amongst her supporting cast.

I think it was through Elsa that I first met Humbert Wolfe and thereafter saw as much as I could of him, though the only one of his delightful 'epitaphs in advance' I still remember is that prepared for 'the Gloomy Dean':

> Hark the herald angels sing
> Doubtfully, because Dean Inge
> Has arrived and seems to be
> *Bored* with immortality.

Being in the Ministry of Labour and perhaps himself a refugee from an earlier purge, Humbert was in a position to help some of those who had to get out of Hitler's way—and help them he did most devotedly, incidentally landing me in due course with a couple of Austrian architects for whom I had to try and find face-saving work of some sort in my already war-shadowed and overstaffed office.

My Ebury Street set-up had convinced me that there was much to be said for the 'common hall' architect's office or studio, where principal, secretary and draughtsmen all work together, in close and constant liaison yet with a feeling of spaciousness impossible in the ordinary series of small and separate offices. At any rate it is what suited me and also I think my sort of practice and my method of working, so far as I may claim to have had a method.

It was this love of spaciousness that had propelled me first from South Eaton Place eastwards and thence yet again up to Hampstead where the desire for bracing air, a garden and good schools for the children, were other factors determining our choice.

From the edge of a plateau high above the dome of St. Paul's we looked southwards from George Romney's old house across the maze of London to where the smooth horizon of the North Downs reassured us that the monstrous huddle of streets and buildings was not after all unlimited. Northwards we had the merciful green spaces of the Heath, beyond which the retreating country then still stubbornly persisted, despite the strings of mean buildings along the great new roads.

The fine old house, much altered and adapted to our curious habits, being far too large either for our needs or means, was proportionately delightful to inhabit, and with two ex-billiard-rooms (it was once a club) at the disposal of the children and their friends, its size had compensations. For myself I had taken the immense old picture-gallery as my studio, and I did not hesitate to play up to the magnanimity of its proportions in my embellishments. I have, as I have confessed, a leaning towards the formal and the grand in certain moods, though my wife was surprised and a little shocked at my choosing to work in what she not unjustly called 'my ballroom', whilst nothing could be further from my noble ideas than the unstudied plainness and intimate disarray of her own chosen workroom.

For the rest, the presence of children, our own and other people's, ensured enough genial disorder to take the sting out of such small splendour as I was permitted, with the result that we all found the place exceedingly agreeable. It was a splendid house for large parties and we gave quite a lot of them—dances every so often, a show by the Ballet Rambert, David Low drawing large cartoons to amuse the company and selling them for charity. We also gave a party to meet the Russian Ambassador, M. Maisky, who made a speech from the gallery balcony, and all sorts of odds and ends of meetings and conferences, mostly vaguely cultural. The large house with its big reception rooms was well adapted for just such activities, but as our children hived off, we shrank it down gradually until, when Hitler's war came and we moved to Wales, we had only the ground floor left, the rest being let off.

Whilst our children were still around, Sir Solly Zuckerman wished one of his research baboons on to us, as he wanted to study its reactions to 'bright, intelligent young society'. He was then writing his rather ambiguously entitled book *The Sexual Life of Primates*—so his Betsy had quarters on the flat roof at the top of the house for several months. Not the social success that we had hoped, unresponsive and dirty, we bade our disappointing little lodger farewell without regrets. The experience may have been good for Betsy, but I don't think our children benefited markedly from the association.

The onset of the war of course meant a re-orientation of their lives for most of our friends as well as for us, and many we were never to see again, partly because we decided to settle permanently in Wales with only a pied-à-terre in London for our necessary and as infrequent-as-possible visits. The perch was a charming little Regency maisonette in Carlton Mews, now alas—and shamefully—all torn down. But throughout the years between the two wars there had been no lack of congenial contacts.

H. G. Wells and Jane were endlessly hospitable both at Easton Glebe, and in London, entertaining a wide spectrum of friends, all of interest.

It was through them that we first got to know Rose Macaulay, Arnold Bennett, Maynard Keynes, and Lopokova, Harold Laski, Baroness Budberg, Charlie Chaplin, Elsa Lanchester, Philip Guedalla, Miles Malleson, the Huxleys, and I don't know who besides.

Lopokova's valient English was incidentally sometimes puzzling as when on returning from a brief country ramble she reported, 'Very nice yes, but not again, my legs were too much tickled and bitten by barristers.' It transpired that what she meant was '*harvesters*'.

The Birleys' circle was less varied, consisting mainly of painters, ballet-fans, Sir Oswald's fashionable sitters, Diaghilev, Lord Duveen, Generals and such. But it was Lady Colefax's glittering gatherings at Argyle House that for years provided the main 'personality exchange', though Mrs. Mathias's salon was also a rewarding rendezvous, as too were Lady Bell's and the Charles Trevelyans' 'evenings' in a more austere and politically-slanted way.

Chapter Eleven

A Spectrum of Clients

I have, it seems, an inborn capacity for attracting eccentrics, cranks, and oddities of all sorts, which fact, I am well aware, inevitably says something about *me*. Yet I never seek them out—they just seem to gravitate towards me and I do rather tend to find them agreeable and sympathetic though too often, in the long run, embarrassing.

I suppose it has been the sensing of a certain kindred oddity in myself that has brought me quite a number of pretty unusual clients, sometimes the result of their accidental discovery of Portmeirion. One such commissioned me to design him a grandiose Palladian mansion in the north of England which I did with delight, but after detailed models had been approved and with the work of building barely started, he decided he would prefer to live elsewhere. In north Wales he bought a romantic property where I have built him a quasi-Tudor manor house which however remains an empty shell until we can decide on its interior finishings. Meantime (1970) he is circling the globe—to return no doubt with all sorts of new ideas for somewhere else.

Another client whose home and estate I have been variously transforming and embellishing for more than a decade has suddenly mothballed the whole splendid set-up and gone off to live abroad. Starting with the reconstruction of the great house itself, we went on and on with gardens, terraces, pavilions, archways, bridges, gateways, monuments, waterworks, swimming pools and planting—the lot—as though back in the eighteenth century and then, of a sudden, full stop. My client, ever brimming with ideas and with an acute critical sense was as deeply concerned in it all as I was, and having created so personal an environment I cannot believe that he can really abandon it for long. Anyway, there it all is, unique, I should think, as the product of this day and age and a display of uninhibited landscape embellishment unlikely to be soon repeated.

I have several times been asked completely to demolish monstrous white-elephant country houses and replace them by more reasonable and elegant successors after various abortive schemes for reduction and adaptation had been abandoned as impracticable. In one case it involved the demolition of a monumental addition I had made for the owner's mother only a decade or so earlier.

This particular monster had, besides two billiard-rooms, one for the French and the other for the English game, also a covered real tennis-court attached as well as a cavernous great 'Tenants' Hall' and a straggling tail of dank and dismal kitchens, still-rooms, brew-houses, game larders, laundry, store-rooms and such strung along dark stone-flagged 'semi-basement' burrows. The servants' hall to seat thirty, looked north into a blank wall, but the cellars were magnificent and are the only part of the old house to survive in or rather under, the new.

It was not difficult in such a case to contrive a transformation that did better justice to a superb setting and that made possible civilized living for *all* the house's occupants.

During the demolition we made an entirely unforeseen discovery—a medieval carved and painted hall-screen and three great oak beams each beautifully graven with loyal tributes to Queen Elizabeth the First, in English, Welsh and Latin respectively. These last now act as a cornice in the new hall and the screen went to the National Museum of Wales.

My client's family had lived in the house for centuries but he had no suspicion that its history went back as far or that his ancestors had been so careless of it as to thus build it up and plaster it over!

In another case the main treasures of the condemned great house were a number of very fine pictures mainly of the sixteenth century that the family aimed to retain in the much-reduced replacement that I planned for them, and that posed quite a problem as some of the paintings were very large.

The outcome was a really fine gallery incorporated in a relatively modest externally symmetrical twelve-bedroomed house with an entrance for outside visitors at one end of the gallery and access to the drawing-room and the rest of the house at the other. In neither of these instances had I the least compunction in completely making away with the old structures, in that they were architecturally vacuous, functionally impossible, structurally unsound and socially and economically quite absurd.

But elsewhere I have generally done my best to keep anything that I could of earlier work, even against my clients' wishes, for the sake of history and continuity, so long as it was good of its kind, no matter what the period, and provided it could be reasonably harmonized with the overall mood of the new deal.

Except in a completely formal setpiece I think there is much to be said for allowing minor stylistic surprises to break a rhythm and coherence that might also be monotonous—something not actually to shock the spectator—but to give his perhaps flagging attention a little jolt and set him wondering just why one had done whatever it was and whether it was justified, aesthetically or practically.

Thus have I introduced white-painted sash windows to light the grand staircase of a big country house where all my other windows were stone mullioned with leaded lights, chiefly because I had designed the stair and its painted walls as a formal Georgian setpiece that I wanted nothing to disturb. Also these sash windows in sudden contrast to the rest gave the house's exterior a certain liveliness and interest that it would else have lacked.

In the same way when restoring a remote old church in the wooded hill country of mid-Wales, instead of installing the usual gloomy heating stove and pipes I built a great open fireplace for the burning of local logs—a departure that some deemed so unorthodox as to be a little shocking. However, this singularity drew just the public attention to the poor old church that it sorely needed—and helped to justify my nonconformity.

A most romantic project that was cut short at foundation level by the Irish troubles was a house on the lovely shores of Bantry Bay—a partly-crouching, partly-towering building of rough masonry on a rocky headland near Glengariff, only just above high-water mark—for Lady Kitty Somerset, who had been captivated, and no wonder, by the magic of the whole setting.

Annan Bryce had already begun the making of his now famous gardens on his nearby island of Garinish where Harold Peto had built him the elegant Palladian pavilion that was to serve as a gazebo to the intended house which, like Lady Kitty's, was never built.

Our own immediate troubles began when the workmen laying the water supply pipes were too much shot at and downed tools. Then the contractor was jailed, I don't remember why or by whom, only that the whole wretched upset was political and apparently quite intractable and seemed likely so to remain. So the project was finally abandoned as hopeless, to our great grief, as we had been so sure we were going to adorn a fabulous site with just the building it deserved. That was the nearest I ever got to building anything in the Irish Republic, a most disappointing ending to our romantic gesture.

One pretty odd client was a woman who suddenly wrote to me out of the blue asking me if I could come along sometime soon and advise on certain estate developments that were being considered.

In due course I travelled down to the designated station by the appointed train and was duly met by a most attractive girl driving a large Daimler who said she was my correspondent's daughter. Dusk was falling as we turned in at the park gates of her home and soon the house itself loomed up out of the mist across a reedy lake, a great rambling pile of indifferent Strawberry Hill Gothick in stained and peeling stucco, all pretty discouraging.

As my driver disappeared to put the car away I was ushered into an enormous very high drawing-room by a cadaverous and sinister-looking butler absurdly like Boris Karloff and speaking in an appropriately deep and hollow voice.

'If you will wait here, Sir, I will tell her ladyship of your arrival.' So wait I did, and for quite a while in dazed astonishment. The blotchy walls were distempered a sort of livid yellow, satin curtains of baby pink hung despondently from slightly crooked bamboo poles and in two corners were stacked, of all things, untidy piles of polo sticks and *bicycles*, the whole unlikely set-up made the more unforgettable by being illuminated by a series of naked unshaded gas jets that the butler had lit before withdrawing. What the furniture was like, I cannot now recall, except that it was as odd, as unlikely, and as generally queer as its background—and therefore appropriate. In due course my hostess came bustling in with profuse apologies for keeping me waiting and we talked of 'the project' until it was time to dress for dinner when she said, 'Oh, by the way, you are sleeping in the old wing, in fact in what is called the haunted room. I hope you don't mind?'

'Not in the least,' I said, and I was conducted up and away to a large and rather bleak room in what was clearly by far the oldest part of the house—Tudor at the latest.

There were only my hostess, her daughter and myself at dinner and spaced out at a vast table in a room almost as big and desolate as the drawing-room. What intrigued me was the curious behaviour of the butler, who, at each course, would carry off a helping on a tray through a little secret door beside the sideboard so hung that you could not see beyond it. Between these mysterious exits a basso-profundo voice would reverberate in my ear and I would jerk round to find that Boris Karloff had padded up and with his sunken face bent down to the level of mine was offering me more wine. As we left the dining-room I noticed that the moon was up, that the mist had dispersed, and that the night was now fine and clear.

'Would you care to see our other house?' asked the daughter. 'It's quite near and I can easily run you over.'

I knew about this other house as a distinguished example of

Georgian architecture and was all for this unexpected chance of seeing it as I should have no time for anything but the work I had come for on the morrow.

This other house, standing high on a wide terrace, was all I had hoped for, serene and beautiful in the moonlight, but it was some time before we got any response to our ringing at the front door. At last the housekeeper appeared, candle in hand, and so lighted us through a succession of fine rooms—holding it up as asked, the better to show details of door-cases, mantelpieces and pictures, there being neither electric light nor gas—nor, apparently, lamps available to illuminate the interiors and furniture in the noble manner of William Kent.

Back in the car for our return, it failed altogether to respond to the starter, and the girl said, 'What *again*?—no petrol as usual!—it's always happening, the worst of being mad I suppose. We are all mad, you know.' This statement she rather belied by soon discovering a motor-mower whose tank she dexterously emptied into her own. The odd thing about the whole place was that though deserted, it was all beautifully kept up both within and without from its polished floors to the cropped lawns and well-trimmed hedges. Why, I asked, had they left so lovely a place for another so far less desirable as it seemed to me and, I would guess, less comfortable. Her answer, 'Oh, just economy', seemed to me implausible—as the house with the haunt was as large as the abandoned one and there they were, *two* needing to be maintained instead of one. Might it be, I wondered, that there was an even worse haunt in the hilltop house, or had some tragedy happened there?

It was fairly late by the time we got back and I went straight up to bed and read for half an hour or so, as I normally do—by an acetylene gas jet rather awkwardly overhead—and then fell asleep.

The next thing I knew was that there was a great weight on top of me and what felt like an ice-cold hand clutched around my windpipe. This is murder, I thought—but how pointless—I have nothing worth stealing—it must be some madman just out for an aimless kill, so clearly my best ploy is to pretend he has done what he aimed to do and that I am in fact dead.

So I lay absolutely still, breathed as little as possible, and after what seemed like a long time but was probably no more than a few minutes, the weight lifted, the hand was withdrawn and in a few more minutes I dared to stir gently and then to move quite freely, light a match and then the gas. Nothing had been moved or disturbed in any way, no marks even on my neck where the pressure had almost throttled me. It was not until I was back in bed and had resumed my reading to forget my extraordinary nightmare before trying to sleep again, that I suddenly remembered my hostesses mentioning that my room was 'supposed to be haunted'. It was then 2.30 a.m. That of course set me thinking and puzzling about the possibility or impossibility of haunts and kept me awake until just before I was called with early tea which was never more welcome.

At breakfast my hostess said she hoped I had had a good night. I replied that it had been the worst I had ever spent anywhere in all my life. As she seemed hospitably anxious to know why, I told her. 'Oh!' she exclaimed, all eagerness and excitement, 'It's exactly, but *exactly*, what happened to our last guest who slept in that room—even the same time—2.30—strange indeed, is it not?' I agreed that it was. So much, I thought for your hospitality! I spent the morning on the site of the proposed enterprise, looking around and making notes, returning to the house for lunch. There the butler repeated his mysterious disappearing tricks exactly as at dinner the night before. We were just finishing our meal when he bent down and said something to my hostess in a low growl of which I only caught the words, 'His Lordship'.

She obviously got the message, whatever it was, for as we rose she said, 'My husband would like to meet you before you go and hear what you think of our scheme so I thought we might join him for coffee.' I was ushered into a small study next the dining-room, and there, sure enough, was the other side of the little secret door in the wainscot—and there, too, huddled in a rug beside a meagre fire sat an obviously very sick old man whose wasted hand, courteously extended, I gently took, but who uttered no word, only a low sort of moan.

'I'm afraid my husband can't speak, but he can hear and understand fairly well,' explained my hostess brightly—and that was all she ever told me about the master of the house who was, I supposed, officially my client. I gave him my views on the project as clearly and briefly as I could and got nods and grunts in return, but of course no questions. Travelling back to London my mind was about equally divided between the sketch plans I had already begun to draft, the extreme oddity of the whole set-up I had just quitted, and my inexplicable night's experience.

I have never believed in haunts or ghosts and was still as sceptical as ever and so remain to this day. I was sure that no human agency could have produced the effects I have described so I was driven back on the assumption that my experience was a purely subjective one. But how and why occasioned—and what too about that other occupant who had had precisely the same experience—or was that a fabrication? I had taken no conscious notice of the mention of the 'haunted room'. I had not even looked under the bed or behind the curtains, I had neither eaten nor drunk anything unusual, and unless the general oddity of the whole background had affected me unconsciously more than I knew and laid me open and receptive to still stranger oddity, I am quite unable to explain away this one and only quasi-psychic happening in my whole long life.

Within a week or so I sent off my report and draft plans which I flattered myself solved the problem set with considerable ingenuity and success and would yield a handsome return on the capital invested, whilst greatly adding to the amenities of the place, both private and public.

Hearing nothing, I wrote after a month had passed to ask whether the report and plans had been received and if so, what about them? I got a letter in reply saying yes, indeed—they thought my ideas were splendid but they had decided that they really couldn't afford to do anything at all. Accordingly in due course, I sent in a very generously scaled-down account for my professional services that ultimately produced a response from my incredible hostess enclosing a five-pound note with the explanation that she was very sorry but that was as much as she could afford.

As it barely covered my train fare and my tip to her butler I returned it with, I am afraid, some slightly ironic comment as to how strangely one can be deceived by appearances and my obtuseness in not having realized how sadly straightened were her circumstances.

And that was the end of the whole absurd affair.

An even more unexpected commission, not even marginally architectural, was to be suddenly asked by a court official to write the speech to be delivered by a Royal at the annual Academy banquet. Sir Edwin Lutyens was then President which encouraged me to slip in some really funny and quite relevant jokes as well of course as a good dose of conservation propaganda—landscapes on the walls of the R.A. all very well, but what about the originals, who was looking after *them*, and so on.

The speech was generously reported and the serious stuff was there all right but, unleavened by any cause for laughter, it all read pretty stodgily. Naturally enquiring why I had been thus cruelly plucked of all my fine feathers I was told by 'the Palace' that they were too obviously out of character to be at all suitable for H.R.H.'s display and that was that. This valuable first lesson in speech writing (to get inside your principal's skin) was wasted on me, as I never wrote another—except for myself whose limitations are only too well known to me—and quite different.

Amongst the top half-dozen of my most unpredictable clients I would rate Mrs. A. pretty high. Her husband was charming, indulgent, very rich and seemingly bewitched by his wilful wife. Large and handsome in a 'flaunting extravagant quean' sort of way, she charmed not me, though she did her considerable best, as with every other man in sight. One had to grant her gaiety, a certain malicious wit, and boundless vitality—but she was utterly self-centred, cared nothing for her husband's mild protests when she behaved too outrageously and not much more for mine when I supported him, her theme song being, 'I wish my Jack may never come back, but is jolly well drowned at sea.'

My first job for her was to alter a Tudor manor house which I had lately restored for the previous owner, but she always wanted things changed around to meet her own particular whim of the moment, and she had a whim of iron.

She was not without architectural sensibility and I could generally thwart any too outrageous a project in furtherance of her 'personalizing' projects by pointing out or inventing insurmountable structural or practical difficulties.

Somewhere she had picked up a great Tudor archway that had probably once given entrance to a forecourt and she thought it the very thing for the new hall fireplace. It could just be fitted in, and I agreed that it really might look rather fine and anyhow, there it was. But I insisted that in such a vast opening no fire would draw and they would have perpetual smoke trouble and no heat. 'Never mind,' she said, 'there's plenty of central heating and it's only for looks, but you *must* make a great big log fire burn brightly on that hearth *somehow*.' And I did, most extravagantly, by fixing a flaring gas torch up the chimney to induce a sufficient upcast draught.

Then as an occasional change from the manor house and Mayfair she romantically saw herself as leading the simple life in a sort of *Cottage-Orne* belvedere—where she would, she said, look after herself and not be bothered with servants except of course for her personal maid and her chauffeur who would run her back and forth in her Rolls. She would give elegant informal little supper-parties in the manner of Marie-Antoinette at the Petit Trianon. All this (though she was not herself a golfer) on the edge of a celebrated home-counties course, where, presumably, gentlemen agog and grateful for a merry evening, would be readily available. Anyhow, up went this curious not-so-little play-house, very much 'personalized' within but disarmingly simple and discreet without. It was, I gathered, functionally, a great success. Then it was a matter of altering one of a succession of town houses because she just had to leave her mark on each before moving on to the next, and unattainable perfection.

The last I saw of her before Hitler's war put an end to all such frivolity, was when she took a very beautiful and famous country house of the highest architectural distinction, for, I think it was, three days, though it was unfurnished and indeed had not been occupied for quite a while.

This rather mad-seeming escapade was partly prompted by genuine appreciation of the house's architectural quality but mainly that she might entertain a large house-party for a neighbouring hunt-ball. Few things seem to be impossible if you are rich enough and for three days and nights this slumbering old mansion was awoken to bustling activity merely by the waving of a golden magic wand inscribed *carte blanche* in the direction of Fortnum and Mason.

They, it appeared, had seen to the cleaning and airing, the lighting and heating, the furnishing and equipment throughout, the linen and plate, the admirable food and wine, and the large staff of attentive servants. But knowing all this, and that the great house would, in a day or so, like *The Lost Domain*, be all forlorn and shuttered and dark and cold again, gave the whole thing a curious feeling of unreality, nothing and nobody seemed quite credibly substantial, but rather part of an unusually vivid dream, or a muddled memory of some story of unexplained revellers in a haunted house by Robert Louis Stevenson or Michael Innes. I cannot now recall a single one of my fellow guests, but I could, at any minute, do a pretty accurate memory sketch of the house's main façade.

Apart from problem clients, there were sometimes also problem jobs. Building by remote control in China had its own special difficulties. First I was sent accurate site surveys giving levels, also photographs of all the surroundings. I was happy enough to design in a generally British Imperial classic mood, which was what my clients Butterfield & Swire required, but I wanted to introduce some small Chinese motifs in polite acknowledgement of its location—but no—that, I was told would be somehow impolitic—so all I was allowed, or rather, all I was able to get away with, more or less surreptitiously, were some of the interior fittings, stair rails, chandeliers, lamp-brackets and such to which I did manage to give a somewhat Chinoiserie flavour.

Plaster casts were sent out for all mouldings, capitals, cornices, bases, panels and architectural details of every kind and were faithfully reproduced as shown by the photographs that accompanied the monthly progress reports sent back to me.

When all was done and the place furnished and occupied, I was sent an elegant great volume filled with large photographs covering the whole achievement inside and out. My clients also generously offered me a free passage out there and back in one of their own ships if I cared to go and have a look at it all myself. I was fool enough at the time to think I was too busy for so long a trip, though I had also done two other jobs for the same firm up at Tientsin which I should also have liked to see—and much more than either—something of China itself. I doubt if I shall ever make it—now.

In those inter-war days contractors could sometimes present problems, too, and architects were then exposed to quite a bit of more or less decently camouflaged corruption from manufacturers and such under the heading of 'public relations' consisting mostly of invitations to expensive parties on some plausible pretext. Perhaps dinner at the Savoy and on to a ringside seat at some crucial boxing match, a special champagne luncheon-car rail ride to Aintree and back for the Grand National, tempting no doubt to some, but with no allure, as it happened, for me.

Then, at Christmas mostly, cases of wine, boxes of cigars, fur rugs or game would arrive 'with compliments' from suppliers of this or that. As this 'softening-up' technique was apparently so well established and so generally accepted—I gave up sending things back with an ungracious and rather pi snubbing letter, and substituted a printed acknowledgement slip that read thus:

> Mr. Clough Williams-Ellis, whilst fully appreciating the generosity that prompted the dispatch of the present received from your firm, has had to make it a rule not to accept gifts of any sort from any business with which he has or may have professional dealings. He has therefore passed on what he cannot enjoy himself to an institution where he knows it will be most fully appreciated, he hopes with your approval.

Whether it was the effect of this rather pompous declaration or that of the much needed anti-corruption act which I think came into operation at about the same time, I don't know, but this particular embarrassment anyhow ceased abruptly and is now only meagrely represented by an annual shower of extravagant but unwanted calendars.

Actually I believe and hope that our would-be tempters were

just following the once perhaps generally accepted custom of an earlier, laxer and possibly jollier time and had failed to appreciate that architects now have to be above any possible suspicion of partiality, and in all my long career I knew of only one who wasn't.

All the same I was once the unconscious accessory to a mild and friendly corruptive gesture by contractors who inexplicably started sending cars to convey me to and from the distant job they were doing for me. When I demurred at this, it emerged that they had been so surprised and touched by my not having demanded a commission from them on their contract that they felt they must show their appreciation in some way! It was a difficult matter to dispose of without being ungracious—but it had to be done.

But to return to clients, even as I write (1970) I am still involved with several pretty fabulous specimens who have refused to take seriously my reiterated declarations that I have really and truly retired from general practice, as should surely be accepted as only decent at my age.

Sometimes a client's absence can be more worrying than his over-intrusive presence as when a most trustful and valued client elected to travel round the world for a year leaving no reliable address and me in charge of comprehensive alterations and embellishments of her very large country house. Everything had been agreed, and all would have been fine, had we not discovered virulent and widespread dry-rot in various parts of the original building that just *had* to be dealt with there and then. Also the main portico was in real danger of collapse and so in need of immediate and extremely expensive underpinning.

These were necessarily day-work jobs with no fixed estimate and the final cost of the whole adventure as totted up by the quantity surveyors at the end of these dismal operations, certainly far exceeded what anyone of us had originally bargained for. Especially not my poor client who returned radiant from her safari to be confronted by this horror. Yet never one word of complaint from her, still less of reproach. One client as understanding and considerate as that can make up for quite a few who may be less so.

One might call that 'negative niceness' but even more encouraging is positive appreciation of one's efforts such as:

> It seems a waste not to tell you—and in writing, so that no one can interrupt—that your building has given me more kick and pleasure than anything that has happened for years. The outside is wonderful and satisfying, and the upstairs passage gave me a lump in my throat and for 2d. I could have burst into tears. Ordinarily I only have felt like this for music, and once, when I first saw Westminster Hall. So really this is to say thank you. I just feel thankful and delighted and rich because it has been built, and I'm glad it was you that built it.

Quite possibly it is only such heartening little yelps of pleasure that have encouraged me to think less doomfully of my countrymen's visual unawareness.

Being primarily a domestic architect with private clients I have probably been less exposed than some to the dingy underworld of financial tricksters with which however I did several times find myself in astonished contact.

My first was when a friend rang me up to say that a financier of whose integrity he was quite satisfied had asked him to act as general engineer to a projected new town for which he had already bought the land in Middlesex, and that he hoped that I would act as his architect and wanted to discuss it with me. The financier and I met, and his general ideas seemed quite unexceptional and indeed most advanced and very much like my own, being all for district heating, segregated traffic, a balanced community and all the other planners' tenets of the time, and withal most eloquently propounded. So I took him to lunch at my club when he said I really must come right away and see his lovely site that he was sure I would approve—which indeed I did when I ran him down to it in my car, his own Rolls, he said, being unfortunately laid up for servicing.

Back again at the club for tea and further discussion, he said, 'Goodness me—I am taking a party out to dinner, I have forgotten to cash a cheque, I shall be late if I go back to the Ritz—could you possibly I wonder . . . ?' He seemed such a nice intelligent chap with all the right ideas that I did hand him a fiver—no more, because a horrid little suspicion had just begun to wriggle in my brain that he had been 'reading me up' so that I naturally thought his ideas were splendid, because they were, in fact, my own only very slightly distorted. Also, he hadn't entirely satisfied me in his answers to some of my nautical questions about his steam yacht being fitted out at Southampton for a cruise on which he said, he would hope for my company.

Of course I never saw him again—though I heard of him—in prison. My engineer friend, being more credulous than I, got off far less lightly, having played along with him for quite a while, wasting his time and advancing substantial sums. It finally emerged of course that the ownership of the land and capital were both pure moonshine. Had it not been so, we might well I think, have produced something pretty remarkable, and long before the actual New Towns had got going.

My next deceiver was the director of a contracting firm with very impressive West End offices, that had clearly grown fat during the Kaiser's war and sought to grow fatter yet by property dealing and speculative building. I was commissioned to plan a large-scale development scheme. This I did and actually designed and got built several 'model' houses which were opened with a gala luncheon, boosting speeches, press photographers and all possible publicity—but no fees. Then a quite ga-ga old peer was made Chairman of this particular enterprise in an effort to give it the credibility it was beginning to lack.

Then the Deputy Chairman who was supposed to be keeping an appointment with me to clear up my growing doubts about the whole set-up, failed to show up. Having waited a while I rang up his flat to be told that he was dining at the Carlton with Mr. Blank. As Mr. Blank was a very well-known character indeed, not of the highest repute, I thought it well to check up on this disquieting tip-off, and did. There, in the old Carlton's main restaurant sat my director with his dubious guest in full view, a magnum of champagne in its ice pail between them and in much too intimate conversation to notice me. I tip-toed away, for if Mr. Blank was going to be in on the act, it was clearly high time for me to be out of it and I forthwith sent in my resignation and with it my bill for professional services so far rendered.

After some delay, and to my surprise, my fees were actually paid before the company was finally wound up, perhaps because I may have been thought to know rather more than I actually did about a variety of dubious fiddles that I had only just come to suspect. Well, out of that particular frying pan it was not long before I found myself in yet another—seduced by the prospect of scenic knight-errantry in rescuing a very beautiful little bay from the threat of unsympathetic and even brutal mishandling.

An ebullient and up-and-coming young London business man had bought the place to develop it as a speculation and was somehow directed to me for advice. He had few ideas of his own so readily swallowed mine. I was able to establish the general lay-out and build several sample houses to set a standard before he and his Rolls, his decorative official wife and his poodle, disappeared to be seen no more—leaving the contractor with the last house unpaid for and me in a like plight.

Still a standard for the development *had* been set and later, an even more ambitious speculator who took over the bankrupt estate, did make some attempt to carry the thing through to a decent conclusion before he too went into liquidation through over-ambitious and less sensible speculations elsewhere. The final result—what might and should have been a model of the discreet and sympathetic use of a lovely setting—turned out to be an only partially mitigated mess, but little better than the norm. A sad waste of a golden opportunity through the stupid cupidity of Philistines who in their anxiety to get rich quickly so often don't even seem to know the rules of their own game.

I have said that I seem to have an unfortunate inborn capacity for attracting eccentrics, and I confess to having a certain sympathy with any agreeable crackpot.

I suppose this kink of mine prompted my rather disreputable response to a B.B.C. invitation to take part in a series called 'Personal Choice' when I broadcast a few subversive passages from *The Almost Perfect State* by my favourite philosopher Don Marquis:

> In the Almost Perfect State every person shall have at least ten years of easy, carefree, happy living before he dies. Personally we look for-

ward to an old age of dissipation, indolence and unrevered disrepute.

We shall indulge ourself in many things that we have been forced by circumstances to forego. We have always been compelled to be prudent, cautious, staid, sober, conservative, industrious, respectful of established institutions, a model citizen. We have not liked it, but we have been unable to escape it. . . .

The people whom we really prefer as associates, though we do not approve their ideas, are the rebels, the radicals, the wastrels, the vicious, the poets, the Bolshevists, the idealists, the nuts, the Lucifers, the agreeable good-for-nothings, the sentimentalists, the prophets, the freaks . . . .

We shall write ribald songs against organized society and address public meetings (to which we have been invited because of our wisdom) in a vein of jocund malice. . . .

We shall know that the Almost Perfect State is here when the kind of old age each person wants is possible to him. Of course, all of you may not want the kind we want. Some of you may be dissolute now and may look forward to becoming like one of the nice old fellows in a Wordsworth poem. . . . The point is, that no matter what you want to be, during those last ten years, that you may be, in the Almost Perfect State.

Any system of government under which the individual does all the sacrificing for the sake of the general good, for the sake of the community, the State, gets off on its wrong foot. We don't want things that cost us too much.

There is a reckless gaiety about Don Marquis's humane philosophizing that I find most endearing and his *Almost Perfect State* stands high on my list of 'desert island' books.

Chapter Twelve

Writing and Russia

Though busy enough in the early twenties, what with contriving elegant settings for private clients and with the master work for Stowe, my nagging concern for a more general nation-wide seemliness still obsessed me.

Work with the Design and Industries Association went on including the small 'black comedies' of our Cautionary Guides, meetings were arranged, lectures sought and given, various Amenities bodies and Civic Societies founded, in fact quite a buzz of gadflies, not without effect.

But experience of such propaganda (which, as is usual, was often mainly a grave sustaining of the already virtuous) seemed to suggest that there might also be another approach.

How would it be to suggest not so much that good design, good architecture and decent town planning were a national duty, but those who tried it, found it fun to concern themselves with such things? Sir John Squire was already running his Architecture Club with its agreeable dinners, but these again were mostly attended by the already saved.

The club aimed at including 'Practitioners, Patrons and Publicists' and under these several headings we did collect a pretty lively membership with G. K. Chesterton, J. B. Priestley, Oswald Baron and of course Squire himself as star performers.

Amabel Strachey arriving at her wedding to the author, with her father, St. Loe Strachey, July 1915

THE WELSH AIRS, SUNG

AT THE

WELCOME HOME MEETING

TO

Lieut. and Mrs. Clough Williams=Ellis,

AT PLAS BRONDANW, LLANFROTHEN,

JULY 31st, 1915.

Rhyfelgyrch Gwyr Harlech.

Harlech, cyfod dy faneri,
 Gwêl y gelyn, enyn, yni,
Y Meirionwys oll i waeddi,
 Cymru fo am byth,
Aed y waedd ac aed y weddi
I bob cwr o'n gwlad uchelfri
Nes adseinia yr Eryri.
 Cymru fo am byth,
Arwyr, sawdwyr sydyn,
Rhuthrwn ar y gelyn,
Gyrwn ef i ffoi o nant
A bryn, a phant a dyffryn,
Chwifiwn faner goruchafiaeth,
Gorfoleddwn yn ei alaeth
Clywir llef ein buddugoliaeth,
 Cymru fo am byth.

Gwaed sy'n gwrido y cleddyfau
Twrw mawr a thincian arfau
Uwch na'r twrw ceir banllefau.
 Cymru fo am byth,
Saethau a phicellau wibiant,
Cyrn udganant meirch weryrant,
Milwyr rhuthrant rhengau floeddiant,
 Cymru fo am byth.
Tanbaid i'w calonau,
Grymus ydyw breichiau
Gwyr yn ymladd dros eu gwlad,
Orenwog wlad eu tadau,
Gwyllt a ffyrnig yw'r ymladdfa—
Gwancus yw y cledd wrth wledda
Duwies buddugoliaeth floeddia,
 Cymru fo am byth.

Bugeilio'r Gwenith Gwyn.

Mi sydd yn fachgen ieuanc ffol,
 Yn caru'n ol fy ffansi,
Mi yn bugeilio gwenith gwyn,
 Ac arall yn ei fedi;
O! pam na ddeui ar fy ol,
 Ryw ddydd ar ol ei gilydd,
Gwaith 'rwy'n dy wel'd y feinir fach
 O glânach, glânach beunydd.

Glânach, glânach wyt bob dydd,
 Neu fi sy'a'm ffydd yn ffolach:
Er mwyn y Gwr a wnaeth dy wedd
 Gwna i'm drugaredd bellach:
O! cwyd dy ben, gwel acw draw,
 Rho i mi'th law, Wèn dirion,
Gwaith yn dy fynwes berth ei thro
 Mae allwedd clô fy nghalon.

Mi godais heddyw gyda'r wawr,
 Gan frysio'n fawr fy lludded,
Fel cawn gusanu llun dy droed,
 Fu'r hyd y coed yn cerdded:
O! cwyd fy mhen o'r galar maith
 A serchus iaith gwârineb:
Gwaith mwy na'r byd i'r neb a'th gâr
 Yw golwg ar dy wyneb.

Tra bo dwr y môr yn hallt
 A thra bo'n ngwallt yn tyfu,
A thra bo calon dan fy mron,
 Mi fydda'n ffyddlon iti;
O! dywed imi'r gwir dan gêl
 A rho dan sêl atebion
P'un ai myfi neu arall, Gwen,
 Sydd oreu gan dy galon.

Welsh Airs sung to welcome the author and his bride
(leaflet damaged by fire at Plas Brondanw, 1951)

The Watchtower, Plas Brondanw

The Garden, Plas Brondanw

Plas Brondanw, an interior, as rebuilt after fire

Plas Brondanw, entrance front

Romney's House, Hampstead

Chatham House, Stowe

Stairhead, the Butterfield and Swire Residence, Shanghai

Llangoed Castle, Breconshire

First Church of Christ Scientist, Belfast

Entrance front, Bishop's Stortford College Chapel (the first building in England by a living architect to be scheduled for preservation)

The Library, Oare House, Wiltshire

Cold Blow, Oare

Paper model for Dunwood House, Yorkshire

Piers by Wren, gates by the author, Wroxall Abbey, Warwickshire

Cornwell Manor, Oxfordshire

New Village Centre, Cornwell

King George VI and Queen Elizabeth at Pen-y-gwryd, with the author showing them the proposed extent of the Snowdonia National Park

Unveiling by the Prince of Wales of the memorial tablet in Westminster Abbey to David Lloyd-George designed by the author, 1970. From the right, the group includes the Prince of Wales, the author, the Sub-Dean of Westminster, Earl Lloyd George of Dwyfor, Sir Dingle Foot, the Right Hon. Edward Heath, the Right Hon. Jeremy Thorpe

The Town Hall at Portmeirion from Battery Square

A crystal goblet, by Laurence Whistler, presented to the author on the fortieth anniversary of the foundation of Portmeirion by its trustees

The author speaking from the Gloriette at the anniversary celebrations

The Lloyd George grave, designed by the author

Telefoto picture of Portmeirion from across the estuary, with Snowdon in the background

The author at work, 1970

The Duke of Westminster lent us his picture gallery in old Grosvenor House for our first exhibition and there were club parties at Londonderry House and Lansdowne House and elsewhere, all jolly enough but inevitably rather inward-looking coterie affairs with little effect on outside public opinion. The club still flourishes as a forum where current questions that are, or should be, of concern to architects are periodically threshed out over the dinner table.

But my wife and I, feeling that all this, though fine as far as it went, was not really reaching out to where enlightenment was most sorely needed, set about the writing and illustrating of a light-hearted propagandist book which we called *The Pleasures Of Architecture*. We suggested to our readers that it was perfectly proper for the layman—the citizen, the voter—to have an opinion about any piece of architecture and we suggested how an untechnical quizzing might proceed:

> A building which is new to us is like a ghost, and we shall feel much more comfortable if we have one or two questions ready to put to it. That was the best of older codes. You could ask the poor thing point-blank. 'Are you pure?' or 'Do you express your construction?' Questions-of-thumb should not be expected to cover all the ground, but as long as their limitations are recognized it seems fair enough to ask a building at any rate these five:
>
> 1. Do you fulfil your function (as house, shop, factory, church, or what not) adequately and with a minimum of friction?
>
> 2. Are you, or were you, for a reasonable period, structurally efficient, so that your doors and windows opened and shut properly and you kept out the weather?
>
> 3. Do you seem beautiful to me, or, if not, did you at any rate seem beautiful—not merely correct or expansive—to those who built you?
>
> 4. Have you got a general architectural theme which you try to express?
>
> 5. Are you a good neighbour, so that your setting or any building near you gains rather than loses by your presence? Candidates for admiration need not necessarily pass in all five questions.

Anticipating Osbert Lancaster, we invented flippant titles for architectural styles—Pimlico Paladian, Gaspipe Gothic, and so on. We indeed tried in all sorts of ways to humanize stone and brick, for instance by suggesting that a fine building not only expresses its epoch—say the scholarly Hubris of the great eighteenth-century magnificoes, but also the character and quirks of a human being, an individual architect. These might be writ large for all to see, expressed unequivocally. Not only façades, but house plans, practical or absurd, and the lay-out of a street or a park, were we suggested, humanly expressive. Take Vanbrugh for instance, who kept such fashionable company and who was a brilliant show-off, as Blenheim and Castle Howard indicate, and as Alexander Pope did not fail to notice. Horace Walpole blames Kent, the architect of Holkham for the same sort of faults, for disregarding purpose and for building only for effect:

> We are left to conjecture whether the noble host and hostess sleep in a bedroom forty feet high or are relegated, like their guests, to a garret or an outhouse or perhaps may have their bedroom windows looking inward on a lead flat.
> All this may suffice to display the perverse ingenuity of the architect in producing a monumental whole; but both the proprietor and his guests would in the long run probably prefer rooms of appropriate dimensions, and so situated as to enjoy a view of the scenery of the park or the fresh breezes of heaven.

As for the great designers of the Gothic cathedrals and abbeys such as that superb master mason Yevele, only their soaring achievements are known. Sir Christopher Wren, we pointed out, as might be guessed from the variety, grace and appropriateness of his achievements in architecture and science, emerges from the scanty biographical information, as an almost wholly admirable character. In a Court full of the coarsest jobbery he remained unspotted:

> A masterly designer, an ingenious planner, an untiring worker, and a shrewd, honest, capable man of affairs, his value as a type is accentuated by his having probably had one social defect which, as hinted, seems to have been—and perhaps still is—characteristic of the profession. Outside his art, and outside astronomy and his ingenious

experiments, he seems to have been somewhat inarticulate. . . . Wren, unable, as we conjecture, to express more than tolerance and good humour along social lines, turned to his art and made London eloquent. His architecture has every grace and displays every human quality in stone and brick, and is universally admitted to be expressive and alive in a most unusual degree. If we see it as the distillation of the whole of an uncommonly rich and vigorous nature, we shall not be surprised.

In our effort to entice a public to whom this sort of brick and stone biography might prove a stimulus, we did not neglect the architects who were then practising, though we kept our contemporaries discreetly anonymous and only designated them by letters of the alphabet.

Nevertheless, one of these did choose to recognize himself (and correctly) in one of our little vignettes, and, though he naturally never admitted that he realized we had been making fun of him—the venomous review he gave the book showed us that we had at least made him feel a little less sure of his fancied pre-eminence. Otherwise our effort was most cordially received and indeed ran through five editions, the last (largely revised) being even now not long out of print.

What is most satisfying is the large number of people we meet, now often prominent in the world of arts or letters, who aver that their interest in architecture was first sparked off by our *Pleasures*.

Amabel being fully occupied with her own writing, both novels and journalism, to say nothing of children *and* books for them—my next effort was a solo—*England and the Octopus*.

This, unlike *Pleasures*, was a denunciatory, angry book, commissioned by its publisher. Its purpose was to give a more permanent form and to bring into focus all or as much as possible of the sort of 'Amenity' propaganda that I had been plugging for years, in season and out, in articles and speeches. After some heart-searching and misgivings I signed on to do it and it was duly published in 1928, with, to my astonishment, immediate and laudatory notices in almost every newspaper and relevant journal. There were reviews by such unexpected eminences as D. H.

Lawrence, G. K. Chesterton, Robert Lynd and others, whilst J. C. Squire gave it two columns in the *Observer* as 'the book of the day'.

All very encouraging as promoting the causes for which I mostly cared. Then followed *The Architect*, for Bles's Life and Work series and next another 'command performance' but again prompted by concern as well as by special affection, my biography of Sir Laurence Weaver.

There followed a couple of 'popular' illustrated books on architecture, *The Adventure of Building* and then *Architecture Here And Now*, a more scholarly effort in collaboration with Sir John Summerson, who along with Sir Nicolaus Pevsner sits as final appeal judge on all historical architectural questions. Then came a truly co-operative book *Britain and the Beast* again suggested by its publisher. The idea was that I should collect a team and myself act as contributor, 'introducer' and editor. It was felt that such an arrangement would more widely cover all the issues, and from the team's own points of view, that I had briefly touched on in *The Octopus*. An ambitious project, but I liked the idea, and soon had my panel of chosen contributors all lined up—over two dozen of them, all of eminence in their particular fields and some of them of more general celebrity. There were for instance, Lord Keynes, E. M. Forster and Sir George Stapledon, Sir Patrick Abercrombie, Lord Horder, G. M. Trevelyan, Sir William Beach-Thomas, H. J. Massingham and Sheila Kaye-Smith, and they all co-operated with the most generous enthusiasm to a big and admirably produced book that was sufficiently well received to be followed up by a much larger and cheaper edition.

A pleasant memory of the whole agreeable exercise was a full-dress dinner-party for all those who had promised to contribute and who could attend, generously given on my behalf by Sir Geoffrey Fry in his spacious London house that I had lately altered and embellished for him.

This preliminary convivial get-together was most fruitful and helped us immensely in our joint effort to give our book all the coherence and relevance possible.

I had hoped that the fact of our host being principal private secretary to Stanley Baldwin, then Prime Minister, who was always talking about the English countryside, might influence Baldwin sufficiently to induce him to write an introduction, especially as I knew him anyway. But not he. He must have have approved our aims, but couldn't be bothered. 'Very well then,' I thought, 'I shall jolly well get commendations from a whole panel of other notables, including your political opponents, so there!'—and I did.

Lloyd George, Sir Stafford Cripps, George Lansbury, J. B. Priestley and Sir Julian Huxley were amongst these, but of course there were good Conservatives, too, including Lords Derby, Crawford, Zetland and Baden-Powell.

Then I was commissioned by *Country Life* to write a practical book on *Pisée Terre* (rammed earth) building, a technique in which my father-in-law was greatly interested and for whom I built a cottage to demonstrate its merits at Newlands Corner where it was something of a nine days' wonder, inspected by landowners and their agents and much publicized in the press. It was hoped that this way of building would greatly cheapen and expedite rural cottage building in the twenties, but though there was a lot of enthusiastic experimentation, nothing very substantial resulted so far as I know. Ray Strachey's cottage, so built, was irreverently known as 'The Mud'. And now I cannot give the book a date. The second, revised edition is still in print, but my copy has not been returned by the last (unknown) borrower. Constantly missing books that I once had, I am reminded of a dark saying quoted to me by Bertrand Russell. A man is proudly displaying his library to an envious visitor: 'Yes, the collection of a lifetime and I guard it well. I never lend! Only fools lend books. All the books on this shelf once belonged to fools.'

Some of my journalistic efforts of that time were directed not so much at a general as at a local public. One of these was a series of twelve fierce articles on 'Our Squalid Towns' for the *Week End Review* commissioned by its editor Sir Gerald Barry, wherein I was allowed to be as bluntly outspoken as I chose so long as I based my reports on my own personal observation and enquiries.

My sample was a variegated one—the subjects for this civic inquest being largely chosen because I happened to know something about the places already, and they ranged in stature from small residential and resort towns to great industrial cities—a pretty wide coverage of urban England and Wales wherein there was then plenty to criticize and very little to commend. And criticize I did, freely and fearlessly, having had legal assurance that 'a *place* cannot sue for libel'. There were threats but these died away when the threateners got the same legal advice that I had already had.

Unfortunately, though almost inevitably, in one case, I did bring in a prominent speculative developer by name. I had let myself go in unbridled denunciation, holding him up to ridicule as well as to hatred and contempt—as was duly and not unfairly claimed by his lawyers. Periodicals are understandably shy of libel actions and consequent damages that are entirely speculative but can be crippling—so there was nothing for it but a published apology and a withdrawal in terms agreeable to the aggrieved party. This public, if perfunctory whitewashing of my prize exhibit of a municipal malefactor (as I still hold him to have been) I found hard to take, but had to swallow as there was no alternative. However, I was able a little later, to work off my righteous indignation at this setback in a couple of long articles exclusively concerned with municipal corruption. These were commissioned by Sir Arnold Wilson, M.P. for his journal *The Nineteenth Century*, wherein I could let myself go all out without fear or favour because all my examples, without exception, were taken from actual and mostly recent court proceedings where all the accused had been severally found guilty of a quite bewildering variety of fiddles. Some of these were of extreme ingenuity, others so stupid as to seem almost innocent. Anyway I produced an impressive rogues' gallery, consisting almost entirely of municipal councillors and officials, each docketed with the date and place of his fall from grace and the particular nature thereof, whether racketeering, bribery, fraudulent conversion, corrupt log-rolling, breaches of trust, speculation, straight forgery, perjury, a too-flagrant nepotism or whatever it might be. I employed a sleuth to hunt out material from the appropriate records and this material proved to be far, far more than I had ever anticipated or could possibly use. In the picture it gave of rottenness, it was exceedingly depressing and it solved many things that had been puzzling me.

During my 'Squalid towns' reconnaissance I had constantly wondered just why this or that was neglected or not done and why this other had come about, so often to the manifest disadvantage of the town and its citizens, and in the course of these articles, I seemed to find an answer, at any rate partial, that genuinely shook me and which I felt I must proclaim. Maybe there is now no need for the sort of exposure that I then felt was called for, which, owing to the outbreak of the Second World War was a somewhat stifled cry. Or is there?

It was when this second war was almost upon us that Sir Arnold used to drop in to breakfast at our Hampstead house to discuss the theme of my articles and things in general. We found him exceedingly well-informed, highly intelligent, but obviously troubled. The fact was that he had had certain Nazi sympathies and indeed contacts, but was undergoing a process of agonizing disillusionment. This needs a postscript. By way of penance for his error and unmistakably to demonstrate his change of heart, though well over military age, he gallantly sought out the most dangerous job that the second war had to offer—that of rear gunner in a bomber. Very soon, of course, he was killed—and our cleansing campaign was forgotten in the welter of greater issues that soon engulfed us.

Naturally in our efforts to improve Britain we of the Amenities brigade had all also had an eye to what was happening in other countries. We were emphatically not so provincial or insular as to overlook the need for this. Sometimes, as with Sir Arnold Wilson, there was a difficulty here. Bitterly as you might dislike the Fascist government in Italy it had to be conceded that it did seem to have a proper architectural pride and the conviction that the State could be both glorified and enriched by its artists, which though an old notion enough, is being but gradually received again throughout Europe, and perhaps more cautiously in England than anywhere else.

For some of my colleagues of the Amenities movement another country had brought the same sort of feeling of ambivalence. This of course was Stalin's Russia. As in Italy, a highly centralized Government had the same wish to build well, the same power to do so. Their admiration was for such architects as Ernst May, Le Corbusier and Frank Lloyd Wright.

Our first visit to Soviet Russia (by the Soviet ship *Smolny* to Leningrad and back) was during the progress of the first five-year plan, when my wife and I accompanied the Commissar responsible for physical planning and reconstruction on an extended tour of inspection by air, rail and road to Moscow, Orel, Leningrad, the new town of Kharkov, the great Dnieprostroi Dam and its attendant new industrial city. We saw much to admire, much to criticize.

When it came to taking to the air during our tour, I noted that the plane though large enough was an only partly converted ex-bomber. I rather mistrusted its battered rustiness, its door only secured by a twisted bit of wire. The Russians were notorious then for their maltreatment of machines of all kinds—especially of cars and tractors which were constantly out of action through mishandling and gross neglect of maintenance.

Anyway, it was with some doubt that we boarded our neglected-looking plane in the chill darkness of a very early start from Moscow, bound for Kharkov. Having lurched into the air, I felt sure that we were on fire, but it was only inordinate flames from the exhausts through something wrong with the fuel control. But about half-way to our destination we ceased to be airborne and found ourselves quite gently stranded in the middle of a wide plain regarding our poor old ex-bomber with a crumpled undercarriage and broken wing.

However, it was fine and warm and we were within sight of a most attractive looking little town (Orel) all a-bristle with white onion-domed companiles. We were told our plane was completely *kaputt* and that there could not possibly be a relief one for some long time—so we set off on a most rewarding exploration, one result of which was that when I came to give my farewell 'thank you' lecture in Moscow, I begged my hosts at all costs to preserve their lovely towers and campaniles even if they could find no new use for their closed churches. Essential, I said, if only to give some liveliness and grace to their street-scapes which they were even then beginning to stultify with lumpish blocks of new construction in drab concrete.

We had scarcely returned to our crippled plane at the time we had been told that a relief *might* be expected, when, to our surprise an elegant though smaller machine did actually touch down alongside us. Quite good service after all, we told each other, until it was somehow explained that the newcomer was not for us at all, but had been sent to pick up the stereos of the *Pravda* newspaper that we had been carrying, and deliver them at top speed to their proper destination.

However, we must, at some time, have been picked up for we were ultimately delivered to Kharkov where we rejoined our Commissar, who had prudently not trusted himself to the air. In explaining the layout of an entirely new industrial town then in an early stage of construction, he endeared himself to me by saying with great emphasis, 'Here of course there will be grass and trees and everything necessary.' If only the Victorian entrepreneurs who built our industrial towns had included grass and trees among the 'necessary' things!

Our host and guide was fortunately English-speaking and as I was genuinely moved by the great works I was so proudly shown and was eager to be helpful, my criticism was as frankly and freely expressed as my admiration for these vast conceptions, and the imagination, faith and drive that was getting them realized despite the most desperate deficiencies and obstacles. But I still recall the chill that crept down my spine when, rolling slowly back to Moscow in our lumberingly luxurious Tzarist *wagon-lit* our commissar suddenly said, 'You have been very critical of much that we are trying to do. I must ask you to be good enough to repeat your words to the Central Committee in Moscow as soon as we return.'

That I did, through a most efficient interpreter. It soon emerged that the committee was essentially technical rather than political and agog for anything I could tell them, so my 'secret-police' suspicions were sufficiently lulled for me to say my say with no punches pulled and even with afterthought criticisms added for good measure. But I was quite unprepared for the outcome of this long session of addresses, questions and answers, which was the presentation of a barrow-load of books, plans and portfolios, and—the offer of a job! And a tempting job it was—

the selection of sites for, and outline planning of, New Towns for the Soviet Union, with my own train that would run me and my surveying and drawing-staff wherever required about the map of Russia.

And, in principle, I accepted, though in the end nothing came of it, for though the offered pay was generous enough, it had to be in unexportable roubles and they wanted a three-year contract. One way and another, by the time I got home and had tentatively recruited a handful of assistants it became clear that there were altogether too many difficulties to justify the adventure.

But I recorded my impressions of Russian building and planning in a series of long articles for the *Manchester Guardian* and *Daily Telegraph* and was sufficiently impressed to return later, and saw the transition from extreme austerity to a positively opulent style of building, with classical orders, marble, carving, gilding and chandeliers wherever possible, including the Moscow underground.

All this, and the huge 'prestige' buildings I was assured were 'in accordance with the will of the people'—though how their preferences had been ascertained was not explained.

On one occasion I was bidden to a banquet at the Soviet Foreign Office and the dazzling old Czarist gold plate was brought out for the occasion and used throughout. But when I tiresomely asked the white-shirted servant behind my chair for mustard, he eventually presented it all right and triumphantly on a golden salver, but in a rusty little tin with a tooth-pick stuck in it by way of a spoon. It seemed to typify the contemporary Russian set-up rather aptly.

My hostess in Moscow was Ivy Litvinov, wife of the then Foreign Minister, an Englishwoman and an old friend, and my visit happened to coincide with that of Lady Astor, Lord Lothian and Bernard Shaw, for whom a number of parties and meetings were arranged to which I was also bidden. Shaw of course was the star of this odd triumvirate and clearly much relished his popularity—saying in effect 'you may think it odd that I, a socialist, should be visiting you as it were arm-in-arm with an American heiress and a ridiculously wealthy English marquis—but I thought it would do them good as well as myself to see what you are up to here and to learn what is cooking'.

Two quite different embarrassments dogged another visit to Moscow for an architectural conference, this time by train. It began in Potsdam whither I had gone to have another look at Frederick the Great's Sans Souci before catching the night train from Berlin to Moscow. Hurrying back to Potsdam station I saw approaching me a large squad of Brown-shirts with polished shovels at the slope, swastika flags aloft and Nazi badges on their arms—singing one of their new patriotic songs as they marched. All the local people were springing to attention shouting 'Heil Hitler' and giving the ordained salute.

I simply could not do that, yet neither could I risk missing my transcontinental train reservation through being detained on some pretext for my nonconformity. I was thinking fast how to dodge this awkward dilemma when my eye caught a fine new and heaven-sent public lavatory just ahead of the marching column into which I dived precipitately, as though in urgent need of its facilities—as any citizen might well be at any time. No one came after me and I simply waited until the singing and shouting had obviously passed my refuge and then emerged to run on to the station to catch my train back to Berlin—which I just did.

I had taken my seat in the dining-car of the Moscow express when the waiter brought along a couple to sit opposite me. I bowed and said 'Good evening' at a venture, and got the same back in very slightly Americanized English. I said I was on my way to the Moscow architectural and planning conference. The man said, 'You are an architect then? So am I.' 'Your name?' I asked. 'Frank Lloyd Wright.' 'Ah,' I said, 'how kind of chance thus to turn a legend into present reality,' or some such civility, acknowledging his fame as I knew would be expected.

We had quite a good talk but when at the frontier we were roused and turned out on to the station platform with our baggage and told to open up for Customs examination, my companion flatly refused to open anything at all and went off into the most uncontrolled fit (or show) of anger that I have ever beheld in a grown man. No, he simply would *not*. Say or do what they chose—rather than have his things pawed over, he would turn back right there and return to America where such barbarity would be unthinkable and so on and so forth. They could take their choice—and the consequences, whatever they might be.

When the tirade was over, I walked him along the platform reviewing the actual facts of the situation and reasoning mildly.

Where there are frontiers, so are there Customs checks—surely he realized that? The local officials could not possibly have the authority to except anyone however eminent unless he held a diplomatic passport, and didn't he realize that his violent refusals to comply with the regulations had naturally aroused the examiners' suspicions as well as their hostility?

'Of course,' I said, 'turn round if you will, but there is no train back until tomorrow and a comfortable night here looks pretty doubtful to me and may be difficult to arrange as you don't speak either Polish or Russian. Also, please, what do I tell your friends and admirers in Russia who will no doubt be meeting the train to greet you? And what will *you* tell those you represent back in America—you, their delegate as I am the U.K.'s? That you turned back rather than have your shirts and socks inspected? Oh, come off it! You can't possibly do anything so utterly silly—come and have a drink and tell these chaps they can get on with it.'

Grudgingly, he did so, and we reached Moscow without further incident. There, sure enough, was a large reception committee especially to do him honour as one of the leading lights of their current architectural revolution. Thus acclaimed, he thawed delightedly into smiles and hand-waving and when a few evenings later we were driving out of the Park of Rest and Culture together after attending a vast outdoor opera performance that involved a squadron of cavalry, he burst out with 'These are the people, theirs is the future!'

But despite all the lavish hospitality, the privileged sightseeing, the gargantuan feasting, the friendly toasts and speeches, the whole atmosphere not surprisingly seemed to me somehow tense and oppressive. This feeling was intensified when I was run into their guard-house and searched and questioned by the Kremlin guards just because I chanced to be at the entrance gate as

Stalin was driven within—with a close-up view of him through his car window only a foot or two away.

Being unarmed and my passport and papers being all in order I was soon released, but a few days later I had another shock. I had been warned that any contact with our embassy would be poorly thought of by my hosts—but I thought it would be safe to see something of the one compatriot in Moscow who I happened to know—and indeed we dined and attended the ballet together. But he was clearly even less at ease than I was—and handed me a sealed letter to take back with me and deliver to a mutual friend —'Just in case.'

I rang him up the next day to make sure that I had rightly understood certain verbal messages and had not finished my first sentence when he hissed down the telephone, 'Are you mad?' and hung up on me.

As arrests and telephone tapping seemed rather to tarnish hospitality, I decided to cut my visit short by a few days. I forget how I explained my defection but was allowed to go—an official of some sort conducting me to the station and seeing me off.

Everything had been for free within the Soviet Union, so I had made the most of this by ordering the finest caviar at every meal from breakfast to supper in the hope of satiating my inordinate desire for it. Possibly, had I stayed out my full time the slight abatement in my eagerness for the stuff might have reached the stage of revulsion, but as it was, my week's over-indulgence had no permanent good effect—I remain a confirmed but deprived addict.

When we propagandists went to see what the Scandinavian countries were doing in our field of design and planning there was of course no ideological ambivalence.

Chapter Thirteen

Island Hunting

Meantime I still itched for a different sort of propaganda. All this writing and speaking and broadcasting was useful no doubt, but not, for me, a sufficient assuagement. I partly wanted to show others what I thought could be done and partly I wanted to experiment for myself.

I bought, about two years after the end of the Kaiser's war, a small Hillyard sloop, *Twinkler*.

I had messed about with the old dinghy on our lake at Glasfryn from about the age of six and learnt to sail her, more or less, with an ill-balanced lugsail, no keel, and an oar for a rudder. Consequently every other craft that I have ever sailed since has seemed a miracle of responsiveness, handiness and stability in comparison and, I think, that the laborious coaxing of that cranky little tub with only occasional capsizes did perhaps give me a certain sense of helmsmanship.

I did not explain the relevance of *Twinkler* to my wife, who luckily soon took with pleasure to the role of deck-hand. Indeed I was perhaps not quite aware of one of my own motives. I had begun to feel that I should try in actual building to show an example of what I meant and that I must find a site, preferably on the coast, perhaps an island, which would provide the sort of remote and unspoilable setting that I demanded for my cherished though still fluid ideas. I was like a sea-bird seeking a nesting place.

Our first cruising area with *Twinkler* was between Holyhead and Cardigan, and thus not extensive. However, there were hazards enough to provide adventures in plenty for the inexperienced so, time and again, we feasted ceremoniously on making harbour just to celebrate being still alive.

For four or five years, whenever I could get away, sometimes sailing *Twinkler* or other shared yachts and exploring in other ways at home and abroad, I actually landed on some two dozen islands. But enchanting as many were, only a fiercely romantic millionaire could have faced the fantastic cost of building on any one of them, and most assuredly not I. So for years, there I was, with a roll of charts, a pile of abortive sketches, plans, and models—but still no site.

Whenever on holiday or otherwise travelling, I was always on the watch for a possible site and for ideas about layouts that might suit this situation or that—ideas for buildings that might suit one that was flat or wooded, another that was mountainous, or one with a sweep of beach or whose outline was fretted with little coves and headlands. Later, while we were visiting a daughter and our New Zealand son-in-law, I had indeed one quite serious flirtation with a disturbingly attractive island off Auckland. I very nearly bought it, and have sometimes regretted not having done so—but I think I might well have had more regrets if I had, because being some 12,000 miles away, I could not really have cherished and embellished it as it deserved.

There were, as I found, plenty of tempting islands off the British coast.

Inch Kenneth was the first Scottish love, and bonnie indeed, but it had its drawbacks (what island has not?)—too much house, too few trees. Then came Gometra off Mull, where I stayed with the owners just long enough to decide that, with all its rugged charm, it was really not for me—only just an island, too bleak and bare, too much a sheep farm, no real trees.

Next it was Giga lying in the sound between Kintyre and Isla and with an actual scheduled steamer service. The owner had, in his absence, kindly put his large house at my disposal, where I slept rather eerily quite alone until fetched next morning by the factor to be driven around the island as far as might be in his dog-cart. It was certainly tempting, but too big, while the great house was of a solidly Victorian-Baronial flavour that I could not have lived with but that it would have seemed wanton to destroy.

I think my next affair was with the smallest of the Channel Islands, Jethou, of which Compton Mackenzie was the then Crown leaseholder. But as president of the Siamese Cat Society he wanted me to take over with the island some three dozen pedigree cats together with I don't know how many thousand gramophone records and his collection of 'by-gone' machines. I had, as usual, got a sufficiently severe attack of island fever to make an inspection both imperative and urgent. Fortunately the Lieutenant-Governor of Guernsey at the time was an old friend and a keen yachtsman, Lord Ruthven, and during a week's cruising and island exploring in his cutter—Sark and Herm as well as Jethou—I returned still fancy free. I think it was lack of sheltered anchorage that tipped the balance against Jethou, charming as it was in its miniature perfection.

But it wasn't only when we sailed in *Twinkler* and then more ambitiously in a later and larger yacht, that I pondered on how to do what I so longed to do, or that ideas came to me about sites or layout. All sorts of travel, including visits to friends, might add something to what was always somewhere at the back of my eyes.

For instance, when we were touring in North Italy with Geoffrey Scott, I was constantly but silently in my imagination re-aligning the elements of some little hill town—the campanile, the various squares and fountains and so on, to see how they might fit some other site.

Geoffrey Scott, author of *Portrait of Zelide* and—most importantly to me—*The Architecture of Humanism*, still, I think, the best book of architectural criticism yet written, was an incomparable guide. I had first met him when contriving a little classical pavilion for him out of an old coach-house at the end of the garden of a Regent's Park house that I had already 'classicised' for a mutual friend. He had been an attaché in Rome during the Kaiser's war and knew Italy well. From his Italian home, the Villa Medici near Florence, he conducted us on a memorable tour, showing us all the most notable towns, churches, houses and gardens within a day's drive and taking us to see Bernard Berenson's Library that he had planned. He incidentally persuaded me to have my portrait painted by an Italian who he insisted was *the* coming man, but Amabel liked it so little that I never even brought it home, but sold it, at cost, to the brewers who bought the Mytton and Mermaid hotel from me—where it still hangs surprisingly alongside Jack Mytton.

When we quit the elegant comforts of the Villa Medici and the company of Geoffrey's wife Lady Sybil, we suddenly turned rugged and, leaving the flesh-pots, set off on our own on a walking tour with our rucksacks. And so it was that one evening in the autumn twilight we found ourselves by the sea, groping our way down a great flight of steps past the open doors of a church whence issued music, incense, and a file of angelic nuns. Soon we were down on the quay of the little enclosed harbour, a full-rigged ship alongside, lights reflected in the still water, the piled-up multi-coloured houses palely visible and one quay-side cafe still open where we sat down to dine at a little table by the water —the only customers. Suddenly there were great plops in our wine-glasses and upon our heads, and in no time we were sheltering inside the cafe from a torrential downpour that increased rather than diminished. We had made no hotel reservation and had no idea where to stay so we asked the cafe if, in its charity, *it* would put us up. 'Alas! the last of the guest beds were put away for the winter only today.'

However, the kind people relented and pulled a couple out of store, which saved us scrambling up the hill through the storm to the only hotel still open, a quite ordinary tourist affair that might have been anywhere. And so it was that we awoke in brilliant sunshine to enchantment—bells ringing, the people just astir, fishing boats setting out, a pervading smell of fresh bread and delicious coffee, *and* a back-cloth of simple, colourful, unaffected southern building huddled all around us. How should I *not* have fallen for Portofino? Indeed its image remained with me as an almost perfect example of the man-made adornment and use of an exquisite site—and a marine one at that, as a sketch shown me by Eric Kennington years before had suggested.

But its charms and indeed the charms of Tuscany only remained at the back of my head, and for a long time sea-faring and island hunting and the exploring of other coasts were what holidays mostly meant.

Twinkler was small, our three children were of an age to make 'going foreign' a practical proposition so, undaunted by the absurdities of many kinds that overtook us, we took to the sea again, this time more ambitiously. A winter of prowling round likely yacht-yards up and down the country at last rewarded me with a most comely old 15-ton Loch Fyne ketch, the *Scott*, hauled up at Poole, which after survey, I bought rather cheaply because of her age and some dubious timbers.

Fitted up, launched and rigged there, by the time our next holiday time came, she lay a picture of sea-kindly grace moored in Poole's great lagoon and reflected in its glassy surface. Lovely, but not a ghost of a breeze and the elderly if honourable engine known to be pretty chancy. And surely wasn't she riding rather oddly low in the water? With her high bulwarks and black hull I had expected more free-board than she was showing—but perhaps she was carrying too much pig-iron ballast? Boarding her, the horrid explanation of her new trim was instantly apparent—someone had left a sea-cock open and down below she was all awash knee-deep with even the mattresses afloat. Had we come a day later, only her masthead might have been showing above the sea. A pretty start for our maiden voyage, especially as we had brought along a Naval Commander friend to admire and to join us! But he was as good a man at the pumps (or with bucket and rope) as we could want, and next day we actually got away, our immediate destination Portsmouth. There we were to lunch with the captain of H.M.S. *Flinders* as indeed we did, after skilfully avoiding collision with the battleship *Hood*. But then we were in trouble again, for we had gratefully tied up to *Flinders* only to be sternly told that civilian craft were forbidden thus to cuddle up to warships.

I forget how we dealt with that one—I think the captain coped for us in some way—but we had barely started our luncheon when a lieutenant appeared with a message that the port Customs Officer wished to see the master or owner of the yacht alongside

Island Hunting

immediately. Our host said I had best comply, excused me, and I found myself being narrowly questioned on my recent movements, my statement that I had *not* 'been foreign' with the yacht recently or at any time being clearly disbelieved. It appeared that he wished to make a thorough search of the vessel. To this I agreed, saying that he and his men could carry on if I could return to my interrupted lunch. After an hour or two's ferreting, the Customs Officer confessed that nothing incriminating had been found, which he seemed to think both surprising and baffling.

'I know all about this yacht of yours and what she's been up to!' were his rather ominous last words.

For months thereafter in and out of Channel ports we had to undergo suspicious interrogations and irritating searches. Sometimes we were all pretty exhausted by a trying passage and in no mood to receive H.M. Customs inquisitors. Clearly our demure and cherished ketch had had quite a notorious career outside the law, a past I had never conceived of. It might well have been one of the reasons for her low price.

Cherbourg was our first foreign port, three grown-ups and three children—a long hot almost windless crossing whilst we read aloud H. G. Wells' *Island of Dr. Moraou* and whistled for a breeze, the engine declining all assistance.

But just at sunset on our second day out, a ghost of a breeze carried us to within a few cables' length of Cherbourg's great breakwater and then utterly died on us. Yet I saw that we were still moving—not through the water but now westwards down channel and past the land and the breakwater end and harbour with the turn of the tide. This seemed a churlish trick of fate, denying us our first intended foreign landing till who knew when, so I decided that the emergency justified the cost of a tow in. Up soared the lovely rockets appropriate for the summoning of assistance whilst I rather fearfully wondered what the cost might turn out to be, trusting that Amabel's excellent French might at any rate save us from unwarrantable claims for 'salvage'. Listening and watching, we confidently awaited the answering tug or launch. But nothing, just nothing at all happened, whilst we drifted slowly further and further past the mole that guarded the harbour entrance. Ten minutes, twenty minutes, thirty minutes, and still no response—it looked like another night at sea off a strange shore, in uncertain weather, with three young children on their first cruise abroad. And then, of a sudden, the saving miracle, a lovely little whisper of a breeze, just enough to ripple the water, gently to fill our idle sails, and to glide us first back to the breakwater head and then close around it across the outer harbour and into the inner.

I expected that someone would come along to enquire about my signal rockets and probably make a claim for having made expensive preparations to respond to it. But I needn't have bothered. No one else had. My rockets had either been unnoticed or entirely ignored. So when, on a later occasion, we again sent up signals to ask for pilotage through a tricky unbuoyed harbour entry and again got no response and had to anchor outside and grope our own way in next morning by the lead, I rather lost confidence in our pretty little rocket rack that had once seemed so reassuring.

After a few days' sightseeing around Cherbourg and a vain attempt to revive the engine, we cleared the harbour one midnight so as to work the tide, though the weather had deteriorated and the sky was as black as pitch.

However, I had to get back to the practice and the children to school, the wind was favouring and we set a course for Dartmouth. But in less than an hour the wind and sea had so risen that we were scudding along under head sail alone with an intimidating following sea, the now wild scene lit by almost continuous lightning, the most impressive display I have ever seen.

But we were both shipping and making water and soon the bunks below on which lay three sea-sick children, were almost awash again—both pumps being maddeningly out of action. We three adults stayed on deck, too anxious to go below, taking turns at the kicking wheel and trying to keep the little ship more or less on course. Certainly, as the skipper responsible, I was worried enough—so much so that at first dawn I clearly saw great breakers cascading back from black and jagged rocks right ahead that I reckoned must be the dreaded Casquets or else some hazard I had forgotten about in Alderney Race. But reference to the wet and crumpled chart made both seem unlikely and a closer view through binoculars showed only a riot of cross seas—spectacular enough, but innocent of rocks. It was all pure hallucination—my first and last—attributable I suppose to anxiety and exhaustion.

In fact we never made Dartmouth at all but eventually found ourselves, battered, drenched and thankful, feeling our way into a sheltered estuary that turned out to be that of Salcombe.

Hardly had we anchored, before ordeal-by-Customs was upon us.

'Yes, certainly we have just made a night passage over from France (just look at us!).—No, we have no contraband hidden aboard.—Yes, we are the same yacht that had been recently searched at Portsmouth.—Yes, of course, search if you must, but as quickly as you can, please, as we all want to go to sleep and if you can find my cap anywhere I shall be glad to have it back.'

This infuriating inquisition was repeated at every port of call right round the coast home to Portmadoc, the lesson of which would seem to be, if you are buying a second-hand yacht, get a certificate as to her moral rectitude as well as a surveyor's report.

A week or so later, having taken the children home and seen to the more immediate needs of the practice, we set out again this time with an experienced woman friend Karen Stephen and a recommended young man, for the rest of the passage round Land's End to North Wales. Once more we came in for a bit of a buffeting our second day out, involving a good deal of wet and arduous deck-work, but no more than routine shipboard jobs that are only dangerous if you lose your handhold or your foothold—or your head.

This last, unfortunately, our young man did, ex-navy though he was, leaving all the heavy and exposed work to the two women and to me. Reminders that he had been brought along to do his fair share of working as well as of eating and drinking had no effect.

Anyhow, selfish and greedy, he now became boastful, in compensation, I suppose, for his pitiful performance as a deck-hand, and as none of the rest of us had at all taken to him anyway—such meals as we managed were by no means feasts of love.

So, when, somewhere off Deadman's Point we really were being thrown about, he asked me weakly, 'What would you do in all this if one of us fell overboard?' I brutally replied, 'It would entirely depend on who it was.' I think he understood. On reaching Falmouth we tied up alongside a famous old Bristol Channel pilot cutter, *The Cariad*, whose owner I knew and who was just about to cast off, bound for Ireland dangerously short-handed, with heavy spars and gear. Joining him for a drink in his cabin, I offered him our reject. *Cariad*'s owner leapt at the offer despite my non-commendation—just as an extra body, at least young and strong. Our unwanted hand transhipped without fuss or remark and that was the last we ever saw of him. Perhaps he was ill, in mind if not in body, or just naturally unpleasant in an extreme degree—or—it later occurred to us—could it be perhaps that he just plain loathed us?

There were other sailing advantures, sometimes with the children, sometimes without. Indeed we got around quite a bit, over to Ireland and the exploration of its little islands, then off the west coast of Scotland and up to Skye where the sight of whales and water-spouts made us feel we were voyagers indeed.

By this time I had acquired the little twin islands of St. Tudwal, only some twenty miles down the bay from my home, not with any idea of development—far from it—but because they had the appealing charm of most small and innocent things from ducklings and baby bears to toy towns and narrow-gauge railways, to two of which I am incidentally 'Honorary Landscape Consultant'. I had known and loved these islands from childhood. What added to the charms at once obvious to the adventurous boy-buccaneer were those of the mature escapist, to whom insulation from posts and telephones and indeed communications of any sort from the plaguey outer world can sometimes seem the highest good attainable. It is wonderful how effectively a couple of miles of salt water can still isolate you where there is no safe harbour or all-weather landing place. The lighthouse on the western island had become automatic and it was the fort-like light-keeper's house that we long used as our sailing base, our yacht being moored off the prim little granite quay whence a grass track loops gracefully up to where the light-tower and its outworks shine high above you like a snow white crown on its cushion of green velvet.

When last there I found men busily servicing the light and generally refurbishing the whole place (the Admiralty had blackwashed the building and doused the light for the duration of the war) in expectation of a call by the Trinity House yacht, with a glittering party of visiting Elder Brethren.

Were I ever, through some signal service to the State, to be offered high official honour, I should be much disposed to say: 'I would like, please, to be made an Elder Brother of the Trinity.' Sir Winston Churchill has demonstrated how impressive is the full-dress uniform, but it is not only that. Nor is it the godlike sonorousness of the title, seeming almost to suggest that the Pope himself ought properly to call you 'Sir' but the fact that this high and privileged order can, whenever so minded, cruise around our coasts and poke at will its noble noses into the loveliest, loneliest, most romantic places of the kingdom, not as idle sight-seers but as a matter of high duty imposed on them by ancient charter as the guardians of all who may sail around our coasts.

In early days, imperilled mariners could only invoke the protection of the appropriate local saint, and from the sixth century Cardigan Bay has been in the guardianship of St. Tudwal, who chose the islands that bear his name as his base. He is now better known to the Catholic sailor boys who come over from Brittany to hawk their onions around North Wales than he is to us, his own people, for he was the next Bishop of St. Malo after that saint himself.

But the religious history of the islands was extended into my own lifetime by the tragically abortive efforts of another Welshman, Father Hughes, to follow in St. Tudwal's footsteps and to resurrect the monastery of which only small fragments and legends still survived. I think the warning bell buoy of Carreg-y-trai rock just south of the islands was there in the Father's time, as the lighthouse certainly was, and, if so, I hope that he found its solemn tolling as agreeable as I always do, especially when accompanied by the singing of the seals that there abound.

But, despite such oral and visible warnings, I have seen a racing yacht, cutting things too fine, run slap on to those shelving submerged rocks in broad daylight, though by great good luck slipping clear again as the tide made. Of sea-birds there are all that you would expect to find on such an island in such a latitude in greater or less strength from season to season and year to year, unless you looked for gannets, as you reasonably might—but there are none nearer than Grassholm across the bay. Puffins used to throng the place in thousands in accordance with their most punctually observed calendar, but of late there are fewer, I cannot guess why, unless it be that the rabbits, whose burrows may have saved the birds the bother of scooping out their own, have themselves mysteriously disappeared. Why?

That certainly is clear gain (except from the point of view of provisioning) for where there is now a long, lush pasture, there used often to be turf nibbled down to the bone and quite clearly too many rabbits chasing too few blades of grass. When there were sheep as well as rabbits, with ten thousand puffins as regular summer visitors in addition, the competition even for mere standing room was intense.

I believe the ecology of islands is apt to fluctuate in this odd way—the population of some species or other increasing beyond the optimum, when a sharp decline or even extinction may supervene and a quite new and different balance be built up that will in turn suffer gradual or sudden change as modifying influences operate, internal and inevitable, or imposed from without, by the vagaries of the weather or of man. The fact that during the war the islands became R.A.F. practice targets for smoke bombs may well have been upsetting, with ecological results that, though in themselves apparently minute—the slight discouragement perhaps of one sort of sea-bird that had maintained its colony exactly at the optimum number, maybe since St. Tudwal's time—none the less started a chain-reaction of readjustments that will continue for as long again.

All the naturalists who visit the islands, of course, have their own theories—their guesses anyway—which are as intriguing as they are ingenious, but nobody really seems to know, which adds an abiding mystery to the islands' more obvious and everyday charms.

One evening as the weather looked threatening, Amabel and I decided to leave the children bedded down, up at the sufficiently provisioned lighthouse, whilst we went to sleep aboard the yacht 'just in case'.

It was as well we did, for, on going on deck for the third or fourth time to make sure that all was well, I found that we had dragged both our anchors in the strong tide and rising wind. We were already close to the breakers along the cliffs of the other island and still dragging.

Somehow we managed to claw round and clear the end of the island to anchor again in relative shelter in its lee, but still 'at risk' owing to the poor holding ground for our anchors—seaweed over rocks.

So, as the weathered worsened with the dawn, we decided to clear out and run to Pwllheli for secure shelter. The children, of course, woke to find themselves entirely abandoned. It was some days before we could get back, to find them interested to know what had happened, but not perturbed. Provisions had sensibly been rationed by them 'just in case' and stretched by the collection of shellfish of various kinds.

Why, some of our more sedentary (or, if you like, more sensible) friends used to ask us, did we consistently put ourselves into such exceedingly uncomfortable and sometimes perilous situations? Why deliberately seek to be wet, cold, hungry and sometimes frightened? Why did our three children agree to play along with us? One of them decided, after experience, that 'toughness is tiresome'. Of the other two, one continued to seek such experiences, and the third was neutral, taking things as they came and weighing advantages and disadvantages. As for us, we continued to feel that a certain amount of adventure is essential as a holiday ingredient, there being much to be said for blood sports—when the blood is one's own.

You have thoughts of nothing else at all beyond your immediate predicament, any and all external problems or worries of your ordinary life being utterly forgotten, while the snugness of home is incomparably enhanced by experience of wet and cold.

However, after some years, the anxieties of a merely amateur and inexperienced skipper responsible for the lives and safety of up to half a dozen others even less competent than himself, often in unknown waters, became too burdensome to constitute a holiday at all, so at last I retired from the sea, thankful to have drowned nobody. The Second World War found *Scott* finally laid up and half-dismantled in which state I sold her to a scrap dealer who used her to pick up old railway metals and such like from abandoned coastal quarries.

Chapter Fourteen

Portmeirion Conceived and Born

During all my searches for a site for my demonstration of development, and in all my brooding on layouts that might suit this place or that, I had always in front of me the fact that a building costs money, and that to build a hamlet, a cluster of buildings, a village, or the smallest townlet would inevitably cost more—a great deal more.

My practice was prospering, our tastes were not extravagant, we were managing to save, but all the same . . . ?

For a time I toyed with the idea that it might be possible to find a sufficiently affluent and whimsical patron who, investing as it were in me and my ideas, would none the less give me my head and turn me loose at some delectable spot saying, 'Well, there is your site, let's see what you can make of it—you just go ahead and build whatever you like and I pay.' I have indeed been most fortunate in having had clients with whom I have had real architectural fun, sometimes involving village schemes and improvements, group manipulations and landscaping—but perhaps not surprisingly, no *carte* quite as *blanche* as that.

So it became gradually apparent that, if the thing was ever to happen at all, I must somehow finance it myself as best I might, out of my profesisonal earnings and, as those surprisingly (though also only gradually) outstripped my modest expectations, I realized that I could indeed do it—yet again, of course gradually —if only I could find a setting, a birthplace, that I deemed suitable for and worthy of my cherished baby-to-be.

Clearly I must be free from all outside interference whatsoever and sole master of all I surveyed, with no tiresome neighbours— hence my island fixation. But I had also made the sobering discovery that there is one curious characteristic that nearly all small islands seem to have in common, and that is that they are almost always sooner or later, for sale. Susceptible romantics like myself fall blindly in love with them only to discover on closer acquaintance that the *affaire* is doomed by the difficulty of ready communication with the beloved. However, within a few years I had as I have said, hopefully landed on some two dozen, though only one seemed even remotely suitable for the purpose I had in view.

'Remotely' is the *mot juste*, and though I did bid half-heartedly for this one, and made elaborate surveys, draft plans and models, I knew myself for a besotted fool and was really relieved when negotiations finally broke down. There are so many daunting disadvantages attached to islands when you get down to practicalities. They are usually inordinately far away, hard to reach, harder still to get away from, have little shelter and no timber, and are fantastically difficult and expensive to build upon. With his own bus and lorry services, a powerful tug and suitable harbour works, a determinedly eccentric millionaire might possibly indulge such uneconomic fancies, but assuredly not I.

Yet I must call my own tune, so I alone must pay the piper— must indeed, soon find money beyond my owner-driver competence if development was to be on a reasonable scale. Therefore the thing had to be so devised that it would not only pay reasonable interest on my small initial investment, but soon begin to accumulate reserves for further capital expenditure on expansion and improvement.

That meant that such a pitch must be found and secured that would by its own intrinsic merits certainly attract the sort of people likely to appreciate and support my peculiar kind of development. In the end—and miraculously—after all my wanderings, I found what I had so long sought in Wales—and indeed almost on my own doorstep.

One day, entirely unexpectedly, an absentee uncle, Sir Osmond Williams of Deudraeth Castle, asked me if I knew of anyone who would care to buy an adjoining secondary coastal property of his, Aberia (renamed by me Portmeirion) which, though only five miles away from my own home, I had never seen except from the sea. His tenant there had been for many years a strange old lady who guarded her peninsula with ferocious strictness against intrusion by any outsider whosoever—even her nearest neighbours.

To penetrate at last within its high defensive wall and see the place for the first time, utter wilderness as it then was, was to know on the instant that I need look no further. It had all and more—much more—than I had ever dreamed of as desirable for my perfect site—beetling cliffs and craggy pinnacles, level plateaux and little valleys, a tumbling cascade, splendid old trees and exotic flowering shrubs: a coastline of rocky headlands, caves and sandy bays. So as soon as lawyers could contrive, I became the owner—first only of the old house, the site of the now existing village, and the tongue of land beyond it, then of more and more hinterland, and ultimately of Deudraeth Castle, its park and avenue, the Gwyllt headland gardens, and the adjoining farms. None of these acquisitions have, I think, been prompted by mere territorial ambitions, but simply by my resolve to keep Portmeirion itself free from any foreseeable encroachment—a tight little knot of controlled development, forever, as now, set in its wide green belt of woods and farmland.

The very first job had to be a great clearing to allow me even to see where I was; to let in the sun, to discover the possible views and the direction of potential vistas.

But after uprooting and burning the obvious rubbish, I proceeded with the utmost caution and tree by tree, only felling those quite obviously in the way of any reasonably coherent layout and sparing even the most dubious ones until I felt dead sure that they would not be wanted.

A pale mansion, a hundred years old, spread its length along a balustraded terrace on the sea's edge—the house (as I first discovered it) was as neglected as were the twenty miles of cliff and woodland rides and the paths that criss-cross the whole headland between high crags. There were great forest trees and the exuberant jungle of exotic and subtropical flowering shrubs with which a succession of devoted owners or tenants had prodigally adorned it. All, as near as might be, the Palace of the Sleeping Beauty with, on top of all else, the uncovenanted blessing of a private port at the very nearest point on the coast to my own Brondanw. Formerly coastal itself, it had been thrust back five miles or so by the misguided enterprise of my eighteenth-century forebears with their embankment; a land-grabbing exercise that later culminated in the mile-long Portmadoc Cob, the whole business being, as I hold, most deplorable. Even the high promise of financial gain from reclamation went unfulfilled—as served the reclaimers right for their high-handed interference. I would, if I could, most willingly return to the sea the poor lands they so industriously reclaimed. Others followed my great-grandfather's lead, the last being William Madocks, who founded little Tremadoc as his New Town on his reclaimed land, and only just contrived to complete his final embankment by sending round the hat, the subscription list being splendidly headed by his tenant, the poet Shelley, with £100 which would doubtless have been most helpful. However, Shelley being bankrupt at the time, it was worth no more than his inspiring name.

Up to then ships could still sail right up to Aberglaslyn where, indeed, many were built and I had (before our fire) a charming old picture showing one becalmed beneath my windows where today are grazing cattle.

All of which is more relevant to Portmeirion than might appear, for what befell the Glaslyn estuary to its north might yet extinguish the Dwryd estuary to its south, human folly being what it is, reducing 'the Peninsula' to a mere fag-end mockery of its former sea-girt self. But happily there are now quite formidable obstacles to any such barbarity: the National Parks Commission, an alert Country Planning department, the Council for the Protection of Rural Wales, and a more civilized public opinion—to say nothing of my own dead body.

It was for Easter 1926, after less than a year's preparation, that the original old house, little altered, opened somewhat tentatively as an unlicensed hotel, with extra quarters added by the building of two new cottages, a reconstructed old gardener's bothy plus the rather crudely converted stable block. Indeed everything was pretty rough, primitive and slapdash; the equipment inadequate, the staff untrained, the management unsuitable and the food terrible.

The fact was that I then knew almost nothing about hotels—but I did know that here, somehow, there had to be one, and not only to find employment for the pleasant old house. However, the invited housewarming weekend party were appreciative and kind about even the most glaring shortcomings—forgiving all for the sake of the place's own natural beauty and for the weather, which was most mercifully radiantly fine. Also it was rather a good self-amusing party, suddenly thought up and consequently agreeably mixed; a prominent political peeress suitably squired by an ex-minister, a dramatic critic and a couple of actresses, a psychiatrist, an editor, a woman magistrate, two novelists and I suppose about a score of others equally various—rounded off by an entirely unknown lone little business man from outer space who, turning up as an ordinary hotel guest innocently supposing the place to be publicly open, could not well be turned away. Being outside the experience of most of the company he was indeed a centre of general interest, and, on leaving, he said he had never enjoyed a weekend more. I thought that reflected well on the manners of all concerned and was of good augury.

But *paying* customers are less lenient than invitees, and when the weather broke, when private water and electric supplies went temperamental, and when culinary disasters were piled on top of a near-hysterical office—a certain murmuring amongst the people was scarcely to be wondered at.

A. P. Herbert happened to be a victim of one of these early crises and he brilliantly lampooned the whole slap-dash set-up in *Punch*. Funny certainly, but also a little unkind, as he later admitted when apologizing—adding that unfortunately he had to try and find *something* to be funny about every week and that anyhow even that sort of publicity was probably better than none. At any rate it gave a salutary jolt to the whole amateurish outfit, though it was not until James Wyllie, the painter, who had run a most successful restaurant of his own in Oxford, took over the management that the project became really airborne and freed me for the whole of his long reign from (nearly) all worry about the domestic side of things.

Year by year, improvements were gradually made within and without in all departments, so that as the news spread, any anxiety about sufficient patronage was soon replaced by embarrassment over insufficient accommodation—resulting in the unavoidable turning away of many notable would-be guests who, in those early days particularly, would have been most welcome. I recall still apologetically Bernard Shaw as one such, though he applied again a few years later—successfully. Arnold Bennett I myself discouraged from coming as I knew he would find fault with the food—and justly; and by the time we had reached his exacting standard he was dead.

By the end of that first summer I was sure that enough people felt as I did about it to justify my going right ahead in the realization of my dreams—not generally in any headlong way but tentatively and step by step, yet often enough because I was impatient to see realized some particularly cherished feature that I considered important to the whole ensemble. Thus would suddenly appear such non-utility items as the campanile, the dome, archways, gateways, belvederes, fountains, statues or whatever, whilst as time went on, honourable architectural offerings for my 'home for fallen buildings', from far and near, could not always be resisted.

Has it all turned out as I intended? By and large, yes, though my 'intention' has never been any hard and fast development programme, time-table, or rigid schedule of priorities. But the total picture in the 1970s is very much what I originally hoped it might one day become, not of course in detail, but in its general impact. It is still changing, and all the time in the direction of my first imagined optimum exploitation of the site.

Nothing whatever has been allowed to stand in the way of that, and in so far as the final result may be judged inacceptable, the fault is entirely my own and nobody else's. As to the place's propagandist effect, whether for good or ill, there can be no doubt whatever about its actual impact. As I have said earlier, I was aiming at winning as yet uninterested and uninformed popular support for architecture, planning, landscaping, the use of colour and indeed for design generally, by a gay, light-opera sort of approach, whereby the casual visitor who had perhaps only turned up to bathe, or to eat, or out of vague curiosity, might be ensnared into taking a really intelligent interest in the things that give some of us fortunate ones such intense and abiding pleasure.

And the stratagem works. I seldom go over without being buttonholed by complete strangers eager to have things explained, to know the why and wherefore of this or that or to express their appreciation (or doubt) of the other. They now come from all over the world, stray individuals as well as organized parties, photographic and horticultural societies, parties of students, groups sponsored by the British Council and such like—a tourist influx of well over 100,000 a year, despite the toll that is levied to keep numbers within manageable bounds and to contribute to the general maintenance.

In spite of this high pressure throughout the summer season (the hotel used to shut down for the winter, but not the Salutation Restaurant and the permanently inhabited houses and self-servicing cottages) there is so much hinterland 'wander room' —and the stream of visitors is so canalized, that it leaves the hotel and other residents in peace. There is seldom more than an agreeable sense of the place being alive and *used*, whilst litter or damage of any sort is minimal. Personally I like figures in my landscape—especially as clothes now tend to be so gay.

Of course many architects come along, again from all the world over, which brings me to their reactions and those of other specially interested contemporaries. Quite a number of those who have been favourably impressed have written about the place—though naturally any dissenters from my notions of 'amenity' would scarcely bother to do so. Frank Lloyd Wright, so far as I know, didn't write about his reactions—but I recorded them at the time of his visit and repeat them here. Understandably, he approved of *Brondanw*, my own old mountain home, with its somewhat austere four stories of immensely solid masonry reared up on its terraced hillside, still much as my forebears first planted it some four centuries ago, and seeming to have the same 'ten-fingered grip' of the earth as its protecting oaks. But Portmeirion, that was quite another matter. Dare I let him loose on *that*? I did, feeling that I would sooner be damned for my so-much-debated escapade than forgo the G.O.M.'s reaction, however violent. And, to my profound astonishment, he took it all without a blink, seeming instantly to see the point of all my wilful pleasantries, the calculated naïveties, eye-traps, forced and faked perspectives, heretical constructions, unorthodox colour mixtures and general architectural levity.

Lewis Mumford, writing in the *New Yorker*, called Portmeirion:

> ... an artful and playful little modern village designed as a whole and all of a piece.... This is still the country of Thomas Love Peacock, and thus what Williams-Ellis has been up to is translating Peacock's conversations into architectural terms. Portmeirion is impish, a gay, deliberately irresponsible reaction against so much that passes as modern architecture. A folly in the 18th-century sense. The effect is relaxing and often enchanting, a happy relief from the grim absurdities of our thermo-nuclear strategists.

Many of the eminent and austere 'modern' architects of impeccable rectitude who come along to quiz the place seem to 'take it' without any obvious discomfort, seeming indeed to be glad that someone could dare to let himself go in so uninhibited and lawless a manner though they would, I expect, sooner die than be guilty of such levity themselves.

Some, I haven't a doubt, find it all insufferably chaotic, contrived, whimsical or out of place, and I would know exactly what they meant were they to say so, but most courteously (on the civilized 'dog don't eat dog' principle) they never have—yet.

But I think there may have lurked a hint of reproof in a remark made by the then President of the R.I.B.A., Sir Robert Matthew, when I last took him round—'Ah, I see, the *mixture*—as never before.' He is an old and valued Portmeirion well-wisher, and I think he feared I might be in danger of stuffing the little place so full of 'features' as to be no longer normally viable—like a Strasbourg goose. I take his point and entirely agree with it. But I don't think he need worry. At eighty-seven I probably shan't have time to do very much more, and, who knows, I may yet reform—and become as austerely orthodox as any of my critics.

James Morris, whose books *Venice* and *Oxford* have so vividly refurbished their architectural images, seems, like Mumford, to struggle with an addiction for the place. He constantly comes back and back to Portmeirion but, writing in *Horizon* admits that the whole thing shocks him a little:

> Fancy is piled on fancy . . . old buildings are replanted, vivaciously new buildings are added—until Williams-Ellis has established an entire village that is like nowhere else on earth. The very first maps that recognised it were the charts the Germans made when they thought of invading these parts. I am not myself much addicted to whimsy in architecture . . . so whenever I go to Portmeirion I have first to overcome certain prejudices. . . . As I drive through the shadowy trees to the peninsula, though, past a monumental mock castle on the right and a sandy glimpse of the estuary on the left, as I pass beneath the severe gatehouse that is the portal of Portmeirion, and find myself once more amidst all its sparkle, grace and illusion, I always have to admit that I am wrong again, and that this little false village is a proper work of art and intellect. The contrived fizz of the place is intoxicating, and we stagger through all this exuberance rather dizzily, until, climbing down the path between the heavenly rhododendrons, we find ourselves restfully on the water's edge, with the long, white house behind us, a high-and-dry ketch beside the harbour and across the water a superb theatre of Welsh hills—Moel Ysgyfarnogod, Rhinog Fawr and Moelfre, rising above Harlech. I can't quite define the effect of Portmeirion; I can only express my own reaction—something between a scoff, a gasp and an ecstasy. This anomalous prodigy is very famous. You can expect to meet almost anyone there, from a retired Prime Minister to a television actor learning his lines. . . . It is hostile only to prigs, bores, and despoilers; its eccentricity is all genial; and its charm is partly the serenity of a lost society with time, money, talent and hospitality to spare.

But I am really quite conscientious about dull essentials such as drains or extending staff accommodation or some such relatively pedestrian need, knowing I shall have my reward and my morale sustained by a concurrent bit of architectural fun, so that gateways and statues, belvederes and fountains are not merely irresponsible frolics, as might be harshly thought, but symbols of good works earnestly and invisibly executed elsewhere.

Every now and then, if I am away for a day or two, it may happen that my wife will be urgently asked to pass on a long-distance telephone message, 'Is Mr. Williams-Ellis still interested in the clock tower in Edinburgh?' or 'That temple in Dorset?' or 'Those Regency cast-iron railings?' Once it was the Euston Arch, but that was a hoax. The oddest offer of all was of an underground shell grotto. How was it thought I could remove *that*? As a rule this will be the first the poor woman has heard of the affair. Surely I am not unique? No collector, no addict I think 'tells all', especially not to the more sensible members of his own family.

The astonishing and now seemingly world-wide celebrity of Portmeirion must I think be largely attributed to its apparently being a photographic and film 'natural'—especially since colour has become so readily recordable. There have been a steady succession of B.B.C. and other feature films of the place and it is constantly being used as a setting or background for a surprising range of subjects, most notably for Patrick McGoohan's mystifying story '*The Prisoner*' in seventeen episodes, which is, so it seems, still showing around the globe and sending us its own quota of the curious from far and near. All this of course is a totally unforeseen extension of my original propagandist hopes, and entirely welcome.

Even more gratifying is the way that the earlier perceptive discoverers of Portmeirion have gradually attracted other likeminded and highly-civilized persons to the place itself and its immediate neighbourhood.

Rupert Crawshay-Williams, our resident philosopher, in his latest book *Russell Remembered* after describing a party of some two dozen more or less notables at his own Portmeirion home continues:

> This is by no means untypical of the kind of party which seems to take place in and around Portmeirion and the Croesor valley. It must I think be something to do with the 'ambience' of Clough and Amabel Williams-Ellis themselves, which attracts interesting people. Indeed

as somebody once complained, one finds an intellectual under every stone in the valley.

One day in 1950, when Elizabeth and I were first looking for a house up here for Bertie Russell, we commented on how many nice people there were in Merioneth; and Bertie said all one had to do—as in the case of the Place de l'Opera in Paris—was to sit in Portmeirion or the Croesor valley and eventually everybody would pass by. We planned a select House Agency to encourage intelligent and/or interesting people to come; and Bertie suggested that we should call it MERIONETH: A NEW CIVILIZATION? LTD.

Chapter Fifteen

Partly Abroad

As Portmeirion has in fact always developed step by cautious step and therefore slowly, some of what I have just told is really anticipatory.

That leisurely organic growth has, I think, been very largely responsible for the general feeling that all the so-different buildings are, none the less, a logical, gradually developing sequence, conditioned by every little quirk and variation of their individual sites, by what has already been done and by what was intended to follow.

A cut-and-dried pre-prepared development plan carried out by an outside general contractor must, inevitably, have resulted in something entirely different that could not possibly have carried the message that I hoped to put across.

As it was, as landowner, clerk-of-works, architect, client, paymaster and builder all rolled into one, I have been able to potter along and realize my ideas and respond to practical demands just as they arose, as well as have time for second and sometimes third and fourth thoughts. With my admirably skilled little building gang, led by a near-inspired master mason (who succeeded his father and has in turn now been followed by his younger brother) and an equally ingenious master-joiner, and, being so constantly on the spot myself, discussing and directing, the Portmeirion ensemble does seem to have a kind of friendly bloom on it that a strictly drawing-board and formal contract approach would have inhibited or rubbed off. Yet there were inevitably occasional gaps in my concern for my project, when I had to attend exclusively to demanding clients who, after all, were really paying for my fun. Moreover, being human, I occasionally caught the 'flu.

It was after a sharp attack of this same 'flu had laid me low in the midst of around a hundred individual Wembley clients yapping for their plans, that it was thought that my taking a fortnight's holiday in the sun would really serve them all better than my staying snivelling away at my desk.

Portugal seemed the easiest option for convalescence and H. G. Wells encouraged us to join him for a bit at Estoril. We went, as we always did whenever we could, by sea and had a merry voyage out with John (later Lord) Davidson and his wife, Joan, full of political gossip.

But we found that late April in Portugal was no warmer than in England and far wetter. Nor did we like the raggedly developed *plage* of Estoril, nor our hotel, but it was fun gambling with H. G. at the casino, though when at the end of our first session we were told that we had lost I don't know how many thousand escudos —we were badly shaken. Then it was revealed what pathetic chicken-feed escudos then were, and we came to. Moving into Lisbon we sought wet-weather diversions, but only found one that was really memorable.

'Perhaps,' suggested our hotel porter, 'you have not yet seen our museum for cabs?'

We had not, so, for want of other attraction, decided that even old cabs might be worth a brief look over and set off as directed to the quay-side address at Belem. What greeted our astonished eyes there was, of course, the magnificent collection of the most sumptuous baroque coaches in the world, of which we were ignorantly entirely unaware—a dazzling riot of carved and gilt gods and goddesses, dolphins, mermaids, cherubs, dragons, rococo scroll-work, heraldry and emblems of all sorts—dignifying I don't know how many beautifully-kept vehicles in which, at some time in the past, poor little royalties and noble nobodies, must have been sorely put to it not to feel—and look—pretty insignificant enclosed in such boastful and gesticulating splendour. Cabs!

We were really waiting for better weather to move out to Cintra, but though it didn't mend we moved there all the same and squelched about under the fern and moss-grown trees that told plainly of the local rainfall.

Owing to that, we soon ran out of the books we had brought to read and were reduced to asking the hotel if by chance it happened to have anything in English. 'Oh yes,' was its proud reply —and we were introduced to a great pile of back numbers of an American magazine called, I think, *The Morticians' Journal—With Which is Incorporated 'The Casket'*, sections of which bore the subtitle, 'The Sunny Side'. So far as it went—and it went quite a way—we found its macabre technicalities, its matey convention reports and snobbish advertisements, together with a page of professional jokes, almost unbelievable. But there they all were, issue after issue, stranded there in our musty hill-top hotel. The management was clearly flattered when I asked if I might take one away to show to a friend and H. G. was so entranced by it that for a year or so he enrolled as a regular subscriber. Evelyn Waugh could very well have written *The Loved One* merely by studying a few issues of this revealing trade journal. Maybe that is just what he did.

I didn't know Evelyn well but staying for a weekend in the same country house with him, Amabel and I happened to be bidden again for the following weekend when our host showed me this:

Dear . . .
 Thank you for my week-end. That your wine should be mediocre in quality is understandable. That it should also be insufficient in quantity is unforgivable.
      Yours Evelyn.

If, for some reason, he did not wish to be asked again, a writer of his infinite invention might, one would think, have found a subtler formula.

My host had been prompted to read me this by my own rueful tale of an apparently equally unwelcome 'thank you' letter, over which I had taken some trouble because the occasion seemed to warrant it. It had brought back on me, to my consternation, a really stinging response from my hostess, Vita Sackville-West.

The occasion was this. We had been spending a golden summer's weekend with her and Harold Nicolson at Long Barn, close to her old home Knole, where we were taken to be shown over the house, or bits of it, and for tennis. It was before they moved to and re-created Sissinghurst Castle.

Knole (now a National Trust possession) is indeed truly great, in size, in architectural quality, in its distinguished history, and the slendour of its contents. I still vividly remember after forty years a magnificent state bed with a superb plumed canopy that particularly took my baroque fancy.

'Yes,' said Vita, 'It's certainly grand enough, but having had complaints from honoured guests who had slept in it—or tried to —that it wasn't all that comfortable, it was overhauled, when we found that the mattress had been entirely stuffed with old cast-off footmen's wigs.'

We returned to Long Barn to get into evening dress to dine with Lord Sackville back at Knole where all was magically and brilliantly festive, as though the penurious war years had never been. On Sunday we were taken over to lunch with the de Lisles at Penshurst Place, another famous house, mostly Tudor, and then on Monday, on our homeward journey, we called in at Mereworth Castle, Colen Campbell's exquisite version of Palladio's seminal villa at Vicenza. I had long known the place thoroughly inside and out from plans and photographs, but had never yet actually seen it.

Well, in my roofer letter to Vita, I, of course, paid due homage to her so passionately loved Knole, added a bouquet for Penshurst, but then really let myself go on Mereworth which I said put the crown on an architecturally unforgettable weekend. That was my undoing: 'What—that mid-eighteenth century upstart bubble of a house, that overblown, under-bred folly to be compared with, and even seemingly preferred to, Knole—well, if *that's* your taste—good-bye.' That was the tenor of her comeback—splendidly and characteristically loyal—but startling—and we were never asked to stay again.

Staying with friends was often worked in with necessary visits to whatever jobs were in progress within reach. An architect's work is not and should never be just at his drawing-board, desk and telephone, nor yet only at home in England. He should sharpen his wits by periodic darts abroad to quiz foreign works both old and new, and to charge his batteries.

Amabel, unlike me, being something of a culture-vulture, was for long addicted to attending conferences that offered discussions and enlightenment in subjects that interested her, such as those of the PEN Club, the international writers' body.

I have tagged along with her on occasions as her guest when the *locale* of the conference attracted me, always on condition that I was let off the actual meetings and only attended such parties and booked for such expeditions as I chose.

Thus have I visited such delectable cities as Stockholm, Prague, Vienna, Venice and Dublin, all under optimum conditions for privileged sight-seeing and the laying on of just everything by our invariably generously hospitable hosts. In Stockholm the PEN club was entertained to an exceedingly gala dinner and party with trumpeters and all in the rightly-celebrated town hall, whose architect, Ragnar Ostberg, I had known from earlier visits. I also met the sculptor Karl Miles whose work I also admired and who had generously given me leave to crib his exquisite mermaid as my Portmeirion emblem.

Because of him I went to visit a sculptor friend of his, Prince Eugene, in his unique waterside studio. There I was greeted by another caller—a very tall man who said, 'I am the president of the Swedish PEN, I hope you are seeing all you want to see.' When, later, I asked who he might be I was told he was Prince William. All Swedish royalty seem to be like that. I ought I thought to have remembered him, as some years before he had, I thought, showed me round the Stockholm Exhibition and I had actually lunched with him at his country house, where he had had the wonderful mechanical scenic effects of his private eighteenth-century theatre set in motion to demonstrate their primitive ingenuity and effectiveness. Then it emerged that *that* one had been the *Crown* Prince. Such is my memory for people— even when really interesting as well as princely.

As to that I recall being introduced to someone who I really knew quite well with our mutual friend apologizing for my vacant stare with, 'You mustn't mind Clough cutting you, he never recognizes anybody, though if you only had a façade instead of a face he would never forget you..'

In Prague we had an equally privileged visit with a memorable outdoor performance of *Romeo and Juliet* in the courtyard of the Presidential Palace, Juliet being beautifully played by the President's wife.

When the Nazis overthrew Czechoslovakia, many of those who had so hospitably entertained us and who we had hoped to see again, tragically disappeared, including a most sprightly political cartoonist who had been particularly friendly. Alas this, as it turned out, was only the first of the bitter tragedies that overcame that country. Or is 'overcame' the right word? Let us hope not.

Vienna we had visited before, though I can't think quite when, but my only clear recollection for some reason was of being at dinner with Sinclair Lewis and Dorothy Thompson at the Hotel Sacher and being there introduced to the almost fabulous Frau Sacher herself and being entertained in her private retreat.

The walls were lined with the signed photographs of Grand Dukes and such, the tray on her desk overflowed with the stumps of her black cigars and the whole set-up very much the Austrian equivalent, writ large, of Rosa Lewis and her Cavendish Hotel in London.

Of our PEN club visit, among the most memorable fixtures in Austria were a ball in the Imperial Palace of Schonbrunn, a party at the Belvedere palace, the very apotheosis of Baroque architecture, and a session with the famous and all but ballet-dancing horses at the Hofburg.

More adventurous (for me as it turned out) was a visit with the PEN club to the great Baroque monastery of Melk, a huge building that stands high on a cliff at a sharp bend of the Danube.

I already knew it well from illustrations and had once glimpsed it from the nearby railway but had never, never visited it. Now we were all being taken to see it by an elegant special train that, before reaching Melk, made a long halt at some pleasant little wayside town where luncheon was laid on for us.

As soon as I had fed, I immediately set off alone to explore the town and the several inviting-looking churches I had spotted. I went on of course to the station to rejoin the party.

But when I got there, there was no train, and it was eventually made clear to me by pantomine—for I have no German and the officials had no English—that the special had left quite a while ago and that there was no other train to Melk for several hours. Nor, it seemed, were there any taxis to be had. I felt quite unusually angry with myself for my folly in missing what was to me the main object of our whole long journey. I had missed this memorable place it seemed, by five or ten minutes and some five and twenty miles.

Then, like an angel from heaven, appeared a young signalman, who beckoned me to follow him to a little nearby shed where, throwing open the door, he displayed a fierce looking motor-bicycle. 'Melk?' he said questioningly, then patting the pillion seat, 'O.K.?' I nodded and grinned, and off we shot on a ride I shall never forget. As we swooped blind round the huge cliffs that edged the road which in turn followed the great winding river, I just managed to keep my balance by clinging to my rescuer, who was clearly most expert, whereas I had never ridden pillion in all my life. I was about equally terrified and exhilarated but, considering my situation, I decided that if I was going to be killed, Melk was better worth dying for than quite a lot of other causes.

Actually we made it without incident, caught up with the rest of the party in time for coffee and frankfurters on the monastery terrace and the formal perambulation, so that, to the amazement and headshaking of the assembled international authors, all ended well.

I was so grateful to my railway man that I gave him nearly all the money I had on me—which was quite a lot. When, on our way back to Vienna that evening, we passed through his station, there he was, first waving and beaming, and then scrambling up to shake hands—a warming little footnote to tack on to my monumental and almost overwhelming memories of Melk itself.

Venice is of course a 'natural' for anything like a PEN club conference, and though we knew it pretty well, the 'special' things that were laid on for us—a party in the Doge's palace and a performance of a Monteverdi opera in the unique little *Teatro Olimpico* at Vicenza which is so fragile and so great a fire hazard that it is scarcely ever used—were memorable 'extras'.

But then Venice can be relied on to surprise and enchant the traveller however often it is visited. One time it was a fancy-dress ball in a fine old Palazzo, and home by gondola in the dawn with bathing parties on the Lido.

That visit must I think have been in the early twenties when staying with the Oswald Mosleys, with Nancy Cunard and Bob Boothby amongst our fellow guests at the hall. Since then we have of course explored most of the obvious 'musts', the great villas along the course of the Brenta canal from the princely immensities of Stra with its staggering architectural vista, to the Palladian refinements of little Malcontenta, more esteemed than obvious, and the main islands of the lagoon.

From Venice we had—with Cynthia Mosley and her sister Lady Ravensdale—taken a steamer voyage down the Dalmatian coast and back and this led, some years later, to the offer of a job that sounded exactly made to measure for me. This was for the building of a Portmeirion-like hotel on a peninsula of the delectable little island of Korčula at which we had touched. As soon as I was given this most alluring commission I at once proceeded to produce sketch proposals that were accepted and arrangements were made for me to fly out forthwith.

But the day before I was due to leave, my travel agents rang me up and told me that not only had my application for a visa been refused by the Jugo-Slav embassy, but that my passport had been returned so heavily endorsed that there could be no possible hope of my being allowed to land on my island. Utterly at a loss to account for this refusal and happening across Ronald MacNeill[1] who I knew held some Foreign Office post, I asked him (1) What it could mean, and (2) What I could do about it?

His answer briefly was (1) 'It means that they evidently don't want you' and (2) 'Nothing at all.'

'But,' I persisted, 'they give no reason for refusing me entry. They can't have anything against me. It must all surely be some silly mistake?'

[1] Later Lord Cushendun.

He explained that any country could, at will, exclude any foreign national without giving a reason—as we ourselves constantly did, but added that he would none the less ring up Vansittart at the F.O. and see if *he* could get anything out of the Jugo-Slav embassy.

Ultimately I got the message, 'Sorry, they decline to say anything at all except that you are quite specially *non grata* and that you will most certainly be turned back if you attempt to enter their territory.' Utterly mystified, I had to resign myself to giving up all hope of the island project and so informed my would-be employer.

It was not until some while later that the reason for my unacceptability emerged. Unknown to me, Amabel had, along with Shaw and Wells and others, sent a cable to the Jugo-Slav government protesting against the imprisonment of certain of its political opponents.

Disappointed as I was, it was really a providential let-off as things turned out, for the outbreak of the second war and the general upheaval would probably have caught the hotel less than half-finished and so abandoned for years thereafter, if not for ever, with me not only unpaid, but probably financially implicated as it had been broadly hinted that it was hoped that I might 'take an interest' in the venture. Still, when once more I passed close inshore to the lovely island a year or two ago, I did rather wish that I had some stake in it.

Being incurably sea-minded we try whenever we can to do some part of our travelling on shipboard even when all logic and the travel agents are dead against it. So it was, that about this time we wilfully decided to include a reconnaissance of the Zuider Zee in a middle Europe motor tour, and, as it turned out, we were viciously punished for our eccentricity.

We chartered a large 'Botter Ark' auxiliary sailing barge with an odd nervous little man as our pilot. He could talk no English and we no Dutch and it soon emerged that though, as arranged, all the proper charts had been put aboard, he could not read them. However, he was quite a good deck-hand which was a help as all the boat's gear was extremely heavy, as were the great lee-boards that had to be raised or lowered as we tacked. Actually with her broad beam and bluff bows, though a fine vessel to look at or to paint (if in a seventeenth-century mood) she was an utter pig at beating to windward—butting and crashing into the waves, the larger ones bringing her up almost to a standstill. And besides head winds we had more than our share of fog, when our little gnome of a man would squat up forrard and toot most pitifully on his mournful horn with which he also warned lifting bridges of our ponderous approach. Though several times completely lost in the fog, we did find and land on the curious and rather sinister-seeming fishing island of Urk and duly made the various little ports we aimed to see. Our ship's complement apart from the gnome and myself consisted of Richard Hughes, Amabel and our three children, all really *en route* for the Schloss Wernberg in Carinthia—there to stay for a week with the Von Zeppelins in the course of an Austrian tour in the car we had brought over and left at Rotterdam.

Salzburg was an obvious 'must' on our way (more or less) to Wernberg but, being innocently unaware that we had reached it on the opening day of its great musical festival, our successive refusal at a whole string of hotels of mounting splendour was rather a facer for our party of six, including three tired children.

However, we did in the end find just one large bedroom in which we were invited to bivouac, such being the pressure that our eager acceptance of the offer was taken for granted. Determined to exploit our unlooked-for luck in thus stumbling headlong and unawares into the festival, I rushed off to the Opera House to see if by any chance we could wangle tickets for that night and was miraculously rewarded with three front stalls that had that moment been returned.

Heady stuff, but still more memorable to me was my first discovery of hard-by Heilbrunn—the magical baroque ensemble of miniature palace and sparkling pleasance, all contrived by an ingenious this-worldly Prince-Archbishop as a birthday surprise for his current mistress, where pretty garden toys, worked by falling water, still tinkle out the music of Mozart.

But most unwisely (as it transpired) we had (all except Amabel) bathed in some of the canals through which we had passed and within a few days of reaching Wernberg our eldest daughter

Susan was in the Krankenhaus at Klagenfurt dangerously ill with mastoid, being nursed by Amabel and fluttering and inexpert little quasi-nuns, while I too was being carried off delirious in an ambulance that lost its way but did ultimately deliver me unconscious at the same Krankenhaus. So there was poor Amabel with two cases to cope with, both on the danger-list—and two young children miles away in a strange house with Diccon, in nominal charge, himself also laid low. Penicillin and the other antibiotics still lay in the future.

My trouble was diagnosed as double pneumonia and pleurisy of which I very nearly died as the hospital staff were confident I surely would and so assured Amabel. But neither she, nor I, nor the admirable doctor agreed with them—and I didn't. My delirium seemed to last a long time, but when it abated Diccon was himself recovered enough to come over and read to me whilst Amabel coped with Susan and the two other children.

I had to stop him reading Evelyn Waugh's *Vile Bodies* because I found laughing too painful to be borne.

Eventually we were all able to reassemble at Wernberg where —bidden for a week—we had outstayed our time by a month or more and one way or another had been the most tiresome guests imaginable.

There was no difficulty about *accommodation*, the castle being very large and built around a courtyard on a rocky bluff above the rushing river Drau with cone-topped towers, winding stone stairs, a vast empty and echoing 'Prälaten-saal' with frescoed walls, surviving from its religious past and great wolf-hounds prowling around—a fairy-tale castle if ever there was one. And what of our long-suffering host and hostess? Kindness itself in their different ways, the count, Leo, a lively, muscular little man usually in national green hunting dress, leather shorts, feathered hat and so on—extrovert and pleasantly eccentric. For example, attending an auction whilst we were there to buy a bull for his farm, he came back with a lion cub he had taken to instead. She, on the other hand, was a highly sophisticated English intellectual, tall and elegant and an old family friend, whence our ill-starred visitation. Yet, to our confusion, we found that she had unconsciously absorbed some of the, to us, odd ideas of the

Austrian aristocracy as witness her shocked surprise when we asked if we might invite the charming and highly-qualified doctor who had undoubtedly saved my life, to tea. Amabel, though a student of folk-customs, is no slave to etiquette, and she carried her point with considerable firmness.

As rumours that I had actually died were fairly rife and had indeed reached at least one newspaper, I was concerned to demonstrate their falsity by getting back into circulation as quickly as might be. My recovery was certainly much accelerated by a most kind invitation to spend a week or two with the Dorrien-Smiths at Tresco Abbey in the Scillies (islands again!) where the spring comes early and where, before I left I was able, somewhat feebly, to help in the daffodil harvest, a most healing therapy.

But there were some two months of arrears awaiting my return to work—urgent professional work—as well as catching up with all the committees with which I was conscientiously but always reluctantly involved.

Far more to my taste than formal committee work were the perhaps more useful and certainly more hilarious activities of Peggy Pollard's 'Ferguson's Gang'.

I think our orbits must have first crossed over some National Trust project, a cause that she espoused a generation or so ago and has aided nobly and anonymously in endless odd ways, in any way, in fact, in which solid financial gain could be salted with surprise and humour.

Well over twenty years ago I find that I ended my book on the National Trust thus:

> It is fitting here, at last, to pay tribute to Ferguson's Gang—a benignly melodramatic secret society that has brought off a number of COUPS on the Trust's behalf in what can only be called a spectacularly stealthy fashion.
>
> One day the title-deeds of some notable little property will be handed to the Trust's Secretary with the compliments of the Gang by a masked man who will not speak—another day will come a registered envelope full of bank notes—the Gang's own contribution to some special acquisition fund.
>
> The Gang has most sedulously guarded its anonymity—though I still

have my suspicions that I was once in company with one of its members from a certain unguarded reference in some verses that presently appeared, almost certainly inspired by the Gang.

How they raise their money is not asked. Indeed, there is no one TO ask—or to answer. One hopes it is by fair means rather than foul—though in any case the results are equally beneficent, for one should not, I suppose, say equally welcome.

One only wishes there might be other such gangs, for there need be no rivalry save in well-doing, and it is agreeable indeed to find a Hidden Hand for once intent upon good works instead of crime.

Well, it turned out that I was right in my guess, as Peggy herself at last confessed and later gave me leave to reveal, though I have become privy to other equally anonymous and beneficent ploys that are still under the seal of secrecy.

But she isn't quite as expert at disguise as her deviousness really demands—her prose, laced with classical quotations, biblical allusions and words from half a dozen languages including Cornish and Russian, is an unmistakable as her typing, whilst her verse, in which she is apt to address me, sometimes on postcards, could come from no one else. Thus when she thought I was over-stressing the claims of landscape as against the basic needs of my fellow-creatures she sent me this:

> Pomona loves the orchard,
> And Liber loves the vine,
> And Clough he loves an old façade
> And an unspoilt skyline.
> But the citizen wants gasworks
> Electric wires on high,
> And light and drains and telephones
> God help me, so do I!

Or again, when I was campaigning hotly against ribbon building she gave me great aid and comfort by contributing a splendid tirade, a long and searing ballad that ended bitterly:

> They threw out a grand new bypass
> When the first was a chock full street
> And the glorious day isn't far away

> When London and Liverpool meet,
> And nothing remains of England
> Where the country used to be
> But a road run straight through a
>   building estate
> And a single specimen tree.

You never know in what guise she will clothe her next utterance, in that of a poet intensely sensitive to natural beauty, or that of a robustious Cornish fish-wife full of strange and splendid oaths.

I gather that her dabbling in witchcraft only ended when her success as a practitioner really rather frightened her, or at any rate her neighbours, and that she has now embraced (more or less) orthodox Catholicism with her usual contagious fervour.

When as general editor of a series of regional books I invited her to deal with Cornwall, she only consented on the condition that she might quizz it as through the eyes of a goat, and so report, and that the author's fee should be paid to charity. Of course I agreed, and her contribution was just as entertaining and 'different' as I had guessed it would be. She is forever embroiled in movements to promote this or prevent that and often with singular success, as she will never take NO for an answer. She has lately told me that I have got to help her raise £6,000 for a landscape salvage project that she is perfectly right in insisting is truly important. I have told her that I really can't, but I know it's no good. I almost certainly shall.

Chapter Sixteen

War Again

Nothing about the economic blizzard of the early 1930s? No. And little about the gradually darkening world thereafter. It was bad enough just to live through it all with the nagging suspicion that Hitler and Mussolini might and should have been halted.

The suspicion too that our newspaper proprietors as well as the politicians were deluding themselves and us by their unrealistic wishful thinking, with editors not choosing to believe (or at any rate to print) the menacing dispatches of their own correspondents, some of whom, however, found unofficial vehicles for their rejected reports in privately circulated sheets such as Claude Cockburn's deliberately hair-raising mimeographed *The Week* which nonetheless did much to sustain our morale throughout the war.

Foreseeing the coming nightmare, we paid a brief farewell visit to Europe before, for the second time, its lights would be put out, to be relit—when? North Wales was designated as a 'safe area', safe that is from the expected bombing from the air, so we prepared Brondanw as well as we could for its share of the trainloads of children and their teachers that were sharing the railways with the mobilizing armies. My practice was already beginning to shrivel and was soon to be all but dead, and reckoning that what survived could be perfectly well carried on from Brondanw, we decided to let Romney's House which served us as both home and office. This we quickly did, though to a very odd person—a mysterious foreigner—who turned out to be the leader of some curious religious sect that revered him as their mahatma. Though he claimed to be able to reincarnate himself in any part of the world at will, London was his and his movement's headquarters, and our gallery and big rooms were, so he said, just what were needed for the ceremonies of his 'Temple of Service'. It all sounded to me so exceedingly bogus and, in the circumstances, so suspicious, that I went to see the appropriate person at Scotland Yard, suggesting that investigation of my tenant by MI5 might prove rewarding.

However, though I had had private warnings and hints of pro-Nazi activities, he was cleared by the authorities and in fact stayed on until some time after the end of the war, when I sold the house to Raymond Russell, the collector of musical instruments, the attraction for him being the great gallery in which to give concerts.

Down in Wales with a house full of evacuees—there were seventeen children from Birkenhead's dockland at one time—Amabel, with her other local wartime responsibilities, was more than fully mobilized, but I was not. Applying for military employment I was directed to Shrewsbury for a medical check and interview. Everything was as good as could be—no trouble at all, until my age was revealed. Then I was more or less told to go home and not be silly, though I was then only fifty-seven and had been passed as fully fit by all the doctors.

I pulled such strings as were within my reach, but they all seemed only to lead, if anywhere, to staff jobs in an office where I knew I would be a pretty useless misfit as well as miserable. In the end my second war service amounted to no more than undistinguished membership of the local Home Guard, first as a private and finally as a captain under the zealous and unflagging command of my younger brother Martyn, who as a gunner, had had an exciting 1914–18 war in the Middle East and was full of ingenious dodges for the discomfort and defeat of the then expected enemy invaders. My only microscopic spell of quasi-active service was when I was called upon at first dawn to man a post established at our lodge, armed, with orders to stop all passing cars, check identities, hold any suspects, and immediately report anything the least suspicious to H.Q. So there I sat on a camp-stool for the best part of a day, my shot-gun across my knees and a book in hand between my checking of the astonished occupants of the infrequent cars.

How or where it all began I don't know, but from somewhere there certainly came a signal that there had been a German landing on the north-east coast and that individual infiltration must be expected and effectively dealt with wherever detected.

After some hours of conscientious though sceptical vigil, I was told that the invasion was off, for that day anyway, that I might go home and leave the passing motorists to proceed in peace without being alerted or alarmed.

But almost at once a group of officers suddenly and mysteriously appeared from where they wouldn't say, were billeted on us for a day or two and then melted quickly away, admitting only that there had been 'something'—yes, possibly a false alarm or a mis-read signal—but that anyhow all was now normal again. Was it just a mare's nest, a communications mistake, or a testing exercise to gauge our alertness? I still don't know. Maybe no one does nor ever will.

Meanwhile, either through some underground leak or tip-off or from an actual official German threat, my brother-in-law, John Strachey, was warned that his name was on Hitler's special black-list of those British citizens who would be of particular interest to the Gestapo when it took over responsibility for the internal security of our country after its successful occupation by the Wehrmacht. He was there as a leading anti-Nazi propagandist with a wide public following through his writings and broadcasting as well as his growing political influence. Hitler was of course perfectly right to include John in his catalogue of those held to be oustandingly *persona non grata*, but just how his curious cousin Lytton Strachey came to be granted the same honourable distinction is not so clear, though the very name may have been enough to arouse the Gestapo's hostility.

It was as well perhaps that Amabel had elected to write under her married name and not as a Strachey, as she had aided and abetted her brother and had indeed been on a challenging anti-Nazi mission to Germany just before the war—a mission which had been by no means free from unpleasantness and even danger. John, of course, stuck to and stepped-up his anti-German activities, but knowing full well the methods of the Gestapo, he had no intention of leaving his wife and two young children at risk, if and when he might be forced to continue his resistance underground if the threatened invasion succeeded. Foreseeing the possibility of an agonizing choice between giving himself up and with it all his potential usefulness as a *saboteur* and having his family held for 'treatment' by the Gestapo, he decided to send them off to Canada, where they remained for several years.

Before they could be got right away, we harboured them in a little old seventeenth-century cottage, next to our lodge, that I had fortunately just restored and fortunately *not* let to any of the car loads of passing strangers, foolishly offering quite ridiculous rents for anywhere so attractive and so (apparently) 'safe'. But with Amabel's own past and her dangerous Strachey connections, we didn't feel all that safe ourselves and thought it only sensible to make some slight arrangements for at least a temporary vanishment should the Germans actually reach Merioneth, take over the village and be after us. So, after some prospecting, we discovered and selected as our hide-out a secret little cave overhung with fern and ivy in the cliff-like wall of a narrow gorge down which a sounding waterfall leapt from shelf to shelf in a mist of spray with no apparent approach to it save up the bed of the stream itself which we reckoned would protect us even from bloodhounds. The cave, almost certainly an ancient copper working, ran in from the cliff face for some twenty feet, was high enough to stand upright in and about as wide as it was high and only reasonably damp and drippy once you got well inside. Anyhow we reckoned that it would harbour us and the children well enough in no more than tolerable camping discomfort for the duration of a moderately long hue and cry, against which we accumulated a basic stock of tinned provisions and iron rations of various sorts. Though we revealed our intentions to no one and kept the whereabouts of our hide-out a close secret, we did confidently rely, should we outlive our supplies, on being sustained by food deposited in unlikely places for us to collect by night, agreed with loyal and friendly tenants. We did not very seriously expect that we should in fact have to put this 'Operation Vanish' into actual execution, but if the emergency *did* arise with no effort at survival made or plans laid, we should look pretty silly. Also, it was of course rather fun, when any other was singularly lacking.

Years later, reading David Lane's book *The Last Ditch* in which he describes the preparations made for an effective resistance throughout Britain in the event of a successful invasion, I found a long extract from the official German 'Gestapo Arrest List for Great Britain' reproduced in reduced facsimile. It contained this:

SONDERFAHNDUNGSLISTE G.B.
51. STRACHEY, JOHN. SCHRIFTSTELLER, VERMUTH., ENGLAND., RSHA,. IV. B4.

According to the key index the symbol IV.B. stands for 'Party measures, special cases. Security measures. Attempted assassinations. Economic affairs. Press Questions.'

Wonderfully thorough and well-organized those Nazis and their chosen implement, their abominable Gestapo!

From time to time various war jobs were sought or offered me —one a quasi-naval one—but none ever actually got fixed up, so that, there being apparently no place for me in the armed services or indeed in recognized war work at all, I felt free to devote myself to my affairs at Brondanw and Portmeirion which at least kept me usefully employed. For some months I acted as host to an Indian Mountain Artillery brigade camped on my land up the valley that added greatly to the local gaiety and colour of our immediate wartime setting.

Its mule-trains carried out exercises to the very summit of Cynicht where, however, the peak is so steep and sharp that it was found impossible to dismount the guns strapped on top of the mules' backs, high up against the sky above the heads of the little gunners. One of the officers, passionately devoted both to his men and the mules, was a most winning talker, and particularly entertained us with stories about an old aunt of his who was a strict Jane whose eccentricities he obviously greatly relished. One of his tales described how, finding some insect in her house whose proper habitat was in some dense and distant part of the jungle, she despatched a servant to carry it thither lest harm should befall it, this at the very real risk of the man being eaten by a tiger.

Then at Portmeirion there was plenty to do in contriving ways of dealing with fluctuating military demands, the shortages of men and materials and in general in backing up Jim Wyllie, the manager, in his efforts.

When the invasion of Britain seemed imminent there was a school of thought that expected it to be made by way of neutral Ireland. A military Command was established at Portmeirion and took over the incomplete 'Town Hall', fitting it out as offices complete with a web of telephones.

Might not the sands of our tidal estuary be used for the landing of 'planes or of parachute troops? Some such landings had indeed, as everyone knew, been made in France, so thousands of timber stakes were driven in at low tide by the Royal Engineers.

If, in spite of stakes, armoured vehicles were parachuted down, what more likely than that they should be set rolling up our drive from the no doubt already captured hotel? So, half-way up the steepest part of the drive, monumental granite tank blocks appeared, which soon seemed to be growing into veritable towers twenty yards from the front door, with only just room to walk between. Now the hotel is built against a cliff, and there is no back drive. So how was the laundry van to get in and out? How were stores to be delivered? The military was numerous, the officers usually had their meals at the hotel, and there were many guests to be fed as well as the staff. I protested to the young engineer officer in charge that it was surely unlikely (with many far less inconvenient landing places along the coasts on either side) that the Germans would in fact want to use our drive, and meantime what about those large, heavy laundry hampers?

He was proud of his twin granite monuments and refused to halt their construction.

Now, as Jim Wyllie presently pointed out to me, this zealous officer loved not only his anti-tank defences but also a quiet mug of beer on his surprisingly frequent inspections.

So one evening, before the granite impediments were quite finished, he was met with the sobering news that, alas, there was no more beer. Jim Wyllie went on to explain most mournfully that this was because the brewers' men could not drive down to deliver it and had declared that they neither could, nor would, manoeuvre their large, heavy barrels through the narrow gap between his obstructions.

After a decent interval it was decided that these particular anti-tank precautions were not after all as militarily important as at first had been supposed. Gratefully, I asked if the fine granite blocks of which they had been constructed could be dumped at the top of the cliff where the dome now rises. Its massive terrace wall is the memorial of this incident.

After a while the tides of war carried the whole military set-up elsewhere and then it was the turn of the Air Ministry.

It had been decided, they wrote, to requisition the whole of Portmeirion as a rest centre for airmen on leave. Though apprehensive of the likely result of such a military occupation we could naturally only cooperate. I had to keep going up to London for consultation, officials had to keep coming down to verify plans, and to check on accommodation, water supplies, electricity and drains.

After a week or two of this, and a cancellation of all future bookings by old and new clients, there came another letter from on high. It had come to their notice that the place was a full day's journey from London, and that to go back and forth would shorten an airman's rest period by two whole days of travelling. I was certainly relieved for we knew all too well what occupation by the Forces could do to even the most solid structures. Without any malice on their part, 'service personnel' seemed to have a power of almost literally dissolving buildings and furniture.

All the same, we were determined that fighting men on leave should always somehow come if they wanted to, and that Portmeirion should not become just a hideout for nimble, food-ration-dodging civilians in search of comfort in a safe area. Unless non-combatants were actually bombed out or were entitled to 'points' on some other valid ground, priority was always given to men on leave from the Forces. Jim Wyllie was good at this sometimes awkward kind of discrimination. He agreed with me that some such arrangement was only right, resisted pressure from people we considered unworthy, and moreover agreed that we should 'for the duration' take the untried step of keeping open all winter.

So it came about that Portmeirion did, but unofficially, become a leave centre. I remember how two of the most gallant of our airmen spent what (alas) turned out to be their last leave there, 'Dam Buster' Guy Gibson and Ian Gleed, author of *Arise & Conquer*, who amused themselves dinghy sailing or flying model 'planes from the cliffs across the sands.

Sir Kenneth Clark with some of his experts and assistants were among the civilians who had, we knew, every right to be there, though what constituted that right we were not at the time at liberty to explain even to surprised members of the staff, or to jealous would-be clients who had to be refused. The secret was of course that the most noted pictures from the National Gallery had been unostentatiously transferred to certain carefully prepared air-conditioned chambers built inside underground slate workings deep in a nearby mountain. These irreplaceable pictures had to be tended, light as well as temperature must be right.

But there were some odd juxtapositions and I especially remember the stern frock-coated figure of Mr. Gladstone at the end of one great gallery glaring down its length as though in deep disapproval of some of his less decently clad neighbours.

Meanwhile, as the war dragged along, Portmeirion got shabbier and shabbier. Not only were my masons, painters and joiners successively called up, but all materials for repair and maintenance were strictly rationed. Rightly they were only doled out in minute amounts to any would-be customer who could not claim to be going to use them for something essential to the war effort.

Our two daughters were called up, one, a biologist, to do agricultural research, the other, a painter and designer, first to teach in a school and later to work in the offices of the Admiralty. Our son, Christopher, was in the Welsh Guards.

Meanwhile it was rightly deemed that Universities and other centres of learning should carry on, and as this had to be done with depleted staffs, there was a demand for outside lecturers. Among the speaking jobs that I was myself called upon to do was to address students, staff and public, at Queen's University, Belfast, on the occasion of the opening of a planning exhibition. There were formalities enough even to get my journey officially authorized, but when the Dublin architects got wind of my Irish trip they asked me to come and talk to them there and the paper work became prodigious. The Belfast Planning Exhibition duly opened and I did slowly and uncomfortably reach Dublin.

Dublin was certainly startling after blacked-out London, for it was all ablaze with lights and not only that, it was strange to see the Nazi's swastika flag floating serenely over the German Embassy.

On my first Dublin evening I was entertained to a dazzling party at the Gresham Hotel, all white ties, tail-coats and tiaras—I alone in crumpled tweeds. It was a very merry evening, the neutral Irish so convivial and hospitable that one could not do other than respond, and any doubts or hard feelings were soon drowned in the flood of champagne.

Towards the end of the party, in the small hours, someone said, 'Our Lord Mayor would like to meet you—do you mind?' 'Delighted,' I said, 'but remember that I too am a mayor—of Portmeirion.'

This nonsense must have been passed on before we actually met for, when we did, he advanced beaming with both hands extended saying, 'Welcome, your Worship, you are the first of my colleagues from England to visit my city and I am delighted to have you here—I hope you will lunch with me at the Mansion House tomorrow.'

This was carrying the stupid joke too far, so I said that I couldn't manage lunch but might I perhaps call in during the morning, when I intended to confess and apologize for my silly false pretences.

But the municipal butler must have been forewarned of my coming for, as he flung open the great folding doors of the reception room, he bawled out like a toastmaster, 'His Worship the Mayor of Portmeirion.'

Well, I thought, better leave it at that and hope for the best, so we settled down quite cosily and I successfully warded off any questions about my municipal responsibilities by eagerly demanding enlightenment about his.

My main attraction in visiting the Mansion House had been the chance of seeing the fine portraits which I knew were there, some of them by Reynolds, but what my host was most anxious to display were the miscellaneous contents of various cabinets which seemed to me of no great interest until he told me that they had all been made by himself—whilst in prison.

'*In prison?*' I echoed. 'Why yes,' he said, 'and for quite a while —and what's more, if the armistice had been delayed by only a few days, that would have meant the end of me. I was very lucky.'

On the second evening I was taken by my architect hosts to the Abbey Theatre to see Synge's *Playboy of the Western World*. It was then the custom to seek refreshment between the acts at some neighbouring bar—a different bar for each interval.

At the first of these, someone at the far end of the counter leaned across and shouted (she had to) 'Aren't you Clough?' I admitted it, when she continued, 'Then come and stay with us for the weekend.'

Having identified the speaker and taken down the address—a castle about a hundred miles from Dublin—I accepted gladly, as I am apt to do if an invitation is unexpected enough. This was certainly such a one but soon explained by my hostess-to-be telling me that she had heard from mutual friends in Wales of my probable visit to Dublin and had recognized me from their description, which must have been a good deal better than those usually circulated by the police for those 'wanted'.

Eventually reaching my destination for what I supposed would be a quiet and informal country weekend, I was taken aback to find a house-party of some twenty, assembled for a celebrated woodcock shoot. The food, the wine and the service, to say nothing of the setting, far outdid even the splendours of the Gresham Hotel that had so dazzled my war-conditioned eyes. Again, evening dress for everyone except my scruffy self, though I did have with me a pair of Oxford shoes so that I was able to join in the dancing. They were beautifully polished, their laces loosened and their tongues turned back for me by the pitying but friendly footman told off to valet me and to see to my bedroom fire and bath, just one of twenty-two indoor servants as I was at pains to discover.

There was much agitated telephoning back and forth between Dublin and the Castle that ended, I was told, with a total prohibition by the fuel controller of the use of the fleet of motor cars standing by to take the party to the shoot some twenty miles away.

Fuel of any sort and petrol in particular were about the only real shortages that were obvious in Ireland, and I was asked if, owing to this harsh and unexpected prohibition by the authorities, as I could not stay for the shoot, I would very much mind being driven to the station in the stable dung-cart by a very old man with a very old horse? All the other vehicles, horses and men, would now have to be mobilized for the shooting expedition.

The harness was clearly older than even the horse or the driver, and was only held together by odds and ends of string that looked inadequate, and were.

Sure enough, we had several halts for wayside repairs and so reached the station some ten minutes behind the train's departure time. But it didn't matter. As my driver had cheerfully prophesied, the train was later still.

After having an excellent lunch in the dining-car I noticed that we were travelling ever more sedately, and presently came to a standstill, but not at a station. After we had so remained for what seemed a very long time, I asked what was the matter, to be told that the engine had run out of fuel (I suppose peat) but that someone would soon be along with a load. As I had an appointment to keep in Dublin I asked a little crossly how such a thing could happen, to be blandly told that, naturally, it was always a near thing with the fuel shortage and that today the restaurant-car kitchen had managed to pinch more than its proper share.

However, I eventually reached Dublin and thereafter London, where I am now a little ashamed to say (or am I?) that I went on the air with a B.B.C. broadcast on *Ireland Now*, wherein I dwelt on the carefree luxury of that country as contrasted with our own embattled privation and suggested that when the war was over, and the maps of the sinkings of our shipping round Ireland's neutral coasts were published, we might come to feel less tolerantly of my late hosts' non-participation.

Not, I am afraid, a very cordial sort of 'roofer' for what after all had been a most refreshing interlude, a coming-up for breath from the deep dismalness of wartime England.

I certainly felt what I said at the time, though my strictures may well have been partly prompted by a trace of envy, but I think it was the sight of that Swastika flag that did it.

I broadcast every now and again throughout the war—on subjects as far away from it as ever could be—the only hindrance being that you had to adhere precisely to an already censored and approved script with no single word added or omitted and also to time yourself exactly, to the split second.

The idea behind all this strictness I gathered was that something harmful to the allied cause might somehow be conveyed to enemy listeners, either inadvertently or even treacherously and anyhow no chances were being taken.

I was asked by the B.B.C. to do a Wren feature in celebration of some anniversary of his, for which I tried to collect 'atmosphere'. I had already spent a night with the fire-watchers in St. Paul's, almost all architects and surveyors, and so zealously efficient that though the great church was showered with fire-bombs, almost no damage was suffered until a land mine caught the north transept. Anyhow, dimly and fitfully seen during the blitz, the Cathedral's vast interior did powerfully reinforce one's feeling that here genius and magnaminity had triumphed indeed, and there was no question but that most of the devoted band of watchers with their headquarters down in the crypt (where I joined them for beer and smokes) felt their high responsibility and the same sort of awe as I did. Still in search of atmosphere I thought I would try to talk to Edwin Lutyens.

Though I never knew him really intimately (I doubt if many did save only Gertrude Jekyll) because of his impish elusiveness, he certainly influenced me architecturally more than did anyone else. Being the consummate artist I still hold him to have been, I could rarely get him to talk about his own work, or, if I wanted to consult him, about the matter in hand. Everything had to be made a joke of, often quite a funny joke, but seldom what I wanted to hear. He was a persistent and quite shameless punster, often uniquely funny by giving his sally an unexpected finish as when asked at a dinner of high ecclesiastical dignatories to propose a toast he rose and said:

> Here's to the happiest years of our lives
> Spent in the arms of other's men's wives.
> Gentlemen!—Our Mothers!

Or, of the banal huddle of imperial Simla he said, 'If one had been told that monkeys had built it, one would have said, "What wonderful monkeys BUT—they must be shot at once, in case they might do it again".' Or, on making up a quarrel with the Vicereine over some trouble at Imperial Delhi, he wrote:

> I bathe your feet with my tears and dry them with my hair. True, I have very little hair, but then you have very little feet.

His reluctance to talk seriously about architecture generally or his own part in its revivification seemed to be explained by something he once said, I think on our very first encounter: 'All this *talk* about art is dangerous, it brings the ears so forward that they act as blinkers to the eyes.'

It was therefore for the stimulus of his company that, with this broadcast to compose, I went to talk to him about Sir Christopher Wren, whose spiritual heir I held Lutyens to be, seeking him out at his house in Mansfield Place.

But Lutyens, though interested in what I told him about the fire-watchers and though cordiality itself, was also at his most perverse and whimsical. As we sat by his fire eating buttered buns with our tea, he just would *not* discuss Wren, though he too revered him and habitually spoke of the 'Wrenaissance'. He would instead only talk about Inigo Jones—why, I don't know. On him he was eloquent and illuminating, but it was not what I had come for, so after looking over some of the drawings he was then hopefully working on for various projected buildings including a ceremonial annexe to Westminster Abbey, about which he made his usual schoolboy jokes, I departed.

The broadcast scene was set on the great west steps of St. Paul's where I stood (supposedly) in the midst of the blitz in back-and-forth conversation with Sir Christopher, or rather his ghost, played by a brilliant actor who through his voice alone, at once old, authoritative and slightly pedantic, contrived to conjure up precisely my conception of the Master. It went out on the air of New Year's Night, 1943.

I have found a contemporary press cutting from *Country Life* wherein I was dealing with an architectural query that I answered by quoting from the broadcast script:

> WILLIAMS-ELLIS: ... and I hold it a great honour that I was invited to design the wrought-iron gates to go between the piers that *you* had built all ready for gates, at the place you gave your son in Warwickshire—Wroxall Abbey.
>
> WREN: Ah! Wroxall, yes! They pulled down the house I knew, and put up a great pile they hoped was Gothic. But indeed, 'twas neither convincing nor convenient—a silly business, though, mind you, I was never against change so long as it was a change from worse to better, and so according with good sense. One way and another I did a deal of pulling down myself, but only when I could justify it.

There is one more celebration, one more gaiety besides the Dublin jaunt that belongs to the anxious, dismal, tedious and, for many of us, tragic years of the war. 'Unique' is a much misused word, but it may I think be justly applied to a 'happening' that we contrived deep in the bowels of the earth. This was on the occasion of our daughter Charlotte's twenty-first birthday party which we determined must be celebrated memorably in spite of everything.

We are a somewhat fireworks-addicted family and we found that we had quite a good stock of left-overs, particularly of rockets, the normal letting-off of which would have violated the strict blackout regulations and probably landed us in gaol as being in breach of the Defence of the Realm Act. To dodge that little difficulty I asked my brother Martyn who was chairman of the family slate quarries up at Blaenau-Ffestiniog (which at one time were said to have the greatest underground workings in the world) whether we could have our display in one of his vast subterranean chambers?

No difficulty at all, he would let us down the incline in trucks to the deepest and highest chamber of all, where our rockets could safely soar up in the darkness and, if happening to hit the roof, would certainly not bring it down on us.

So down we all went with our hamper of wine and saved-up delicacies, up went the rockets with deafening bangs echoing and re-echoing through the workings, round buzzed the Catherine wheels, and coloured flares cast our enormous wavering shadows on the drifting smoke.

It was not very long after this notable party that we welcomed our future New Zealand son-in-law, Lindsay Wallace, a fellow biologist of Charlotte, and not so very long after that they were married at St. Martin-in-the-Fields, an occasion that could have been gay if it had not been for the doodle bugs, V_1 and V_2 that threatened London and for the fact that Christopher had been posted as missing.

It was on the day after the wedding that I was asked to go round to the Welsh Guards Headquarters, there to be told, very gently, that he, our only son, had been killed in action before Monte Cassino.

He had joined the regiment straight from his brief wartime course as an undergraduate at King's, Cambridge. His roommate in the Gibbs building there, Euan Cooper-Willis, who, as an economist, was in the Adjutant General's department at the War Office (his eyesight disqualifying him for active service) subsequently married our elder daughter Susan. The armistice was thus a time of both pleasure and of almost unbearable pain. We soon had grandchildren to add to the pleasure. We decided that since we, Christopher's parents, were alive, we should try to be so properly, and to keep the wound to ourselves.

Chapter Seventeen

Butlin, Stevenage, Travel and the Fire

When the war against Hitler was over and a Labour Government got in, we planners wondered if the chaos, the 'non-pattern' of the First World War aftermath was going to repeat itself?

Clearly, in view of a new element, the immense bombing destruction in our cities made everything in the way of building materials for desperately needed houses the more desperately short and they had to be severely rationed.

It was at this point of time I was concerned with a local but in some ways typical controversy in our corner of North Wales. It split the hitherto harmonious advocates of physical amenity into two factions, and spilled out pretty widely. This was a wrangle as to whether there should or should not be a Butlin Holiday Camp near Pwllheli. But it implied the question of how much and what sort of *tourism* a district can absorb.

After the fall of France and the consequent prospect of invasion, there had been a flurried scurry to rush up service training camps in remote and supposedly 'safe' areas. Mr. Billy Butlin had already got a site for one of his holiday camps earmarked on the south Caernarvonshire coast and his standardized plans were all ready for immediate realization. The very place and the very thing, thought the Admiralty—'Go right ahead full steam', they told him, 'rush it up for us—and when the war is over and we have done with it, it will be all yours and ready for your holiday-makers at a bargain price.' That, in a nutshell was the arrangement and an economical and sensible one it seemed until, at the war's end and the prearranged hand-back was duly made, a great cry of protest arose from most members of the planning and amenity bodies on the grounds that statutory planning permission had never been sought or given (the Admiralty, of course, needing no such approval) and that, anyway, an alien holiday camp of such a size in such a place would be in every way a disaster, economically, socially, culturally and scenically.

I was at the time both chairman of the Council for the Preservation of Rural Wales and also Planning Consultant to the Caernarvonshire County Council and was called to give evidence as such.

The Ministry Inspector presiding—as it happened an old friend, Sir George Pepler—said, 'I presume you are representing both Councils', to which I replied:

Strictly speaking I would say rather that I am *mis*representing them, as I myself flatly disagree with both their attitudes and am one hundred per cent in favour of the camp. This was, after all, primarily designed for holiday use (despite its temporary wartime deflection) and I hold that it should be allowed to fulfil its intended and most excellent purpose—granted of course all reasonable safeguarding conditions.

Are we already forgetting that throughout the long years of war most of our countrymen and women have been at full stretch and virtually without holidays at all and that they now deserve and ought to be given facilities for well-earned relaxation and that without such new large-scale facilities such as this camp is tailor-made to provide— the very granting of holidays (and remember they are going to be extended, and with pay(will, with nowhere to go, be no more than a heartless mockery?

There have been hysterical letters in the press lamenting the threatened 'desecration of Snowdonia'—but what has a rather dreary stretch of pebble beach whose proper address is Afonwen Junction got to do with Snowdon a good 20 miles away?

Pwllheli I gather objects on the score of not wanting to be swamped by strangers. That will scarcely do from a town that for more than half a century has been straining every nerve to attract summer visitors—not to be sure, altogether, successfully. If it is afraid that the camp's chalets will be preferred to its own rather grim lodging-houses and the allure of their concrete promenade, that is a challenge to be met and a well-directed response might yet transform the town. As to the hostility of the amenity lobby of which I am generally a vocal member, I think that on this occasion it is wrong. Certainly I too would have wished that the camp might have settled elsewhere—much as Miss Muffet felt about the spider—but there it is and there I say it should remain if the greatest happiness of the greatest number means a thing to us.

We are warned that we shall find ourselves swamped and overrun by hordes of undisciplined strangers. I believe that to be sheer nonsense. I have inspected the camp and talked to Mr. Butlin and my impression is that the whole set-up is most ingeniously contrived to the one end that his holiday-making thousands will elect to spend all their time *and* all their money on the delights provided within his own camp perimeter without much noticing where they are—except that it is 'sea-side'—of sorts.

I would agree that it is a pity that they are likely to be oblivious of the natural beauty of our countryside and incapable of appreciating and enjoying it—as yet, but that is one of the sad results of our over-urbanization that the more fully civilized are trying to correct. And anyway, what is the alternative to the camp's designed purpose? No one has suggested another use that could possibly be viable and only dereliction and demolition are left. Abandoned airfields and other service establishments soon become scenes of desolation indeed—acres of concrete and rubble and weeds and general wreckage even when the 'demolition' has been officially completed. Would you prefer *that* on your door step and on your conscience to a well organized establishment where thousands of your fellows and their families can innocently enjoy themselves? If so—go right ahead and kill the project dead.

That, broadly, is what I said—and with some heat as well as full conviction.

It made me pretty unpopular in several quarters—including,

surprisingly, with Thomas Jones (T.J. of the Cabinet Office and Coleg Harlech), who even attacked me, indirectly, in the press as a turn-coat saboteur, though all was harmony again in the end. I still think that I was right—on balance. Or was I? In return for my support, I had persuaded Mr. Butlin to promise me (or persuaded myself that he had done so) that he would introduce a certain amount of culture into his camp curricula as an alternative to his rumbustious fun and games—concerts of classical music, picture exhibitions, operettas, lectures and so on—and he *did* make a fleeting gesture in this direction and indeed Amabel and I were invited to witness a most spirited production of *The Barber of Seville* at his Skegness camp where we spent a weekend experiencing the camp's so popular delights. I conceived it my duty as a town and country planner to study this strange new development, though as it emerged, the sample was not quite a fair one, as apart from the specially laid-on opera there was also a special V.I.P. train and other trimmings.

It was in a final (and vain) effort to swing Mr. Butlin towards culture that I invoked the help of Lady Clark (Sir Kenneth's wife) with the aim of getting selected modern paintings exhibited. His response was to invite us both to discuss the project with him at dinner at his house in what I believe is called 'Millionaires Row' in Highgate. All very dazzling—we ate quails off gold plate —but I cannot recall that we achieved our original object to any worthwhile extent.

When Mr. (later Lord) Silkin suddenly invited me to become chairman of the corporation that was to build his first New Town —Stevenage—it was not as either planner or architect that I was asked to act, but as an *administrator*—which we both decided after some time I was not. Essentially I am and have always been, a building animal.

At first blush, the whole New Town idea was an intoxicating one—I visualized a New Model where everything from the layout to the lamp posts would be a pattern of sense and sensibility, where special priorities would hasten into being a generous exemplar of post-war urbanism at its very best to set a standard for the whole country, of which it stood in parlous need.

But though the early exploratory months were exhilarating

enough, the looming financial crisis soon began to cast its creeping shadow over our brave new thinking, making too much of it seem idealistic and unrealizable and even an early and adequate beginning of mere bread-and-butter housing less and less likely.

Indeed the pattern of my post-first-war disillusionment seemed to be repeating itself with almost nightmarish fidelity. Shortly before I left, E. M. Forster had written to tell me that the original of the house that he so affectionately describes as 'Howards End' in his great novel was in fact a manor farm house called 'The Rook's Nest' that had been compulsorily purchased by the Government as part of its large-scale acquisition for Stevenage. He was greatly concerned lest its quiet charm should be overwhelmed and obliterated and its views obstructed by a heedless urban development. I sought to persuade him of our good intentions by a joint inspection and we travelled down together by train from King's Cross from where so many 'Howards End' journeys had been therein described and together we drove out to 'The Rooks Nest'.

He showed me all round, no detail was omitted, he recalled his boyhood's memories, took me to favourite viewpoints and readily won my agreement that the whole place, though in no way grand or remarkable, was indeed lovable and, with its distinguished literary association, most worthy of preservation. Happily I was able largely to dispel his fears by showing him, on maps and plans, that the place had already been zoned as an open space *not* to be built upon and to persuade him that, so scheduled, his beloved shrine would have a far better chance of permanent preservation unchanged, than if left out in the cold and at hazard in the open market.

Reassured, he took me to tea with the current tenants of the place, an unforgettable experience, as never in all my life have I been received with such implacable hostility. It was as though I, and I alone, were directly responsible for the whole idea of New Towns, for the inclusion of Stevenage in particular, and for the consequent invasion of their accustomed and cherished privacy.

I admitted that I had long campaigned for New Towns, that I was certainly hotly in favour of the whole policy, but that as administrator and Chairman I had had nothing whatsoever to do with the choice of Stevenage—my only responsibility being to do my best to assure that the whole project was carried out with all possible efficiency and grace. Unfortunately it was inevitable, I said, that some old inhabitants would be disturbed, some even dispossessed, but if a hitherto fortunate fifty had now to give up something for a long-deprived fifty thousand was there anything very wicked about that?

Apparently there was, and nothing I could say in any way abated my hostess's indignation that blazed away at me across the startled tea-cups. To my surprise I got no word of support from Forster who sat silently throughout the long tirade. I could only suppose him to be so equally torn between his democratic principles and local loyalty as—for once—to be unable to find words to match the complexity of his thoughts.

Nor did he in any way explain or try to excuse the astonishing gruelling to which he had exposed me. Possibly he had foreseen that his introduction would touch off just the explosion that it did, had perhaps also felt that such was precisely what his friends needed to reduce the internal pressure of gnawing anxiety and apprehension and that it would be best for them to let themselves go all out—and so, maybe, have done with it.

Anyway, though I left both bewildered and shocked, I felt quite sure that Forster's part in the strange affair could not possibly have been other than well-intentioned and right, and I was just as certain that *I* had been right to stick to my beliefs and state them boldly but as politely as I could. That is why, at the end of the confrontation I felt no embarrassment, only astonishment. When, years later, at Bertrand Russell's ninetieth birthday dinner party, I asked Forster how he then felt about his 'Rooks Nest'–'Howards End', I was delighted when he told me that he was very well content.

As a most agreeable spare-time diversion between other ploys I undertook an ambitious illustrated two-volume book describing all the chief National Trust properties, called *On Trust For the Nation*, a commission that took me to all sorts of interesting places that I had long known about but never yet seen, and involved incidental meetings with people sometimes no less memorable.

This went pre-eminently for Sir Winston Churchill as the vivifying essence of Chartwell. Arriving in mid-morning I was taken up to the master's room where he lay in bed under a top-dressing of papers and telephones with secretaries discreetly popping in and out, but without interrupting our talk.

Later, after I had seen his library, his several studios and his astonishing output of paintings, he took me into the garden, especially to introduce me to his pet fish and black swans. On parting, as he handed me a prodigious cigar some eight inches long with his name on the band, he said, 'I wonder if you would mind letting me see anything you write about this place before it's published?'

Of course I said I would and did—and this is the interesting and characteristic thing about his reaction—he returned my typescript entirely untouched except for a few alterations where he had, in his own hand, given some word a synonym he preferred or changed its position in the sentence. The paragraphs to which he might well have taken exception and have struck out, he left exactly as they stood, recognizing with his usual fair-mindedness that I had as perfect a right to hold strong views and to express them fearlessly as he had himself. Here they are:

Chartwell still provides a congenial setting to their immensely active living. I suppose it is no more, on average, that an hour's drive down from Westminster, but WHAT a drive! I can pay the place no higher compliment than to say that it is worth it. Worth the dingy squalor, the mean ineptitude of the Croydon Road, or, rather, the distress of spirit that the sight of that ragged Via Dolorosa must cause to anyone who can fully savour the graciousness of Chartwell.

I should have expected the dramatic violence of the contrast to have made Sir Winston an out-and-out advocate of town and country planning; but, most certainly, seeing both Chartwell and the ends of the earth with intense interest and clarity, it would seem that the middle distance of home affairs interested him much less than either, and that he can do his driving back and forth without excessive anguish.

Yet once beyond the tentacles of the Metropolitan Octopus, once you have entered the avenue of ancient beeches that ends on the brow of the great down that looks down on Westerham, still little, still tree-girt and self-respecting, your pride revives again and you see below you an England worth preserving.

That reflection had certainly sustained me, when, at the beginning of the First World War, I sweated away with my blue-uniformed convict-like Fusilier Battalion scarring these self-same chalk downs with defensive trenches and parapets, our band in attendance for music while you work—or walk; we had scarcely learned to *march*. But the Battle of Britain for which we were there and then preparing with such naïve resolve, was to be fought and won not by us, but by our sons a generation on in time, and in the spaces miles high above our unwise heads.

We always honoured Westerham and its (we hoped) admiring citizenry by marching through it at attention, which meant 'eyes front', but an architect can even so, see, note, and thenceforth forever remember, every building of the least distinction within his disciplined vision. So that after more than a generation's interval the town was still completely familiar to me—General Wolfe's Quebec House gravely presiding, exactly as I recalled it, over the southern entrance to the town.

My car was delayed on Chartwell's short drive by a great pantechnicon that had just preceded me, out of which, whilst I admired the flag of the Lord Warden of the Cinque Ports floating high against the sparkling blue above the house's piled up mass of mellow brickwork, presently emerged a great terrestrial globe.

It was that presented during the war by President Roosevelt, now reaching its (I hoped) final destination after its long, useful and admired service at Greenwich. Being due to fly to Baghdad next day, I could not forbear to chart out my own presumed course with the curved perspex scale provided for great-circle measurement, feeling that my journey was thereby somehow placed under the very highest auspices. Certainly it proved well starred, but I wonder what high matters of top-secret strategy that transparent measuring slip may not have suggested or decided.

As for that fabulous cigar, having popped it into my breast pocket, I clean forgot about it until undressing that night, when I found the poor thing broken in half and neither fit to smoke nor to cherish as an heirloom.

Freed from my Stevenage responsibilities, Amabel insisted that it might well be a now-or-never chance for me to slip away with her to see our daughter Charlotte in New Zealand who, we had just been told, was expecting her first-born. By damping down all other activities I reckoned I *could* escape for a month or two without disgrace or disaster. The question then was how—with all transport still disorganized and at full stretch after its wartime attrition. Indeed, but for the fact that I had built in China for Butterfield & Swire, we could never have made our get-away. On to one of its admirable ships we were somehow smuggled, thus, I am afraid, quite shamelessly jumping the queue.

That got us as far as Australia where we whizzed around for a few weeks seeing all the places and people that we possibly could, from academics and sheep-ranchers to tycoons and, of course, architects. But the country, as a whole, despite a quite inadequate group of first-rate technicians, I found most dangerously 'un-planning' minded. Being asked by an enquiring reporter with pencil poised, on embarking at Sydney for New Zealand, for my reactions to 'our great city and wonderful harbour', I replied, 'Only if you undertake that whatever I say shall appear unedited.' That being promised, I dictated my brief valedictory message:

> By God what a site!
> By man what a mess!

And he kept his word—as subsequent press reverberations made abundantly clear.

In New Zealand a welcoming party given by the Prime Minister started off a blazing and exhilarating row between myself and his highly bellicose Minister of Housing, which crackled in the newspapers for days with the utmost gaiety.

But the P.M. took the affair seriously and, fearing I might be offended by his colleague's unparliamentary language and uncouth debating technique, laid on a second placatory reception and generously put an official chauffeur and car at the disposal of Amabel and myself for as complete a reconnaissance of both islands as we cared to make.

In our tour of New Zealand's South Island, we made a point of

SEMPLEWOCKY

"When he spoke of Comics of the State Housing Programme, as snivelling Snufflebusters, he did not intend his remarks to be taken as personal by Mr Clough Williams-Ellis, the English Architect, said Mr Semple —"

'Twas Housig and the Semple Gove
Did Ire and Mumble in the Blab;
All snivel were the Adjectoves,
And Aussie the Vocab.

"Beware the Snufflebust, my son!
The Jaws that Gripe, the Claws that Scratch!
Beware the Semplebob, and shun
The Propagandasnatch!"
— Through the Looking Glass (Sort of)

February 18th, 1948.

staying a night at Queenstown, an attractive little place as New Zealand towns go, on the banks of a great lake of memorable beauty which we explored by launch having a barbecue supper in a wooded bay.

Retiring tired and early, we were awoken by a sudden hubbub and commotion to find our bedroom full of jolly fellows holding mugs and glasses aloft, toasting us and each other and singing odd snatches of comic songs—all manifestly more than a little drunk. The odds against us being about ten to one, we pumped up sufficient cordiality to be accepted as members of their party and once that was understood our only difficulty was preventing them from bringing us drinks—our only fear that they would spill theirs over our bed, or worse, start being sick.

When it emerged that they were a Morticians' Convention having their annual beano, we forgave them everything, and, from our studies in our Cintra hotel of those unforgettable trade journals, I think our technical knowledge of their craft almost persuaded their fuddled minds that we were indeed fellow practitioners. Anyhow at long last our revellers moved on elsewhere and left us in peace with many hiccupped expressions of profound regard.

Our tour took us even to little Stewart Island away to the south where indeed I planned a house in a setting and climate resembling that of Scotland, but with penguins parading about amongst the palms, just to confuse and to remind us that Antarctica was the next stop south. Our hostess was the daughter of New Zealand's first surveyor-general, who had at one time been Samuel Butler's partner at Erewhon, so naturally had an interest in planning as well as in Utopias such as she had heard Butler himself discuss. The reason for my planning her a new house was the fact that she was presenting her existing one and her estate to the New Zealand Government as a sort of off-shore Chequers and as an example of scrupulous care for 'rural amenities'—including the preservation of the flora, fauna and timber of the original primeval bush. Of course I met architects and planners wherever I could, all over New Zealand, but naturally mostly in Wellington and Auckland—both casually and at formal get-togethers.

When I left, in return for so much fraternal friendliness, I thought my most useful gift would be a sort of testament, a planning credo and commentary with special reference to New Zealand's many problems. So this I left in the form of six recorded talks which it was arranged should be fired off at the same time on successive Monday evenings, the reactions of the architects being arranged as a follow-up on two further Mondays. What, in fact, I said I don't now know; for though I was generously presented on ship-board with a copy of each recording, they were all on enormous discs that, at that time apparently, no machine in this country could cope with and they are anyhow now burnt.

Nor do I know what was generally thought of my delayed-action legacy—but as the New Zealand architects, like the Australian, subsequently elected me to honorific status in their Institutes, I conclude that they were mostly with me. All the same, as the successive Monday nights came and went as I crossed first the Pacific and then the Atlantic oceans homeward bound, and I knew that my poisoned shafts were being punctually discharged, I did feel a little cowardly at not being around to take the come-back. Still, as my concern and my criticisms all arose from a warm affection and admiration for New Zealand, I took it for granted that that would be understood, as I think it was.

I was really just trying to pass on the fruits of experience and the consequences of our own mistakes in our increasing efforts to manage our own national estate at home.

From time to time I have contributed to various encyclopaedias and omnibus books, edited others, and kept up an irregular output of booklets and pamphlets as well as of newspaper articles and press letters—nearly all related to my ruling interests, in short, hobby-horsical. Though an all too ready controversialist, I am afraid it is my innate impatience that makes me so poor and reluctant a committee man and the hours spent in conference the slowest to pass in all my life.

Indeed, the only thing that enabled me to sustain all the committee work, formality, delays and frustrations of a professional planning practice of any sort, with even such patience as I did, was, apart from my deep interest, the perpetual carefree planning spree that Portmeirion afforded me—where as I have said, I was landowner, planner, architect, developer and paymaster all in one.

Elsewhere, once the delights of the preliminary reconnaissance and the draft proposals were behind me and one began to be impeded by the dead weight of public lethargy and official slow-motion brakemanship, I found it hard to sustain my initial enthusiasm or to persevere with whittled down schemes with the necessary patience.

For some years, however, I was reasonably persistent, sometimes collaborating with Sir Patrick Abercrombie, sometimes with Lionel Brett (later Viscount Esher), but the actual physical results on the ground—for all our hopeful work on paper—remain pitifully small. Indeed, inevitably it would seem, the planner's role must ever remain less satisfying than the architect's, and frustration his vocational malady. Yet our hopes about our architectural future were at least temporarily raised by one splendid happening. In the gallantly conceived and valiantly achieved 1951 Festival of Britain. I had but a minor part as a member of the Welsh Committee whose originally ambitious projects gradually dwindled to near-insignificance through lack of patriotic fervour and adequate financial support, to no one's particular surprise.

But the imaginative forward-looking show so brilliantly mounted on the South Bank by a free-wheeling team of *avant-garde* architects recruited and led by Sir Hugh Casson in a mood of gay adventure and daring innovation really did come off to a miracle, and put new life and spirit into our rather jaded designers that, modified and developed, well or ill, is with us yet.

Higher up the same bank of the Thames, in the Pleasure Gardens at Battersea, beauty unrestrained bubbled up even more excitingly, magically transfiguring a slice of prosaic metropolitan public park into a dancing thing whose sprightly elegance seemed to have been inspired by Xanadu and Eglinton, Harun-al-Rashid and Lord George Sanger, and to owe something to the Tivoli Gardens in Rome and their frolicsome namesake in Copenhagen as well as to the Brighton Pavilion. What really entranced me was the reflexion that the whole of this gigantic joke was ordained by Parliament and (if indirectly) 'run by Whitehall' at the Government's expense, which (Oh, I know) was the taxpayer's, yours and mine, which again was why the Calamity Howlers so furiously raged together. Well, I don't care. This was just precisely one of the things I had always hoped that a Government would one day do—act the princely patron of the outdoor visual arts on a really grand scale, give our brightest young architects and designers and artists a chance to spread their wings in a big way—not in solemn self-conscious academic flight but just for once to frivol with inspired levity, and as high as they could, just to show us.

That is the sort of thing I like to see my money spent on; it's the sort of thing indeed on which—in my own small way—I should spend it myself if the Government didn't take it away and lay it out (for once) thus handsomely and so much more to the public benefit. And, just because it was done with such imagination and magnanimity, I didn't grudge a penny of it, even though the thing did seem to have cost us dearer than it should.

I would say that it was the most significant and distinguished thing in the way of pure *spectacle* that we have attempted since the Field of the Cloth of Gold, far more important as an eye-educator, vastly more effective in influencing public taste through its very popularity.

Tudor England, of course, excelled at display and pageantry as it began to do in architecture, though not in town-planning and still less in landscaping; and right down to the end of the Regency, design went on evolving and being refined hand in hand with a developing civilization, its increasing grace matching the general elegance of life as lived by a fortunate minority. What seems so strange to us today in our different social mood is that such sensitiveness to and delight in visual beauty, the insistent demand for it and the brilliantly answering supply, should have co-existed along with such appalling callousness and injustice, with the bland acceptance of slavery abroad and cruel poverty at one's door, with dirt, disease, ignorance on the one hand and savagely repressive laws, and (to us) indefensible privilege on the other, as an ordained and tolerable way of life.

The lace-ruffled hand of the Regency squire offering the

elegantly enamelled snuff-box so gracefully to a suitably civilized recipient of the compliment might well have written, not an hour before, a magisterial sentence of death for some poor neighbour for stealing a hen to feed his starving family. Certainly we have advanced in the past century or so, but certainly, too, we have retreated—retreated from beauty, blindly, needlessly and, I would say, to our immeasurable loss in happiness.

Yet though we now have more than a century's accumulation of ugliness around us so that being blind cuts out a deal of anguish as well as of pleasure, and although we have acquired many bad habits that are still fatal to visual beauty, from gimcrack jerry-building to crudely blatant advertising—we were in much worse case only fifty, even twenty years ago, before the tide began effectively to turn in favour of better designing for things that are, after all, the essential practical background of our lives.

It was in this same festival year of 1951 that our own budding hopes for a new general responsibility towards our environment were severely nipped and our immediate Welsh prospect over-clouded by a monstrous threat.

This was an official proposal to imprison all our rivers, streams and waterfalls, great and small, in pipes and compel them to earn their living by turning turbines to pump electricity into a linking network of overhead cables.

This we decided had to be combated by all possible means and our own attack took the form of a satirical Peacockian 'send-up' called *Headlong Down The Years*, mostly written by Amabel, who cast me in the role of Squire Headlong. Richard Hughes' prologue thus described it:

> No doubt it is very edifying when someone who came to scoff remains to pray; but it is not very amusing. For the onlooker it is a good deal more agreeable when the opposite sort of thing happens: when someone who came to preach tears up his script, and remains to dazzle and entertain.
>
> A metamorphosis of this sort seems to have overtaken the authors of the cheerful display of fireworks you shall now witness. Being filled with wrath (as I am) against certain statutory proposals, they had set out to marshal their arguments according to the convention of philosophical dialogue. Wisely, they took Thomas Love Peacock for

their model, and even borrowed his Headlong Hall for their setting. Then something seems to have happened. The personified Points-of-view, the stiff little stylised puppets they were handling began to wriggle between their fingers with a life of their own, turned into living characters (often in the literal sense, and wearing disguises so diaphanous as to be scarcely even . . . decent). The bare framework of story burst into leaf: the talk proliferated, till it far exceeded the bounds of the original set theme. Don't suppose that then the gunpowder *all* ran out of the heels of the Authors' boots. Their anger was not dissipated; but it was, most of it, transmuted into wit and slapstick.

But I am to say something more in an epilogue: for the present I must not stand any longer between you and this eloquent, absurd little tale.

In so far as our 'absurd little tale' did focus attention on the disasters to Welsh amenity that the then North Wales Power Company's hydro-electric projects would entail, and contributed to their abandonment—much of the credit for this happy issue ought to go to this same epilogue wherein was marshalled the damning evidence, technical, social, economic and scenic, with all the forensic skill and force of a prosecuting Q.C. It is pleasant indeed when an exercise so agreeable in itself turns out to have also been effective.

That was a battle we claimed to have won. But, as we prophesied in our little satire, the attack is even now (1970) being renewed, though far less barbarously and with the defence far better organized. In our story, when Sir Hercules Megawat, the hydro-electric boss, tried to convert the opposition to his grandiose 'progressive' views, Squire Headlong's response was a blunt, 'We shall fight again'. And so we shall.

Now I am recklessly launched on quite another David *v.* Goliath contest where my defeat seems certain, though I cannot believe that the architectural 'Brutalism' that I am tilting against can survive for ever, and I seem to be no longer alone in my disenchantment, but now supported in my revolt by various eminencies who too appear to be on the recoil from continued submission to de-humanized technology.

I think there will soon be more, even the *Architectural Review* being now apparently in the throes of an agonizing reappraisement. In America Lewis Mumford has long been with me; in France, François Spoerry, with his Port Grimaud, and with Peter Shepheard, the President of the R.I.B.A., also taking a new look at the architectural status quo, I begin to feel that my own gloomy assessment is not just senile grumpiness.

On the other hand, Lionel Brett's important new book *Parameters and Images*, dealing brilliantly and in depth with the reaction between men and buildings throughout history down to today, displays a philosophic confidence in the future that I should dearly like to share.

Meanwhile I stubbornly go along with Goodhart-Rendal's: 'In buildings made for the service of man, architecture begins where utilitarianism leaves off, endowing practical contrivance with aesthetic significance.' I would also subscribe to Edwin Lutyens' aphorism: 'Architecture, with its love and passion, begins where function is achieved.'

On 10 December 1951 I was due to travel up to London for some fixture that involved catching the early morning train and the reluctant setting of our alarm clock for 5 a.m.

That may have saved our lives, for once awake, Amabel sniffed and said, 'Someone must be burning paper—do have a look.'

What was only a smell in our bedroom became palpable smoke on the landing and when I opened the door of the drawing-room and switched on the light, I was met by a blast of heat and smoke so dense that the chandelier only showed up as a diffused red glow. As there were no flames, I dashed down through the smoke to the library immediately below and flung open the door on a blazing furnace, my well-loved terrier, Pennant, lying dead on the threshold.

Both floor and ceiling were alight—one of the pair of gilded caryatids that supported a main beam already prostrate and ablaze, as was the beam itself (built into the chimney as we afterwards discovered) and most of the furniture. Making for the telephone at the far end of the room I fell into a hole burnt in the floor, but not right through it into the old brewhouse below, and reached the instrument only to find its cable already gone

While a messenger ran off to the village to ring up the Portmadoc fire-brigade from there, the rest of us did what we could with extinguishers and a chain of buckets, mostly antique leather ones, but to little or no effect.

Fanned by a full gale, the fire raged through the house with frightening speed, feeding eagerly on the old timber floors, panelling and partitions, so that from miles away the fire-brigade saw the old Plas lit up in all its windows against the night sky and its dark hillside as though for some great festivity. But despite the assembly of five brigade appliances and their crews, it was soon clear that the fire would win, the hiss of the water jets pumped from the fountain pool being drowned by the roar and crackle of the flames, the crash of falling timbers and the whistle of the cruel wind.

As the windows were one by one consumed, the inrush of air soon sent the fire leaping up through the attics and then through the roof itself which collapsed on the ruins below, each section sending up a great fountain of flame and sparks—the signal of our final and utter defeat.

For by mid-morning nothing remained but the massive three-foot thick outer stone walls, or almost nothing, because we had too loyally yet vainly concentrated on striving to save the house itself instead of salvaging its contents, much of which we might otherwise have rescued. As it was, all we saved were a few odd pictures and a few pieces of furniture from the dining-room in the sixteenth-century wing, which was not utterly destroyed, whereas from the main four-storied seventeenth-century block all was lost save for one table and one book (Bickham's *Universal Penman*) from the library.

So there we were with the pyjamas and dressing-gowns we were still dressed in as about our only surviving possessions—even my spectacles and false teeth having perished as well as of course all files, papers and records of all sorts.

Our memories for engagements being anyhow shockingly unreliable, we put a notice in *The Times* saying that as the fire had destroyed our home and with it all letters and engagement books, we begged indulgence should we fail to keep any fixtures made but not remembered.

Fortunately I had deposited the more valuable and interesting family papers on permanent loan with the National Library of Wales, but our best and seldom-used eighteenth-century silver was stored in the attics, and all we have now to remember it by is a great sheet of metal formed by the molten silver dripping down through the house from top to bottom to form a pool on the slab floor of the brewhouse, there to solidify.

When later, I saw a photograph in *Country Life* of the twin brother of our own Paul de Lamerie tea-urn which had brought £5,000 at auction in London, I felt even sadder about our silver puddle, scarcely worth a fiver.

Most foolishly, I had done nothing about the insurance, since I had only partially occupied the house as a bachelor before the first war, so that our cover was derisory, less than a fifth of what it should have been. However, so much anyway needed doing to the house in the way of internal improvements and modernization and I so much enjoyed the opportunity of at last carrying out my long-cherished ideas, I might well have been suspected of arson had the insurance been anything like adequate.

As it was, there were all sorts of difficulties; building of any kind was still subject to strictly enforced licences and cost limits, whilst materials of all sorts were still very scarce and expensive.

Scouring Britain, I was only able to find just two suitable steel joists, the rest of the reinforcement for the new floors (now to be all of concrete with oak parquet) being most luckily available in the form of old tramway rails from long-abandoned slate quarries on the estate, of which we managed to recover a hundred or so.

The reconstruction was carried out by my own estate building gang under my direct supervision. It took a full two years and involved scraping together suitable materials and components from wherever I could find them—dressed stone for new chimney stacks presented by a neighbour whose house I was rebuilding, roof timbers and slates from Llanfrothen's old National School that I bought and demolished, a truck-load of old eighteenth-century doors and mantelpieces from Crowthers in London, also panelling pilasters and cornices from my own store of architectural oddments gradually accumulated over the years and stored at Portmeirion.

Luckily, too, we had quite a bit of our furniture there on loan as well as with friends in London, so that by recalling all these scattered pieces we had a good nucleus of old and familiar things with which to soften the impact of the necessary new acquisitions.

As to ourselves, we first took refuge in our daughter's house, then with Patrick Blackett[1] hard by, then in our cook's cottage only across the courtyard (no kitchen, no cook), and finally in the Chantry at Portmeirion, occupying the studio I had built for Augustus John.

The whole episode gave me a very proper pretext for a monument—surmounting a mound of debris carted up from the ruin—which I raised at the end of the avenue facing the house and on the edge of the chasm, thus inscribed:

THIS FLAMING URN RAISED ON THE ASHES OF THEIR HOME BY CLOUGH AND AMABEL WILLIAMS-ELLIS CELEBRATES THE REBUILDING OF PLAS BRONDANW 1935 TWO YEARS FROM ITS BURNING AND THE NAMES OF THOSE TO WHOM IT OWES ITS RESTORATION, VIZ:
WM. DAVIES. TOM DAVIES. OWEN EDWARDES. HARRY PIKE. HUGH OWEN. ROBERT JONES AND R. O. WILLIAMS.

[1] Now Lord Blackett, O.M., C.H.

Chapter Eighteen

Kaleidoscope

Although eightieth birthdays are nowadays entirely unremarkable, mine did nonetheless provoke, and for no good reason, considerable celebration. Partly I think because though suspected (rightly) of being ripe for our Golden Wedding, we had refused to confirm all such rumours lest kind friends who couldn't afford it should embarrass us with presents we did not want. It also let us off giving or attending a party, which, we later gathered, was considered as verging on the fraudulent.

As birthdays could not be similarly hushed up, three quite formidable parties were in fact separately organized necessarily but rather confusingly on three different dates, so that it even betrayed *The Times* into error in its 'Birthdays Today' the following year.

First came a very large, rather daunting dinner in the Harcourt room at the House of Commons, organized by Bobby Carter, Director of the Architectural Association, but secretly abetted, as it emerged, by Amabel. Then an open-air hilltop 'View party' given by Christabel, Lady Aberconway, at the Drum House I had built for her up our valley and finally a vast affair at Portmeirion, given by its Trustees—bands, fireworks, flood-lighting, gala dinner and a ball—the lot—most happily in perfect weather again, as at the Drum House.

In order to have a dinner given in the House of Commons at all, the host (officially) must be a Member, a function admirably fulfilled by my brother-in-law John Strachey, who made the first after-dinner speech followed by Sir Robert Matthew, President of the R.I.B.A., and half a dozen others, all wonderfully entertaining and to the point considering their theme, and indeed anyhow. How I wished I had had the enviable and apparently effortless wit and eloquence of Sir Alan Herbert or Bernard Darwin (far and away the two best and most entertaining after-dinner speakers I have ever listened to), wherewith to respond. But all the other warmhearted birthday speeches were far above the norm for such occasions, as one would expect from such contributors as Lord Holford, Dilys Powell, Peter Shepheard, Lord Esher, Christopher Hussey, Maxwell Fry (who declaimed a long ode) and Amabel. The proceedings concluded with the presentation of an elegant miniature Japanese conifer in its appropriate vase, symbolic only of the fine weeping elm tree standard that in due season followed it, and was planted on the quay at Portmeirion with an appropriately inscribed plaque. It flourishes exceedingly, which is held to be of good augury.

My chief trouble with speeches is my capricious memory which, though retrospectively well enough, can sometimes let me down utterly when attempting an extempore—especially an important one. I still vividly recall one such at a big Oxford Conference where I was struck down with a sudden and violent attack of 'flu and begged the Chairman, Lord Samuel, to let me off. Sympathetic and kind as always, he said, 'I am terribly sorry, but I have no one else at all to put up in your place—you must do the best you can.'

I was pushed to the rostrum, my legs wobbling, the audience a mere blur, my voice a croak, and my mind a complete blank, except (by some freak) for a fragment of verse from a recent *New Yorker*.

So I began, 'Will you please bear with me if I start by reciting a little poem, the relevance of which will be apparent as I proceed, if indeed I proceed at all?'

> Forgotten, forgotten, forgotten,
> Are the things I fain would recall
> My memory always was rotten
> But now it holds nothing at all.
>
> They picked up a man with amnesia
> I read in my paper today
> He said he had been in Rhodesia
> And spoke in a scholarly way.
>
> He knew a few phrases in Finnish
> He was wearing a little goatee
> His hair was inclined to be thinnish
> Good gracious—Perhaps it was *me*!

It worked. . . . The audience having expected solemnity, were startled into laughter and shocked into puzzled attention whilst I, for my part, found that I too had, in my anguish, been somehow jerked out of my amnesia and back into adequate consciousness. But it was so nearly a fiasco that it still haunts me faintly, and I keep those verses in mind ready for use again at need, like a life-belt that once had served me well.

But now, approaching ninety, I accept forgetfulness as a perfectly natural first failure of my faculties, not altogether without its advantages. Anyway I have given up apologizing. I just remember, or I don't, and say so. Not that I was ever in Lord Inman's class, he, so he told me, having got into trouble, through having an apparently fadeless photographic memory that enabled him to reproduce whole pages of the set books in his written tripos examination word for word, a faculty that had to be explained and demonstrated to the not-unnaturally suspicious examiners.

But that there are worse than me is suggested by the 'joke' on the back of a matchbox I picked up the other day:

> PATIENT: I have lost my memory.
> DOCTOR: When did you lose it?
> PATIENT: Lose what?

It is the *capriciousness* of mine that puzzles me. Why for instance does Max Beerbohm's seventieth birthday party stand out so crystal clear in my mind's eye—and ear—amongst all the welter of more 'memorable' happenings during the last war? It must have been something in Max himself.

There he was, standing up at a lectern responding to the felicitations of our committee of 'Seven Men' and the seventy guests, conveyed through our spokesman Desmond McCarthy, thanking us for the nostalgic little Victorian music-hall show we had contrived to mount for him and for a case of quite tolerable wine that had, by then, been even harder to come by. Amongst many other typical self-depreciative asides I most vividly recall: 'I know that I am accused of not caring about causes, but that is quite untrue. I *love* causes, but, you must concede, the effects are often lamentable.'

It is of course my memory—my capricious memory—that has largely dictated the actual contents of this book—childhood and youth being now more clearly remembered than yesterday, and anyhow only bits and pieces of a long life's experience can be compressed within the covers of a book of reasonable length and I am well aware that my selection of themes has been governed by no very logical scheme.

There are indeed plenty of significant or enjoyable episodes omitted that I might just as well (or better) have referred to than those I have in fact included. Not descriptions of odd places visited around the world which can be tedious indeed, but of some of the adventures and misadventures incidental to foreign travel that are still vividly remembered. Especially when seafaring whether in home waters, around the Caribbean or in the Mediterranean, all fraught with happenings, happy, cautionary or, occasionally, dangerous.

Twice we chartered the same fine 30-ton schooner yacht *Oronsay*, the first year to explore Corsica and Elba and the adjoining Italian coast, the next to circumnavigate Sicily—ourselves and our guests as crew under an admirable professional English skipper. On both cruises the weather was capricious. Once we were driven back under virtually bare poles a whole day's sailing in a full gale that rated us honourable mention in the Italian press and sensational coverage on the local radio.

Seeking shelter for the night before this buffeting, we ran

gratefully in to the harbour of a little island only to discover that it was a penal settlement, and landing utterly forbidden. The harbour-master would not even allow us to lie alongside the quay until our ever-resourceful skipper somehow managed to persuade him that Lionel Brett and I were both English noblemen of the very highest distinction, who he would disoblige at his peril. This inspired deception brought the island's governor on to the telephone and we were after all graciously permitted to spend a secure and peaceful night, though still not to land.

Then one placid moonlit night cruising under power off the southern coast of Sicily we were suddenly boarded by a vociferous mob of piratical looking fishermen who claimed we had over-run and destroyed their tunny nets. And so it seemed we had, as our propeller was all fouled up and took hours to free. Our skipper patiently pointed out, as best he could with his meagre Italian and even less Sicilian, that it was all their own fault for having failed to mark their nets with the regulation lighted buoys—but without effect; it was ten of them to six of us. So we had to agree that two of these pirates should sail on with us to the next port where the dispute could perhaps be justly settled before the British Consul—as it was. I have since been back to Corsica on a professional ploy, where we were caught by the French General Strike, but it is to Elba that I should most like to return for a more thorough exploration.

A. P. Herbert maintains that had the allies not bilked Napoleon of his promised subsidies, he would have been perfectly content to remain as the improving landlord of his idyllic little kingdom. He certainly did wonders in his nine months' residence, but I wonder. Certainly *I* should have found it heaven but, apart from our shared interest in building and town and country planning, the Emperor and I have singularly little in common.

A lecture tour of the British zone in Germany soon after the end of Hitler's war had its moments. Under high auspices I was able to see a lot of what the defeated Germans were already doing in the way of reconstruction and *new* construction too, with beaver-like industry and ingenuity and a care for detail and craftsmanship that astonished me as I reported at length in the *Manchester Guardian*. The scale of destruction in places like Hamburg and Hanover that I had known, and in Essen and elsewhere was truly appalling and one little town where I had delightedly sketched long ago, had completely disappeared. And yet, here and there, new beauty was already valiantly reappearing, which greatly lightened my depression.

Often I was put up at one of the palatial *Luftwaffe* headquarters where the airmen had clearly been the country's favourite sons and given every amenity including fine architecture and—rather startlingly—vomitoria.

I was allowed to visit the French and American zones, but not the Russian and in the first indeed, found myself, of all things, nostalgically gambling amidst the faded Edwardian splendours of the Baden-Baden casino with a Russian Grand Duke—about equally faded—now a teacher of languages.

My visit ended at the Channel ports, and I had been so scared by my uncomfortable flight out in an unconverted bomber that I elected to return home by sea—which, standing on deck, as we did, shoulder to shoulder in our life-jackets and drenched with spray in a fresh gale, was no great improvement.

A subsequent Middle East lecture tour under War Office and British Council auspices found me astonishingly snowbound in Damascus for a whole week, which somewhat crippled my programme though I did manage to keep my Kurdish fixture at Mosul. At Baghdad a helicopter was put at my disposal from which to study the tangled complexities of the old town's lay-out before meeting the relevant authorities to discuss town-planning. I had got into some trouble with the British Council for thumbing a lift in a thunderstorm from Cyprus to Beirut in a plucky little 'unauthorized' local plane in an effort to catch up with my schedule. I was sternly told that had it killed me ('serve you right if it had'), my widow would have had no compensation as their insurance cover specifically excluded my poor little aircraft. So much for zeal and enterprise!

For a week or two I was the rather fish-out-of-water honorary civilian member of the Brigadier's mess (a round dozen of them) at Ismailia—whence I was wafted here and there to do my stuff. When I met the C.I.G.S. Field-Marshal Lord Slim at some party he said, 'I gather you are telling my chaps here about the wonderful plans for reconstruction at home—new towns and all that. Fine, of course, but please don't make it all sound *too* attractive. It's hard enough to keep units up to strength here as it is, and you are only making it harder.' Zeal discouraged again!

I was shown all the sights in and around Cairo including of course the pyramids and the Sphinx by moonlight, and the (to me) far more exciting artifacts from Tutankamen's tomb that might well humble us moderns by their sophisticated virtuosity. As a finale the sight of King Farouk at a night club provided a startling anti-climax.

Foolishly setting out late one night to explore the labyrinthine and rather sinister old city on my own and without a map, I was very soon completely lost and had to accept an offer from a pestering and unpleasing youth to get me clear of a riot that had erupted, out of the maze, and back into recognizable civilization. Instead he conducted me to an outlandish and evil-seeming shop, where it was made pretty clear that I should get no further unless I spent an adequate sum and handsomely overpaid my devious guide. They tried hard to sell me an extremely expensive aphrodisiac that they said they sent every fortnight to an English duke whom they named, but I managed to get off with a few bottles of scent. I wonder if His Grace knows or cares that he is being thus advertised as a satisfied customer.

My last visit to the USA was rather oddly via Fiji and Mexico, where I found Precolumbian artifacts too sinister and Spanish colonial rococo too overwhelming, even for me. Though lavishly entertained by kind tycoons to whom I had introductions and shown many scenic splendours—the political and economic realities of the country rather tarnished one's pleasure, as the desperate poverty of India had certainly clouded my appreciation of its splendours, so that there too any aesthetic judgements of mine must be deeply suspect.

I could not like the so-celebrated ultra-modern Mexico City university buildings though I did like their architect, which made a joint broadcast I was asked to give with him a rather embarrassingly delicate egg-dance.

Flying on to New York, I was soon airborne again, bound for some destination that I do not now remember and in fact never reached—a night flight that I shall never forget. We had soon run into a really full-scale storm with blinding rain and lightning, and were being tossed about by the turbulence in a way that made one think longingly of old-fashioned land-bound travel. When it seemed fully time for our blessed touch-down, an announcement came over the intercom from the flight deck—'Sorry, but conditions are reported as being too bad for landing at our scheduled stop so I am overflying it and will land you at . . . where it's not so bad. All being well, you should be able to get a flight back all right in the morning.'

I think we were all relieved by this confident-sounding official message that the plane was expected to land in one piece *somewhere* even if elsewhere than intended—all, that is, but one hulking sore-head of a sea-lawyer who, as soon as we were safely down, started to accuse the captain and navigator of incompetence and/or cowardice and to threaten that he would sue the airline for breach of contract as well as for damages for an important missed appointment. He was so unreasonable and offensively unfair that for once—perhaps because I had myself been frightened—I did rather lose my temper and took him on in single combat—not by fisticuffs when he would probably have downed me—but by a loud and fierce denunciation of his primitive selfishness and disregard for others, many of whom were doubtless just as much inconvenienced as himself, but whose lives he was blandly prepared to have put at hazard for his own private ends. Surrounded by the rest of the gaping passengers, I asked those of them who agreed with me to raise their hands. All did, and our trouble-maker slunk muttering away. If I ever encounter the creature again it will probably be as a hi-jacker—when angry rhetoric would be unlikely to prevail.

My eager determination to see Williamsburgh as against any of the modern wonders they wanted to show me, seemed to shock and surprise most of the American architects I met—but I insisted, and I shocked them all the more on my return by declaring it to hold lessons for all of them that they badly needed to learn.

It is indeed a most masterly and scholarly restoration and re-creation of the little regional capital as it was in the eighteenth century and, despite its many fine original buildings that survive, it is to that extent artificial. But for its quiet and leafy serenity, its architectural good manners and refreshing adherence to the human scale—I found its ambience almost magical.

My various American adventures both by air and sea had little architectural significance, but my continued island hunting had. Crete, Cyprus, Rhodes, Malta, Capri, Corfu, and other lesser Greek and Italian islands all contributed something to my stored memories of harmonious building.

Greece itself I revisited at the invitation of its government as one of a four-man delegation led by Lord Crawford to advise on conservation and development. King Constantine seemed to be the only one at all alive to the very real and special amenity problems facing the country, and though I wrote a long report and a broadcast script, both translated into Greek, as well as a *Times* article—the looming political crisis that ended in the King's departure, ended too our hopes of getting our advice accepted, let alone acted upon.

Tunisia on the other hand seemed to need no advice. It appears to know exactly what it is doing in the way of development and town and country planning and is already reaping the rewards of its enlightened policies, as it deserves to do as (from my own point of view) the most progressive and civilized of all Mediterranean-fringing countries.

But even the poor old Côte d'Azur that has suffered over a century of gross misdevelopment now has at least one redeeming feature, the quite new and independent little town of Port Grimaud that the French architect François Spoerry has founded and is even now completing. Here, on hitherto disregarded saltmarshes at the head of the gulf of St. Tropez, M. Spoerry has planned and built an almost Venice-like town where all the traffic routes are canals and lagoons excavated to a brilliantly conceived plan, the individual houses in terraces and clusters each with its miniature patio garden and little quay for the mooring of its yacht or boat. There is no internal motor traffic, public transport is by a sedate motor barge, a marine bus, that quietly circumnavigates the whole complex all day, picking up and setting down at the various little jetties—for free. All the houses are different each from each though with an overall Provençal family resemblance, the detailing sensitive, the wide colour-range harmonious. Already a discreet hotel and a score or so excellent restaurants and little shops are serving the place while the town hall and church share a central island to themselves reached by an elegant high-arched bridge.

What is really encouraging about this whole gay adventure is that it is immensely successful economically, there being evidently enough people to appreciate its well-bred simplicity and serenity as against the gross vulgarity of most of the rest of the Riviera.

M. Spoerry and I of course exchange visits—each watching the other's doings, he envious of what he calls Portmeirion's 'verticality', its dramatic changes in level, I of Port Grimaud's perpetual high tide.

Now whenever I need cheering up I just remind myself of this unlikely and so civilized happening on that otherwise dishonoured coast, when I immediately feel that all is not yet lost.

Chapter Nineteen

Adding It Up

Well, there it is, a hop, skip and jump sort of log-book, the equivalent of nearly three generations of variegated activity—but what is there to show for it all? Little enough that matters—except to me.

Children and grandchildren certainly, a dozen or so books, but ephemeral articles, reviews and speeches galore. And what of my proper ploy of architecture? How many actual buildings of what sort and where?

At one time I had a wall-map of the British Isles and a large-scale one of London into which I stuck red-headed pins, as on a war map, to show wherever I was or had been working. It was amusing to see little clusters sometimes forming here and there, never knowing where this welcome clotting might next appear.

Then I had all the counterfoil stubs of my standardized architects' certificate books right from the beginning which automatically registered every single job, the clients' and contractors' names and its final cost—but they perished together with all other records when our home was gutted by fire.

So now it's a matter of memory only and an unreliable one at that. But the buildings listed in the appendix I can vouch for—and as being very roughly in order of date.

There are quite certainly some omissions and smaller items have been intentionally left out such as odd cottages here and there, church furnishings such as pulpits, fonts, altar ornaments, memorials and vestments as well as specially designed domestic decorations and furniture. The record for what it is worth starts *about* 1905, and carries on chronologically as near as may be.

All my adult life I have been acutely conscious of my country's visual impact—often despairingly but after our return from our last tour abroad I had in no way foreseen how much I could still be moved by the gracious seemliness of England. Even the very drive to London from Heathrow showed a certain civilized concern for environment that London itself also seemed to do, as few other great cities I have seen in recent years could really match. Even the train journey across the Midlands down to Wales displayed a countryside still marvellously unsullied, whilst back at home the appealing beauty all around cast its spell more powerfully than ever. Yet for half a century and more I had been crying havoc and chanting Milton's dirge: 'Farewell happy fields where joy for ever dwells, hail horrors', as though we were already doomed to become a race of mechanized men in a macadamized desert, our one hope of salvation the emulation of less prodigal nations. Now I am not so sure. I almost feel that we British have perhaps at long last set a new course away from crass barbarity and may even yet lead the world towards a livelier respect for the setting and background of our life on earth which could yet be made so beautiful if we cared to have it so. Quite suddenly, in short, I am (at this moment) no longer a despairful Jeremiah but a-bubble with new-found hope.

Just the effect of a brief holiday abroad? Perhaps. But still (again for the moment) 'Sursum Corda'!

All very well, it may be said, as regards my own small sector of public concern whether I am right or wrong—but what about the far greater problems that are now looming up to confront and menace all humanity—everywhere?

The population explosion, ultimately threatening global famine, violence and actual wars whether nuclear, chemical, biological or not, the prodigal waste of natural resources, the pollution of land, rivers, sea and air and now, it may be, of outer space itself.

From the terrifying evidence of man's reckless behaviour towards his natural environment presented to us by such disinterested observers as Lewis Mumford, Lord Ritchie Calder, Prince Philip, Dr. Fraser Darling in his Reith lectures, and the rest, ultimate catastrophy seems certain *unless* we react to all these threats, intelligently, vigorously and *soon*.

If we don't—why then my little amenity ploys will have been no more than frivolous fiddling whilst Rome burnt.

All the same—if it's to be extermination anyhow I should certainly prefer to die in some flowery fell than in a befouled and stinking ditch.

But forgetting all that, I am (at this moment) trying to think more objectively and kindly of present-day London—essential London that is, as apart from its monstrous outgrowths. But it is difficult to be fair where old affectations are involved, and to allow for all the pressures and new conditions that have sometimes made change inevitable even when undesirable. Its architectural balance sheet has of course undergone violent fluctuations, both the gains and losses within my memory having been enormous. Hard as I find it to admire the generality of modern buildings, I at any rate prefer the negative impersonality of what has gone up since the Second World War to the mongrel elaboration of that which mostly followed the first. On balance and despite certain crass barbarities (e.g. the slaughter of Nash's Regent Street) and the criminal negligence that has resulted in blazingly flagrant missed chances (e.g. the new Kingsway) I must nonetheless confess that, including the city, central London is after all more seemly and of course infinitely cleaner both overhead and underfoot than in my Victorian youth. Sir Compton Mackenzie, almost my exact contemporary, insists that no humane person remembering the dirt and squalor of east-end London in the eighties and nineties can be other than thankful for the welfare state.

Here and there the gains have been obvious. The present Ritz Hotel (a most scholarly exercise in the Beaux Arts, Louis Seize style) replaced a grubby old predecessor of no distinction whatsoever which I had condemned as ludicrously unworthy of its superb site at first encounter in the 1890s.

Apsley House, now cleaned and freed from clutter, stands grandly isolated, as it should. On the other hand both Devonshire and Lansdowne Houses with their courts and gardens have gone, also palatial Dorchester House with its Stephens sculptures to make way for the hotel that bears its name. Gone too is Grosvenor House, as also Holland House, where I must have attended about its last party before it was bombed into ruin. Where churches have been restored I would say that the work has been done with scholarly scrupulousness, some interiors indeed having gained far more than they have lost by the elimination of irrelevant clutter.

Though so very far from being a Londoner, the place has a strange way of persistently invading my dreams, and I dream a lot. I have visions of familiar street-scapes purged of all present blemishes, the best buildings still there as though fresh-minted but supported and often surpassed by the new ones I have dreamed up to replace unworthy neighbours. Even more often I am walking down, say, St. James's Street, and suddenly, to my delight, I discover that the turning westwards next to Brooks Club leads into a noble avenue at the end of which I am in honest-to-goodness English countryside borrowed from some painting by Constable or Crome or Richard Wilson or specially invented for that night only. I explore and admire and of course plan meddlesome 'improvements' about which I get so excited that I wake up and gradually realize that the city of my dreams is not yet, nor ever will be.

Yet exhilarated by my vision and still not fully awake to harsh reality, I wander on imagining so many citizens having my sort of dreams that one day they resolve to see them actually realized, and do.

It will not be for a long time yet, but being obstinate, I refuse to believe it will be never.

Appendix

Commissions (from about 1905 in approximate sequence)

OXFORD AREA:	A small institution. 4 small and 1 largish house. 2 medium-sized alterations and additions. Sports pavilion (for University College).
CAERNARVONSHIRE:	Aberuchaf Cottage, Abersoch. New farmhouse (Glasfryn Estate).
CAMBRIDGE:	Steam laundry reconstruction.
BUCKINGHAMSHIRE:	Village Hall (Stone, nr. Aylesbury).
SOMERSET:	Cottages in the park (Cricket St. Thomas, nr. Chard).
SURREY:	New farmstead (Byfleet).
ESSEX:	Restorations and alterations (Moynes Park).
SURREY:	Alterations (Normandy Park).
HEREFORDSHIRE:	Alterations, additions and new lodge (Burton Court).
KENT:	Princess Christian's Farm Colony.
ANGLESEY:	Rectory (Nr. Pentraeth).
CAERNARVONSHIRE:	Rectory and church (Pentrefelin).
BRECONSHIRE:	Rebuilding on old site and general estate works (Llangoed Castle). Church restoration (Crickadarn).
CO. ANTRIM:	Village square (Cushendun).
CARMARTHENSHIRE:	Hunting box and stables (Brechfa).
ANGLESEY:	Sham ruins (on islet off Holyhead).
CAMBRIDGESHIRE:	Old People's Homes (Swavesey).
WARWICKSHIRE:	School reconstruction, farmhouse, monument and new gates (Wroxall Abbey).
MERIONETH:	Restoration (Plas Hen, Dolgellau).

WARWICKSHIRE	Cottage group (Guys Cliff).
SURREY:	House (Nr. Woking).
	Cottage group (Compton).
LONDON:	Entire replanning and rebuilding of Battersea Dogs' Home and of country quarantine quarters.
MIDDLESEX:	House (Stanmore).
	House (Nr. Uxbridge).
BUCKINGHAMSHIRE:	Hunting box and stable alterations (Nr. Finmere).
OXFORDSHIRE:	Restoration and alterations (Wardington Manor).
MONTGOMERYSHIRE:	Alterations and restoration (Llechwyddygarth Hall, Llangynog).
HERTFORDSHIRE:	Additions (Markyate cell).
WARWICKSHIRE:	Small industrial hamlet (Nr. Leamington).
NORTHAMPTON-SHIRE:	Alterations (Stoke Bruern Park).
	Alterations (Dower House, Easton Neston).
	Entrance gates (Gayton House).
KENT:	Alterations (Cleve Court).
WARWICKSHIRE:	Reconstruction and additions (Wolverton Court).
OXFORDSHIRE:	Further alterations and additions (Wardington Manor).
ESSEX:	*Country Life* competition house (Gidea Park).
BERKSHIRE:	Ridgeway House (Nr. Wellington College).
KENT:	Alterations (Strawberry Hill).
MERIONETH:	New Lodge, orangery and gardens (Plas Brondanw).
SURREY:	*Spectator* competition cottage (Marrow Downs).

1914: Over 4 years' gap in practice whilst away at the war and 3 months thereafter as a civil servant.

MERIONETH:	War Memorial Tower (Garreg).

Appendix

MIDDLESEX:	Co-ordinating architect to the Palace of Industry and designs for various pavilions and some hundred individual displays (British Empire Exhibition, Wembley).
ESSEX:	Alterations (Gilwell Park).
CO. ANTRIM:	Rebuilding after destruction by fire (Glenmona House).
	Further additions to Cushendun village, Lord McNaughton Memorial Hall and School, Giant's Causeway.
	Bushmill Central School.
FLINTSHIRE:	New Youth Hostel (Loggerheads).
GUERNSEY:	Alterations (Government House).
CAERNARVONSHIRE:	Alterations (Portmadoc Memorial Hospital).
SURREY:	Alterations to pottery.
	Ex-Servicemen's housing scheme (Ashtead).
MERIONETHSHIRE:	Hospital (Blaenau Ffestiniog).
HAMPSHIRE:	Alterations (St. Cross Mill, Winchester).
SUSSEX:	Restoration (house nr. Ticehurst).
CAERNARVONSHIRE:	Restoration and additions (Carregfelin).
LONDON:	House, studio and garden (Swiss Cottage).
	Group of 3 houses (Hampstead).
BUCKINGHAMSHIRE:	Restoration and additions (Savoy Court, Denham).
	Alterations, restoration, additions and new buildings (for use as public school). (Stowe).
BERKSHIRE:	Alterations, restoration, additions and new buildings for use as Bonar Law College, with new hamlet adjoining (Ashridge Park).
OXFORDSHIRE:	Cumnor House.
HAMPSHIRE:	Gardens and temples (Eaglehurst).
	Farmery (Avon Tyrel).
CAERNARVONSHIRE:	Summit station (Snowdon).
BELFAST:	Church of Christ Scientist.
	House.
	School.

HAMPSHIRE:	House (Nr. Romsey).
CHESHIRE:	Reconstruction and gardens (Bolesworth Castle).
	Cottage group.
MERIONETH:	Initial alterations. Conversion of old house and buildings to hotel use and erecting first new houses. Angel, Neptune, etc. (Portmeirion).
SOMERSET:	Alterations and restoration (Kilve Court).
HAMPSHIRE:	Country house (Nr. Andover).
KENT:	House (Littlestone).
MERIONETH:	Conversion to hotel (Deudraeth Castle).
HAMPSHIRE:	House (Nr. Burley, New Forest).
DEVON:	House (Nr. Ashburton).
SURREY:	House (Stapledown, nr. Shere).
	House (Nr. Walton Heath).
HERTFORDSHIRE:	Alteration and additions to house (Royston).
MERIONETH:	Doctor's house and surgery (Penrhyndeudraeth).
	White Cottage (Nr. Portmeirion).
SURREY:	Girls' boarding school (Nr. Guildford).
BUCKINGHAMSHIRE:	Alterations and additions, new lodge and gardens (Great Hundridge Manor).
SURREY:	Restoration (Milton Court).
SOMERSET:	Alterations (house nr. Burnham).
SURREY:	Extensions, alterations and conversion to hotel (Newland's Corner).
	New country house and cottage (Harrowhill Copse).
CAERNARVONSHIRE:	Store (Pwllheli Co-op).
	House (Pencaenewydd).
OXFORDSHIRE:	Alterations (Cross Hill House, Adderbury).
SHROPSHIRE:	Alterations (Attingham Park).
	Alterations (Aitcham House).
	Alterations (Layton Hall).

Appendix

LONDON:	New Ladies' Carlton Club and adjoining swimming pool. Grosvenor Crescent (partly bombed and now demolished). English Speaking Union Club, Charles Street. New Ladies' Annexe to Oxford and Cambridge Club, Pall Mall. Bladen Lodge, The Boltons (Complete reconstruction and embellishment, including gardens—entirely obliterated by a land-mine and now occupied by a new school). No. 8 Hill Street (reconstructed with new ballroom, mews annexe and garden). Leicester Square: Marcel Boulestin's first restaurant). Sloane House (alterations). Hampstead: Romney's House, reconstruction. etc., etc.
DENBIGHSHIRE:	Alterations and reconstruction (Coed Coch House).
CHINA: Shanghai:	Palatial official-commercial residence.
Tientsin:	Two smaller residences.
KENT:	Extensions and alterations (Leigh Coppings Farm).
CARMARTHENSHIRE:	Alterations (Laugharne Castle).
MERIONETH:	Brondanw Tower.
ESSEX:	Reconstruction and additions (Hubbards Hall).
HAMPSHIRE:	Two houses (Chichester Harbour). Alterations (Funtington Lodge, Bosham).
HERTFORDSHIRE:	Alterations and additions (Little Cassiobury House).
BERKSHIRE:	New house and gardens: demolished 1967 to make way for a housing estate (Caversham Place, nr. Reading).
LINCOLNSHIRE:	Enlargement and embellishment (Laughton House).

CAERNARVONSHIRE:	New Methodist Chapel (Llanstumddwy). New farmhouse (Pentrefelin).
CARMARTHEN TOWN:	New trunk road bridge for Ministry of Transport.
BERKSHIRE:	Additions (Caversham Heights House).
ESSEX:	New hall and chapel (Bishop's Stortford College).
SURREY:	New House (Plovers Field, Newland's Corner). Restoration (Maids-of-Honour Row, Richmond).
OXFORDSHIRE:	Reconstruction and additions, new gardens and park lay-out, rehabilitation of whole village and upgrading of 3 or 4 lesser country houses on the estate, also church (Cornwell Manor).
HERTFORDSHIRE:	Reconstruction (Hartsbourne Grange).
KENT:	Restaurant (Laughing Water, Cobham).
CAERNARVONSHIRE:	Lay-out and 3 houses (Llanbedrog). Doctor's house and surgery, recasting (Pwllheli).
HERTFORDSHIRE:	House (Nr. Brickenden).
DENBIGHSHIRE:	House (Rhos-on-Sea).
WILTSHIRE:	Alterations and additions (Salisbury Close Training College).
CAERNARVONSHIRE:	House (Deganwy).

1939 and on: Virtual standstill during the years of Hitler's war and thereafter.

MERIONETH:	Maintenance work to make good wartime neglect (Portmeirion and Brandanw Estates).
WORCESTERSHIRE:	Bewdley Town Planning Report.
SOMERSET:	Weston-super-Mare Town Planning Report. House for doctor (with Lionel Brett).
WORCESTERSHIRE:	Redditch Town Planning Report (with Patrick Abercrombie and Lionel Brett).

Appendix

CAERNARVONSHIRE: New post office.
Restoration, Gegin Fawr (Aberdaron).
Restoration (Plas-yn-Rhiw).
New house (Nr. Llanfaelrhys).

BERKSHIRE: Gardens.
Home Farm House (Aston Tirrold Manor).

MERIONETH: Beudy Newydd reconstruction (Civic Trust Award).

MONTGOMERYSHIRE: Alterations (Glanddyfi Castle).

MERIONETH: Total demolition of old mansion and replacement by new (Rhiwlas).

DENBIGHSHIRE: Total demolition of old mansion and replacement by new including picture gallery, garden and pavilion (Voelas).

CAERNARVONSHIRE: National Forest Park Hall.
Warden's House (Beddgelert).
Beach Cafe-Restaurant (Criccieth).

DENBIGHSHIRE: Restaurant (Conway Falls).

PEMBROKE TOWN: Alterations (Old Bridge House).

CAERNARVONSHIRE: Restoration and alterations.
New Lodge (Ty Newydd Llanstumddwy).

MERIONETH: Rebuilding after gutting by fire (Plas Brondanw).
The Drum House, Croesor (Civic Trust Award).

CAERNARVONSHIRE: The Lloyd George Grave, Memorial and Museum.
Memorial gateways and site preparations for County College.
Restoration and additions (Tyn-y-rhos, Brynkir).

DENBIGHSHIRE: Wholesale demolitions and reconstruction, terraces, pavilions, gateways, bridges, new farmhouse, additions to inn, etc. (Nantclwyd Hall). (Civic Trust Award.)

CAERNARVONSHIRE: Reconstruction and enlargement (Nant-y-Glyn).

CO. ANTRIM:	General rehabilitation of the Giant's Causeway surroundings on being taken over by the National Trust.
FLINTSHIRE:	Entrance gates and monument (Bodrhyddan Park).
OXFORDSHIRE:	Crown House and gardens (Barford St. John). Gardens (Prescote Manor).
MERIONETH:	New house (Porth-y-Castell).
YORKSHIRE:	Large-scale enlargement and embellishment and new park lay-out, only partially realized (Dunwood House).
MERIONETH:	Transformation and enlargement (Cwm Bychan Gerddi Blwog). Further new buildings, as intermittently throughout the past forty years and more, doubling the size of Plas Canol, etc. (Portmeirion).
WESTMORLAND:	Complete demolition and replacement (Dalton Hall.)
SHROPSHIRE:	Temple in park (Hatton Grange).
LONDON:	Lloyd George Memorial (Westminster Abbey).
DEVON:	Monument to Caroline Thorpe (Nr. Cobbaton).

In addition to the works listed above, there were perhaps a score or more of schemes, town and country planning, or architectural that, for one reason or another, never got further than the drawing-board, and have, therefore, not been included. Some, however, were almost as time-consuming as if they had actually been realized.

The compiling of the list has borne in upon me the curious geographical limitations of my practice. Nothing whatever in Scotland or Southern Ireland, very little in Northern England, not much in the west, but a heavy concentration in the home counties and in Wales.

I usually had jobs on in London, of which I have mentioned a few, but I never built a block of flats or offices or a shop, nor a factory or a cinema anywhere—nor wanted to.

Index

Abbey Theatre, Dublin, 237
Aberconway, Lady, 263
Abercromby, Sir Patrick, 138, 180, 255
Aberglaslyn, 206
Aberia, *see* Portmeirion
Abersoch, 12, 13, 27, 50, 51
Adlon Hotel, Berlin, 99
Adventure of Building, The, 180
Agenda Club, 96–7
Allen, Clifford, (Lord), 149
Almost Perfect State, The, 174–5
Amlwch, 21
Annan, Lord, 141
Anwyls of Parc, the, 22
Apsley House, 276
Architect, The, 180
Architectural Association, the, 65–6
Architectural Review, the, 258–9
Architecture Club, 176–7
Architecture Here and Now, 180
Architecture of Humanism, The, 192
Arise & Conquer, 235
Arthur of Connaught, Prince, 131
Arundel House, 77
Ashridge Park, 143–4
Astor, Lady, 186
Athenaeum, the, 55
Attlee, Clement, 129

Bach-y-craig, 19
Baden-Powell, Lord, 37, 126–7, 181
Bagnold, Enid, 137
Baldwin, Earl, (Stanley), 144–6
Bardsey Island, 38–40
Barry, Sir Gerald, 181
Battersea Pleasure Gardens, 255–256
Beach-Thomas, Sir William, 180
Beerbohm, Sir Max, 265–6
Bell, Lady, 158
Belvedere Palace, 219
Bennett, Arnold, 158, 208
Berwyn, Catherine de, ('Mam Cymry') 19
Birley, Sir Oswald, 158
Blackett, Patrick, (Lord), 262
Blenheim Palace, 178
Blood, General Sir Bindon, 110
Bonar Law College, 143–4
Boothby, Lord, 221
Brett, Lionel, (Viscount Esher), 255, 259, 264, 267
Britain and the Beast, 180
British Empire Exhibition, Wembley, 151
Brownlow, Lord, 143
Bryce, Annan, 162
Brynkir Hall, 40–1
Buchan, John, (Lord Tweedsmuir), 144
Budberg, Baroness, 158
Burn, Michael, 18
Butler, Dr. Montague, 57–8
Butler, Samuel, 253
Butlin, Sir Billy; and Pwllheli, 243–6; and Skegness, 246

Butterfield & Swire, 169, 251

Cairo, 269
Caledonian Market, the, 100–1
Campbell, Colen, 217
Campbell, Mrs. Patrick, 87
Carlton Club, the Ladies', 146
Carson, Lord, 146
Carter, Bobby, 263
Casson, Sir Hugh, 255
Castle Howard, 178
Cavan, Lord, 118
Chaplin, Charles, 158
Chartwell, 249–50
Cherbourg, 195–6
Chesterton, G. K., 176, 180
Chiswick House, 105–6
Churchill, Sir Winston, 249–50
Cintra, 216
Clark, Sir Kenneth, (now Lord Clark), 235
Clough, A. H., 67, 69
Clough, Annie, 19
Clough, Arthur Hugh, 19
Clough, Sir Richard, 18
Clynnog Fawr, 9
Cockburn, Claude, 228
Cole, Horace de Vere, 58, 78–9
Colefax, Lady, 158
Connaught, Prince Arthur of, 131, 143
Constantine, King of Greece, 271
Cooper-Willis, Euan, 242
Côte d'Azur, 271
Council for the Preservation of Rural England, the, 138
Country Life, 97, 129, 181, 241
Courtauld, Miss, 143
Crawford, Lord, 138, 181, 271
Crawshay-Williams, Rupert, 212–213

Cripps, Sir Stafford, 181
Croesor Valley, 212–13
Cumberland, Duke of, 22
Cunard, Nancy, 221
Cushendun, Lord, 146, 221–2
Cynicht, 95

Daily Telegraph, the, 130, 186
David, Bishop, 141
Davidson, John, (Viscount Davidson), 144, 146, 215
Dawber, Sir Guy, 138
Debatable Land, The, 18
de Lisle, Lord, 217
Derby, Lord, 181
Design & Industries Association, the, 138
Deudraeth Castle, 205
Devonshire House, 276
Diaghilev, 158
Dorchester House, 276
Dublin, 236–7
Duveen, Lord, 158
Dwryd estuary, 206

Easton Glebe, 158
Easton Lodge, 149
Edinburgh, 98
Elizabeth, Queen, (the Queen Mother), 95-96
Elles, General Sir Hugh, 125
Ellis, Archdeacon Thomas, 10, 11
Emerson, Ralph Waldo, 9
England and the Octopus, 179
English Speaking Union, the, 145–146
Esquilbec, Château, 120
Estoril, 215
Eton College, 142
Eugene, Prince, (of Sweden), 218

Falmouth, 198
Farouk, King, 269
'Ferguson's Gang', 225–6
Festival of Britain, 255–6
First World War, the, 108–33
  (*references to events, places, arms of the services, and individuals are to be found under relevant headings*)
Fleming, Ian, 151
Forster, E. M., 150, 180, 247–8
Fort Belan, 38–9
Fraser, Claude Lovat, 137
Fry, Sir Geoffrey, 146, 180
Fry, Maxwell, 264

Gayton, Northants, 2, 3
Geddes, Sir Patrick, 98, 138
George VI, King, 95–6
Gibson, Wing-Cmdr. Guy, V.C., 235
Gidea Park, 97
Giga, 191
Gillett, William, 80
Glasfryn: the home of the Ellis's, 4; described, 10–13
Glasgow, 98
Glaslyn estuary, 206
Glynllifon, 33–4
Gometra, 191
Goodhart-Rendel, H., 259
Grace, Dr. W. G., 54
Grant, Duncan, 78
Gray's Inn, 73–4, 77
Greaves, (Dick), 35–7, 41
Greaves, Miss, (Aunt Hilda), 18, 34–5
Greaves, John Whitehead, (author's grandfather), 21
Greece, 271
Griffin, Sir Herbert, 138

Grimaud, Port (near St. Tropez), 271–2
Grosvenor House, 276
Gwyllt headland, 205

Hankey, Sir Maurice, 123–4
Headlong Down the Years, 257–8
Headlong Hall, 19, 20
Heal, Sir Ambrose, 77
Hellbrunn, 223
Herbert, Sir Alan, 207, 267
Higginson, General Sir George, 54
Hohenzollern Redoubt, the, 115
Holford, Lord, 264
Holland House, 276
Horizon, 211
Hotblack, Major (later General), 'Boots', 127–8
Household Cavalry, the, 108–9
Hughes, Father, 199
Hughes, Richard, 223, 257
Hussey, Christopher, 264
Huxley, Sir Julian, 181

Imperial Light Horse, the, 109, 110
Inch Kenneth, 191
Independent Labour Party, the, 149
Inman, Lord, 265

John, Augustus, 88, 262
Jones, Jonah, 148
Jones, Thomas, 246

Kaye-Smith, Sheila, 180
Kennet, Lady, 87
Kent House, 89
Keynes, Lord, 158, 180

Kharkov, 185
Kirby Hall, 48
Kitchener, Lord, 109-10
Klagenfurt, 224
Knole, 217
Korcula, island, 221-2

Lanchester, Elsa, 155, 158
Lansbury, Rt. Hon. George, 181
Lansdowne House, 276
Laski, Harold, 158
Last Ditch, The, 232
Laughton, Charles, 155
Lawrence, D. H., 179
Leech, 9
Lewis, Sinclair, 219
Lindsay, Vatchell, 152
Lisbon, 215-16
Litvinov, Mme. Ivy, 186
Llechwyth quarries, 21, 36
Lloyd George, Earl, 146-8, 181; Memorial (Westminster Abbey), 148
Lopokova, Lydia, 87, 158
Lothian, Lord, 186
Loved One, The, 216
Low, David, 157
Lutyens, Sir Edwin, 73, 79, 167, 239-41, 259

Macaulay, Rose, 158
McCarthy, Desmond, 266
MacDonald, Rt. Hon. Ramsay, 149
McGoohan, Patrick, 212
Mackenzie, Sir Compton, 192, 275
MacNeill, Ronald, (Lord Cushendun), 146, 221-2
Maddocks, William, 19, 34, 206
Maisky, M., 157

Malleson, Miles, 158
Manchester Guardian, the, 124, 156, 267
Marquis, Don, 174-5
Marsh, Sir Edward, 153
Massingham, H. J., 180
Mathias, Mrs., 158
Matthew, Sir Robert, 210, 264
Maxton, James, 149
Melk Monastery, 219-20
Mereworth Castle, 217
Merrow Downs, 90
Mexico, 269
Miles, Karl, 218
Ministry of Agriculture, the, 128, 137
Moelwyn, 20, 95
Morris, James, 211
Morticians' Journal, The, 216
Mosley, Sir Oswald, 146, 149, 151, and Lady Cynthia, 221
Mumford, Lewis, 147, 210, 259
Mytton and Mermaid Hotel, 60, 193

National Parks, Government Committee on, 95
National Trust, the, 95, 105, 143, 225-6, 248
New Yorker, The, 147-8, 210, 264-5
New Zealand, 251-4
Nicolson, Sir Harold, 217
Nightingale, Florence, 19
Nineteenth Century, The, 182
9th Lancers, the, 109
Northumberland, Duke of, 153-5

On Trust For the Nation, 248
Orel, 184
Oronsay, the yacht, 266

Osburg, Ragnar, 218
Oundle School, 43–9

Parameters and Images, 259
Parc Plâs, 95
Parys Mountain copper strike, 21
Pavlova, 87
Peacock, Thomas Love, 19, 34, 210
'Pelmanism', 125–7
PEN Club, 218–20
Penshurst Place, 217
Pen-y-gwryd, 95–6
Pepler, Sir George, 244
Peto, Harold, 162
Plâs Brondanw: as Mr. Williams' family home, 19; in 1908, 92–93; its rehabilitation, 93–5, 100; and Frank Lloyd Wright, 209–10; during the Second World War, 228–9; destroyed by fire, 259–60; reconstructed, 261–2
Playfair, Nigel, 137
Pleasures of Architecture, The, 177
Pollard, Peggy, 225–7
Portmadoc Cob, 206
Portmeirion: and the Scandinavian Venus, 142; is acquired by author, 205; the place is opened, 206–7, and developed, 207–9; Sir Alan Herbert, 207; Frank Lloyd Wright, 210; Lewis Mumford, 210; Sir Robert Matthew, 210; and James Morris, 211; Patrick McGoohan's *The Prisoner*, 212; and Rupert Crawshay-Williams in *Russell Remembered*, 212–13; during the Second World War,

233–5, and the National Gallery's pictures, 235
Portofino, 193
Potsdam, 187
Powell, Dilys, 264
Prague, 219
Prendergast, Sir Thomas and Lady, 22
Priestley, J. B., 176, 181
Princes' Skating Club, 101
Punch, 8, 53, 207
Pwllheli, 243–6

Queenstown, New Zealand, 253

Ravensdale, Lady, 221
Raynham Hall, 102–3
Reconnography, 127
Reilly, Sir Charles, 138
Rhys-Williams, Dame Juliet, 150
Ritz Hotel, London, 275–6
Robertson, General Sir William, 141
Rolls, Charles, 60
Rolls-Royce, 60
Roosevelt, President Theodore, 123
Rosmer, Milton, 155
Royal Fusiliers, the, 110–11
Roxburgh, J. F., 141
Ruskin, John, 9, 57
Russell, Bertrand, (Lord), 54–5, 152, 181
Russell Remembered, 212–13
Ruthven, General Lord, 192

St. Martha's Chapel, 114
St. Tudwal's Islands, 13, 198–201
Sacher, Madame, 219
Sackville, Lord, 217
Sackville-West, Victoria, 217

Salcombe, 197
Salzburg, 223
Samuel, Lord, 264
Sanderson, Frederick, (headmaster Oundle), 43-7
Sandow, Eugene, 101
Schloss Wernberg, 223-4
Schönbrunn, Imperial Place of, 219
Scott, (yacht) the, 194, 202
Scott, Geoffrey, 87-8, 192-3
Sert, Paul, 89
Second World War, the, 229-39
Sexual Life of Primates, The, 157
Shaw, George Bernard, 186-7, 208
Shelley, P. B., 206
Shepheard, Peter, 259, 264
Sheridan, R. B., 34-5
Silkin, Lord, 246
Slim, Field-Marshal Lord, 268-9
Smith-Dorrien, Admiral, 54, 225
Smyth, General Sir Henry and Lady, (Aunt Connie), 37
Snowdonia National Park, 95
Somerset, Lady Kitty, 162
Spectator, The, 90, 112, 139-40
Spoerry, François, 259, 271-2
Squire, Sir John, 176, 180
Stapledon, Sir George, 180
Stephen, Adrian, 78
Stephen, Karen, 197
Stevenage New Town, 246-8
Stewart Island, 253
Stockholm, 218
Stowe, 139-43
Strachey, Amabel, *see* Williams-Ellis, Mrs. Amabel
Strachey, Rt. Hon. John, 149, 230-2, 264
Strachey, Lytton, 230

Strachey, St. Loe: and cheap cottages, 90; and *The Spectator*'s infantry company, 111-12; and 'The Surrey Guides', 112, 123; *Pisée Terre*, 181
'Surrey Guides, The', 112

Tank Corps, the history of the, 128-9
Tanrallt, 34-5
Teatro Olimpico, Vicenza, 221
Thompson, Dorothy, 219
Thompson, Professor J. J., 61
Thorp, Peter, 96-8
Thorpe, Rt. Hon. Jeremy, 148
Times, The, 98, 142, 263
Tresco, Isle of, 54
Tremadoc, 206
Trevelyan, Charles, 158
Trevelyan, G. M., 143, 180
Trinity College, Cambridge, 56-7
Trinity House, 199
Tunisia, 271
Twinkler, the, 190-1

United Services Club, 55
Unwin, Sir Raymond, 138

Vanbrugh, 178
Venice, 220-1
Vicenza, 221
Vienna, 219

Wales, Prince of, (Charles), 148-149
Wales, Prince of, (Edward), 117, 148-9
Wallace, Lindsay, 130, 242
Walpole, Horace, 178
Ward, Mrs. Humphrey, 79
Warwick, Lady, 149-50

Waugh, Evelyn, 216
Weaver, Sir Lawrence, 96–8, 123–4, 128, 138
Webb, Sydney and Beatrice, 150
Week, The, 228
Week End Review, the, 181
Wellesley, Lord Gerald, (Duke of Wellington), 144
Wells, H. G., 149, 155, 158, 215–16
Welsh Guards, the, 111–14, 148
Wern, 35–6
Westerham, 250
Westminster, Duke of, 177
William, Prince, (of Sweden), 218
Williams, Sir Osmund, 205
Williams-Bulkeley, Sir Richard, 39
Williamsburgh, 270
Williams-Ellis, Mrs. Amabel; meets author, 90, and becomes engaged to him, 110; as Red Cross nurse, 110; is married, 114; co-author of the history of the Tank Corps, 129; and *The Spectator*, 149, 153; and *An Anatomy of Poetry*, 153; and *The Pleasures of Architecture*, 177; and Jugoslavia, 222; and *Headlong Down the Years*, 257

Wilson, Sir Arnold, 182–3
Wolfe, Humbert, 155–6
Woolf, Virginia, 78, 150
Wren, Sir Christopher, 178–9
Wrench, Sir Evelyn, 145
Wright, Frank Lloyd, 187–8, 209–10
Wroxall Abbey, Warwickshire, 108, 241
Wyddfa, 20
Wyllie, James, 208, 233–5
Wynne, Fred, 38–40

Younghusband, Sir Francis, 152
Ypres, 120

Zeppelin, Count Theo von, 223–224
Zeppelin, Countess von, 224–5
Zuckerman, Sir Solly, 157
Zuider Zee, the, 222–3